New Directions in Human Resource Management

Edited by

Chester A. Schriesheim
and
Linda L. Neider

INFORMATION AGE
PUBLISHING

80 Mason Street
Greenwich, Connecticut 06830

Library of Congress Cataloging-in-Publication Data

New directions in human resource management / edited by Chester A. Schriesheim and Linda L. Neider.
    p. cm. – (Research in management)
Includes bibliographical references.
    ISBN 1-59311-098-7 (pbk.) – ISBN 1-59311-099-5 (hardcover) 1. Personnel management. I. Neider, Linda L., 1953- II. Schriesheim, Chester. III. Series.
    HF5549.N374 2003
    658.3–dc22

2003021158

Copyright © 2003 Information Age Publishing, Inc.

Printed in the United States of America

New Directions in Human Resource Management

2003 SOUTHERN MANAGEMENT ASSOCIATION OFFICERS

Past President: Donna E. Ledgerwood, University of North Texas, 2002-2003

President: Kevin Mossholder, Louisiana State University

President Elect: Terri A. Scandura, University of Miami

Vice-President and Program Chair: Christine M. Riordan, University of Georgia

Vice President-Program Chair Elect: Anson Seers, Virginia Commonwealth University

Secretary/Membership Chair: Allison W. Pearson, Mississippi State University

Treasurer: Tim Barnett, Mississippi State University

Past President: Donna E. Ledgerwood, University of North Texas

Journal of Management Editor: Daniel C. Feldman, University of Georgia

Proceedings Editor: Elizabeth Weatherly, University of Alabama-Huntsville

Newsletter Editor: Gary Castrogiovanni, University of Tulsa

Archivist: Dan Cochran, Mississippi State University

BOARD MEMBERS

Gayle Baugh (2003), University of West Florida
Peg Williams (2003), Virginia Commonwealth University
Shawn Carraher (2003), Texas A&M University—Commerce
Wayne Hochwarter (2004), Florida State University
Alan Witt, (2004), University of New Orleans
Michelle A. Dean (2004), San Diego State University
Jason D. Shaw (2005), University of Kentucky
Shaker A. Zahra (2005), Babson College
Sandy J. Wayne (2005), University of Georgia

Affiliations are at the time of office.

CONTENTS

FOREWORD

NEW DIRECTIONS IN HUMAN RESOURCE MANAGEMENT

Chester A. Schriesheim and Linda L. Neider

This is the third volume of the *Research in Management* series, a joint undertaking of the Southern Management Association (SMA) and Information Age Publishing, Inc. We want to thank the officers and members of the SMA for their continued support of this endeavor, along with our publisher, George Johnson of Information Age.

For this volume we decided to commission chapters to deal with new avenues, approaches, and domains in human resources management theory and research. We gave our authors wide latitude in terms of what might be presented in theory and empirical research, asking only that each chapter make an original and interesting contribution toward advancing future research in the human resources management area. We told the authors that full-blown theories were not needed, that we'd rather see a new seed than a wilted old plant. Additionally, empirical research that was more exploratory than is typically published in the usual journal outlets was encouraged, especially if it provided support for a new idea or additional support for a more established point of view.

The result of these efforts is a collection of chapters that are a mix of review, new theory, and empirical investigation. We believe that these chap-

New Directions in Human Resource Management
A Volume in: Research in Management, pages vii–000.
Copyright © 2003 by Information Age Publishing, Inc.
All rights of reproduction in any form reserved.
ISBN: 1-59311-099-5 (hardcover), 1-59311-098-7 (pbk.)

ters should stimulate new thinking and research in each of their respective domains, and we are highly appreciative of the authors for their willingness to share the fruits of their labor with us and readers of this volume.

Our first chapter, "Customer Feedback as a Critical Performance Dimension: Review and Exploratory Empirical Examination," by Christine M. Hagan and H. John Bernardin, briefly reviews the performance appraisal literature and then focuses on customer feedback as a critical element in assessing services management performance. Service provider job satisfaction as a correlate of service performance is reviewed and an exploratory study presented that shows significant relationships between service provider job satisfaction and customer perceptions of service quality, appraisal of service performance, and intentions about repeat business. We believe that this work should serve to stimulate an increased recognition of the importance of customer feedback in the service provider appraisal process, something that has been virtually missing from the literature altogether.

"Accountability in Human Resources Management," by Angela T. Hall, Dwight D. Frink, Gerald R. Ferris, Wayne A. Hochwarter, Charles J. Kacmar, and Michael G. Bowen, is our second chapter. The role of accountability as a construct in human resources management systems is reviewed, leading to the development of a theoretical model of accountability with antecedent and consequent effects. A test of the model is reported, using structural equations modeling and a sample of 311 employees. The results generally support the proposed antecedents and consequences of accountability, and implications and suggestions for future research and practice are discussed. This chapter should serve as a foundation for the development of theory and research on individual accountability in organizations, a topic that is increasingly timely given the serious corporate wrongdoings of the recent past. Since accountability is the foundation for all employer-employee relationships, this chapter may also trigger a closer look at a number of traditional human resource activities (e.g., compensation) with respect to their role in managing individual behaviors in organizations.

Our third chapter, "Ergonomic Training and Organizational Stress: Implications for Human Resource Professionals," by Angela K. Miles and Pamela L. Perrewé, reviews the literature on ergonomic training and formulates a model of relationships between aspects of ergonomic training, person-environment fit, and employee stress outcomes. A test of the model is reported, using respondents from a variety of organizations and linear multiple regression. The findings support person-environment fit as being a mediator of the hypothesized relationships between ergonomic training and stress outcomes, and implications and future directions are discussed. This chapter should provide support for human resource professionals interested in using ergonomics and ergonomic training to lessen employee stress and its attendant costs (reduced performance, medical expenses, etc.). The ideas of this chapter and those of Chapter 1 could be interpreted as suggesting that it might be interesting to explore the indirect effects of ergonomic training on service customer satisfaction, by enhancing the performance of customer service providers. The results of the Miles and Perrewé chapter may be applicable to workers in a variety of jobs and industries, so future research to explore these possibilities seems both desirable and worthwhile.

"New Directions for Research on Political Perceptions: Suggestions and an Illustrative Example," by Ken Harris and K. Michele Kacmar, serves as Chapter 4. The authors begin by briefly reviewing the literature on perceptions of organizational politics. They then present five areas for future research that Harris and Kacmar believe are likely to advance knowledge in this domain. A study is discussed illustrating the utility of one of the authors' recommendations, that of exploring alternative statistical analyses. Using two large samples combined ($N = 1256$), a triple interaction between leader-member exchange, level of organizational information, and perceptions of politics was tested. Significant effects were found for the job satisfaction dependent variable, suggesting the utility of testing for higher-order interactions that are not usually examined in organizational politics research. Given the support for one of the authors' recommended directions for perceptions of politics research, we hope that researchers will be stimulated to not only examine alternate analytic approaches but also explore the authors' other ideas for advancing knowledge in this important research domain.

Our fifth chapter is, "Complex, Nonlinear Relationships between Group Incentive Context, Design and Effectiveness," by Edilberto F. Montemayor. This chapter uses a diverse set of theoretical perspectives to develop and test hypotheses related to group incentive plan effectiveness. Briefly, sociological and economic views of organizations are highlighted, along with "macro psychological modeling" and non-linear thinking to develop not only traditional linear but non-linear (hyperbolic) hypotheses. The results indicate that the relationships examined are more complex than previously assumed, supporting the presence of several nonlinear relationships. The implications of these findings are discussed, including the fact that the heuristics that are commonly offered in practitioner-oriented writings appear overly simplistic at best. Hopefully, this research will stimulate additional research on group incentive characteristics and how they relate to compensation system effectiveness, as well as further encourage researchers to engage in the nontraditional theorizing and statistical analysis advocated by Harris and Kacmar in their chapter on perceptions of politics.

"Evaluating Recruiting Effectiveness in a New Millennium," by Kevin D. Carlson, is our sixth and final chapter. Carlson classifies and reviews the literature on the evaluation of recruiting effectiveness, presenting and discussing the advantages and limitations of each approach. He then offers a new recruitment evaluation approach, based upon some of his earlier work and the application of utility analysis to estimating the value of differences in applicant quality. Examples are noted, using Carlson's new approach, along with the author's characterization of the evolution of recruitment research in organizations. Implications and suggested directions for future theory and research are discussed, focusing on both basic and applied work. We believe that this is an excellent chapter with which to end this volume because it deals with the bottom line issue of "does it (recruitment) matter?," in terms of the universal organizational metric (money). We hope that Carlson's ideas can be extended and operationalized by other scholars in the near future to help us better understand the practical usefulness of different recruiting models and approaches. Since recruitment can be argued to be the beginning of all organizational human resource management processes, providing better new employees or obtaining new employees in a more cost efficient manner is surely a serious concern for most organizations.

In conclusion, we believe that the six chapters included in this volume are interesting, well written, and provide very useful perspectives and ideas for future work in human resources management. We hope that readers will enjoy these contributions and that they will be stimulated by the new directions in human resources management that the authors' works represent. We'd like to end this commentary by thanking Linda Sinkes and Susan Stearns for helping prepare and organize this volume and we want to also thank our loved ones, Linda and Joe Schriesheim and Syle Kinney, and Paul and Rosie Sugrue, for their understanding and support as we worked on pulling this book together.

CHAPTER 1

CUSTOMER FEEDBACK AS A CRITICAL PERFORMANCE DIMENSION

Review and Exploratory Empirical Examination

Christine M. Hagan
University of Miami
H. John Bernardin
Florida Atlantic University

ABSTRACT

The purpose of this chapter is to highlight the theoretical and empirical work that has been directed at customer feedback to date. In addition, we present an exploratory study which focuses on service provider job satisfaction and its relation to both general customer feedback about service quality, and specific customer appraisal of the performance of individual front-line service workers. Limitations of the current research are discussed, along with suggestions for future research in this domain.

New Directions in Human Resource Management
A Volume in: Research in Management, pages 1–27
Copyright © 2003 by Information Age Publishing, Inc.
All rights of reproduction in any form reserved.
ISBN: 1-59311-099-5 (hardcover), 1-59311-098-7 (pbk.)

Performance appraisal is a critically important element of management practices because it relates to the effectiveness of individuals and groups and the organizational outcomes they produce. Yet, performance appraisal continues to be one of the most troublesome areas of Human Resource Management. Based on a survey of its members, the Society for Human Resource Management (SHRM) reports that more than 90 percent of appraisal systems are unsuccessful (Bernardin, Hagan, Kane, & Villanova, 1998). Other surveys describe similar findings. Dissatisfaction with appraisal has been reported by raters, ratees, top management, and human resource professionals. Researchers have criticized appraisals for a variety of reasons, including halo, leniency, intentional manipulation, and race, gender, or age biases (Facteau & Craig, 2001). The growing volume of legal cases concerning performance appraisal leads one expert to assert that at least some element of every firm's appraisal system will probably attract legal scrutiny at some point in time (Malos, 1998).

The widespread failure of appraisal systems is particularly troublesome given the current environment, which finds so many organizations re-positioning and re-configuring themselves due to opportunities and challenges created by the global economy and improvements in information technology. The shift from a manufacturing to a service economy in the US has strong implications for performers and performance management initiatives. Contemporary service organizations are increasingly interested in ensuring that service workers, especially front-line providers, are appropriately aligned with external customers (Susskind, Kacmar, & Borchgrevink, 2003).

The perennial dissatisfaction with traditional performance appraisal also provides at least some explanation for the explosive growth and popularity of multi-rater appraisal programs over the past decade (Dalessio, 1998). In 360-degree feedback programs, target participants (the ratees) typically assess their own performance, then receive evaluative feedback from the full network of relational dimensions: supervisors (above), subordinates (below), internal customers and/or peers (internal horizontal), and outside customers (external horizontal). By contrast, any program in which a ratee receives feedback from at least two of these sources is considered to be a multi-source feedback (MSF) program. Murphy and Cleveland (1995) argue that MSF generally fits better than traditional, top-down appraisal, given contemporary organizational forms and processes.

Against this backdrop, then, it is surprising that customer appraisal of service worker performance has received so little research attention (McChrystal & Steelman, 2003). Indeed, the conspicuous absence of a significant literature on customers within the management field has recently been noted (Bowen & Hallowell, 2002). Villanova (1992) argued that the best index of an organization's performance is the degree to which it satisfies customer requirements. Performance appraisal researchers explicitly recommend the use of customer-generated criteria in the derivation of performance standards and performance management systems (Bernardin et al., 1998; London & Beatty, 1993; Villanova, 1992). A decade ago, some suggested that multi-rater appraisal systems that exclude customers should be labeled 270-degree feedback programs (London & Beatty, 1993). A review of literature since then suggests that little, if anything, has changed. Perhaps it is this ongoing exclusion of customers in the relevant management research that led one group of authors to define 360-degree feedback recently without any reference to customers (i.e., Waldman, Atwater, & Antonio, 1998).

The purpose of this chapter is to highlight the theoretical and empirical work that has been directed at customer feedback to date. In addition, we will present an exploratory study which focuses on service provider job satisfaction and its relation to both general customer feedback about service quality, and specific customer appraisal of the performance of individual front-line service workers.

THE ROLE OF PERFORMANCE IN SERVICES MANAGEMENT

Services differ from manufactured products in three ways: their intangibility (they are performances rather than objects), their heterogeneity (their performance varies from producer to producer), and their inseparability (production and consumption typically occur simultaneously) (Parasuraman, Zeithaml, & Berry, 1985). Because of these attributes, customers often equate services with the employees who provide them (Gronroos, 1982; Schneider & Bowen, 1985). Bitner, Booms, and Mohr (1994) suggest that analysis of the service provider-customer interaction at the individual service encounter level provides the same type of information that manufacturers glean from traditional quality control measures (reject rates, equipment down time, etc.). This heightened emphasis on the importance of service providers and their performance creates key challenges for appraising and managing performance and increases the importance of effective human resource management (HRM) strategies in the overall business equation.

Traditionally, organizations have pursued employee and customer measurement as separate initiatives, and intuitively believed that favorable business outcomes would follow (Bitner, 1992; Ulrich, 1992). Employee surveys were the domain of management and human resource professionals, while customer surveys were part of an organization's marketing efforts. Over the last decade or so, however, management and marketing experts are recognizing that they share significant common space where customers and employees are concerned. In the marketing area, Kohli and Jaworski (1990) assert that a strong, systemwide market orientation on the part of a firm will create three outcomes: a positive customer response, favorable business results, and a positive employee response (including high levels of job satisfaction and organizational commitment). Content analysis of service themes in empirical management research indicates that service initiatives tend to include two components: concern for customers, and concern for employees (Burke, Borucki, & Hurley, 1992; Schneider, Wheeler & Cox, 1992). In their model of service quality, Zeithaml, Berry, and Parasuraman (1988) indicate that three of five possible service gaps occur entirely *within* the firm, and are mitigated through managerial means. Marketing literature refers to employees as "internal customers" (Berry & Parasuraman, 1991, p. 151), while management literature refers to customers as "partial employees" (Schneider & Bowen, 1995, p. 85). Thus, organizations are increasingly being viewed as open systems with highly permeable boundaries, in which customers may actively participate in the production process, may co-produce the service, or may themselves be the end product (Lengnick-Hall, 1996). In such settings, the performance of individual providers becomes inexorably interwoven with the service content and outcomes.

Related to this literature, there is growing evidence that service providers and customers share congruent, or parallel, views concerning service quality. Parkington and Schneider (1979) found significant correlation between employee perceptions about the quality of service offered and customer perceptions about the quality of service received. Subsequent study replicated and extended this finding by demonstrating that employee reports of particularly enthusiastic service imperatives were associated with customer reports of significantly higher levels of service quality (Schneider, Parkington, & Buxton, 1980). The extension of this service climate to include HR initiatives confirmed their significant correlation with customer service quality ratings (Schneider & Bowen, 1985). In these studies, perceptions about practices were also related to turnover intentions for both customers and employees.

This model was extended to link perceptions with attitudes and behavior. Schmit and Allscheid (1995) reported that employee perceptions of four internal climate variables (management, supervisor, monetary, and service support) were significantly correlated with their perceptions about service capability, which were aggregated and hypothesized to represent an affective response, which was correlated (moderately) with customer perceptions of service quality and satisfaction. In this study, favorable customer perceptions were assumed to be a reflection that service provider behavior had, in fact, proceeded from reported perceptions and attitudes. Longitudinal study indicated that employee attitudes, unit performance, customer satisfaction, and turnover were related; "causal analysis" suggested that customer satisfaction led to employee attitudes, rather than the reverse (Ryan, Schmit, & Johnson, 1996). Further study correlated facets of service climate perceptions among employees with facets of satisfaction among customers (Johnson, 1996).

In an extension of this research, "linkage" models are increasingly pop-ular in organizational settings (Pugh, Dietz, Wiley, & Brooks, 2002). These models attempt to extend the understanding of employee-customer per-ceptional commonalities to include organizational and/or specific unit effectiveness measures. Both *Fortune Magazine* and the *Harvard Business Review* highlighted articles describing the business model in use at Sears, called Total Performance Indicators (TPI), which tracks a set of measures involving management behaviors, through employee measures (percep-tions, attitudes, and retention), to customer outcomes (satisfaction, reten-tion, and recommending the organization to others) to financial performance and investor relations:

> Our model shows that a 5-point improvement in employee attitudes will drive a 1.3-point improvement in customer satisfaction, which in turn will drive a 0.5 percent improvement in revenue growth. If we knew nothing about a local store except that employee attitudes had improved by 5 points on our survey scale, we could predict with confidence that if revenue growth in the district as a whole were 5 percent, revenue growth at this particular store would be 5.5 percent These numbers are as rigorous as any others we work with . . . (E)very year, our accounting firm audits them, as closely as it audits our financials (Rucci, Kim, & Quinn, 1998, pp. 91-92).

Two interesting differences seem evident between these real world models and the academic literature. Academic research appears to assume the pos-itive organization outcomes, and focuses its attention on connecting per-ceptions with attitudes with behaviors in service provider-customer exchanges. In contrast, applied linkage models appear to assume the per-ception-attitude-behavior connection, and focus instead on quantifying the value of outcomes.

To date, this line of research has contributed important perspectives in at least three ways. First, it sheds light on employee-customer linkages in service settings, some antecedents and possible outcomes. Second, its focus on the alignment among a variety of elements encourages a systems perspective otherwise lacking in much of management literature (Cardy, 1998; Waldman, 1994). Third, it encourages reconceptualizing the tradi-tional managerial perspective that has been described as "from the top looking down or from the inside looking around" (Bowen & Hallowell, 2002, p. 70). Replacing it is a perspective that involves focusing on custom-ers who are external to the organization, and the way they interact with front-line customer service workers who do not occupy historically power-ful or prestigious positions within the firm (Singh, 2000).

However, it's important to note that all the management research cited above was conducted at the branch office (or business unit) level of analy-sis. In fact, this level of analysis may only apply to certain situations. Firms vary in the approach they take to creating and adding value in the market-ing and management of services. No doubt, different systems give rise to variations in service provider-customer relationships, customer roles, and organizational effectiveness criteria (Lengnick-Hall, 1996). To date, little management research has addressed the organizational, environmental, or strategic contingencies that might influence the utility of various organizational-customer relationship models (Bowen & Hallowell, 2002). Treacy and Wiersema (1993) suggest that organizations tend to choose among customer intimacy, operational excellence, or high innovation as their route to success. Thus, customer intimacy competitive formats in some industries may be evaluated most effectively through monitoring the employee–customer linkage at the individual service encounter level. Operational excellence firms may find general, system-wide customer feedback to be most informative, particularly if they invest in standardizing processes and training front-line workers as their means for delivering consistent quality. Gutek, Groth, and Cherry (2002) distinguish between service encounters and service relationships, asserting that each requires its own management systems and provider structure. Lengnick-Hall (1996) suggests that the nature, intensity, and frequency of organization-customer linkages may tend to be high when services are more personal and customized (e.g., haircutters, fitness trainers), rather than when services are more impersonal (e.g., dry cleaners, trash collectors). Further, she argues that high customer involvement may be appropriate only when a firm and its customers can agree to target objectives and collaborate successfully. Thus, it should be noted that linkage research involving aggregated perceptions and business results may be useful to particular business models but they may not provide sufficient specificity when services are highly customized or when they are delivered in a framework that involves a single provider interacting repeatedly with an individual customer.

To date, management research has focused very little attention on individual service provider behaviors and their differential effects (if any) on customer perceptions, assessments, and behaviors. In the marketing literature, Bitner (1990) used role-playing in a laboratory setting to demonstrate that individual employee behaviors directly influence customer satisfaction, that they mitigate customer dissatisfaction, and that they can convert a disappointing experience into a relatively satisfying one. In the management literature, Pugh (2001) found that emotion displayed by individual employees during service transactions was positively related to customer affect and customer evaluations of the quality of service received.

INDIVIDUAL SERVICE PROVIDER JOB SATISFACTION

The research cited above indicates that perceptions about service resources and capabilities are associated with positive attitudes and satisfaction among groups of service providers and their customers. This raises new issues concerning job satisfaction among service providers and any increased economic value that may accrue to firms if service provider performance is enhanced by such satisfaction.

For many years, job satisfaction has been a central variable in the study of worker motivation and performance (Leong & Vaux, 1992). Job satisfaction has been viewed as a cause of performance (Schwab & Cummings, 1970), as the result of the receipt of performance-related rewards (Lawler & Porter, 1967), and as a moderating variable (Triandis, 1959). Two meta-analyses report significant correlations between worker satisfaction and performance, although the effect sizes were relatively small (Iaffaldano & Muchinsky, 1985; Petty, McGee, & Cavender, 1984). Iaffaldano and Muchinsky's study (1985) focused solely on productivity measures (objective and subjective measures), specifically excluding behavioral outcomes of satisfaction, such as absence, tardiness, turnover, and union grievances. Although reporting a significant relationship between satisfaction and productivity ($p < .025$), the effect size was a low .17 (corrected for attenuation and sampling error; not adjusted for range restriction), thus replicating Vroom's (1964) earlier estimate that the strength of the correlation across twenty studies was .14. The Petty, McGee, and Cavender (1984) meta-analysis found a considerably stronger correlation of .31 (corrected for attenuation; not adjusted for range restriction or sampling error) when global measures of satisfaction were used. Meta-analysis of satisfaction using the Job Descriptive Index (JDI) facet scales yielded correlation coefficients ranging from .27 for satisfaction with supervision, to .15 for satisfaction with pay (not adjusted for attenuation, range restriction, or sampling error).

Explanations for these weak correlations have typically included poor operationalization of the performance construct, or poorly matched variables. Organ (1977) maintained that job attitude measures were designed to maximize variance, while the performance measures used in these studies were too narrowly defined, thus restricting variance. Bateman and Organ's (1983) study relating overall JDI scores to supervisory ratings of citizenship behaviors (a broader and multi-faceted construct) found effect sizes ranging from .39 to .43. Petty, McGee, and Cavender (1984) suggested that rater errors (such as central tendency and leniency), and the homogenizing effects of organizational practices (such as the effects of selection and training programs) restrict the variability of performance evaluations. The net result of such range restriction would be to understate the true relationship.

Interestingly, studies focused on psychologically-based interventions to improve performance (e.g., changes in work structure or method, adjustments to organizational practices) illustrate stronger covariance between job performance and satisfaction than is suggested by correlation research (Katzell, Thompson, & Guzzo, 1992). In their review of 207 studies of the effects of psychologically-based interventions, Katzell and Guzzo (1983) report that 87 percent succeeded in raising productivity in at least one measurable aspect, and 75 percent of the studies reported significant improvements in job satisfaction.

Considering the relationships previously found between employee perceptions about organizations' commitment to service (at the group level) and customer perceptions of service quality (at the group level), as well as the significant relationship between affect and performance demonstrated meta-analytically, we would also expect that satisfied employees would generally provide better quality of service, that customers would detect better service, and that customers would reflect this in their service quality ratings.

H:1.   Individual service provider job satisfaction will be positively correlated with customer perceptions of service quality.

CUSTOMER PERCEPTIONS OF SERVICE QUALITY

Within service organizations, service quality is considered to be an important dimension of performance that is linked to a variety of customer attitudes, customer future behavioral intentions, customer retention, and future organizational profitability (Zeithaml, Berry, & Parasuraman, 1996). Unfortunately, there has been a lack of consensus about the precise definition of service quality versus customer satisfaction, their relationship to each other, and how each is linked to future business performance (Bitner & Hubbert, 1994). Anderson, Fornell, and Lehmann (1994) describe three distinct conceptualizations of quality in the literature. Traditional marketers and economists view quality as one of several attributes of a good or service. In operations management, quality has two dimensions: 1) fitness for use (Does it do what it is supposed to do? Does it meet the needs of customers?); and 2) reliability (To what extent is the product or service free from deficiencies?). Marketing services literature describes quality as an overall assessment, "a consumer's judgment about the product's overall excellence or superiority" (Zeithaml, 1988, p. 3) that is "similar in many ways to an attitude" (Parasuraman, Zeithaml, & Berry, 1988, p. 15). Boulding, Kalra, Staelin, and Zeithaml (1993) distinguish between the customer satisfaction concept as it has been discussed in the popular press and measured by many organizations, and the satisfaction concept that has been used in academic research. The former typically referred to an enduring, cumulative concept; while the latter was considered to be transaction-specific.

Rust and Oliver (1994) identify four distinctions between satisfaction and quality perceptions. First, quality dimensions tend to be more specific than those underlying satisfaction. An extremely good meal at a fine restaurant with a varied wine list might be influenced by parking problems—

in which case, restaurant quality assessments may have been very high, but more general satisfaction judgments may not be. Second, quality expectations are based on ideals while satisfaction judgments may be influenced by a number of non-quality issues, such as needs and equity, or "fairness" perceptions. Third, quality perceptions do not require direct experience with a particular product or service, while satisfaction is purely experiential. Finally, quality perceptions are believed to have fewer conceptual antecedents, while satisfaction is thought to be influenced by a number of cognitive and affective elements.

In spite of such differences in definitions, it is generally believed that customer perceptions of service quality and customer satisfaction are interrelated (Bitner, 1990; Cronin & Taylor, 1992; Taylor & Baker, 1994) and often intercorrelated (Bitner & Hubbert, 1994).

In an attempt to assist organizations in improving service by better understanding the expectations and perceptions of their customers, Parasuraman, Zeithaml, and Berry (1985, 1988) developed SERVQUAL, a 21-item questionnaire which measures the following five dimensions of service quality:

1. Reliability: Ability to perform the promised service dependably and accurately;
2. Responsiveness: Willingness to help customers and provide prompt service;
3. Assurance: Knowledge and courtesy of employees and their ability to inspire trust and confidence;
4. Empathy: Caring, individualized attention the firm provides its customers;
5. Tangibles: Physical facilities, equipment, and appearance of personnel.

A search of computerized data bases suggests that SERVQUAL is probably the most widely-used measure of its kind. In response to ongoing research findings, the questionnaire has continued to be refined with the most recent version emerging in 1994. In fact, we could find no alternative questionnaire that would be theoretically rooted as well in the marketing services literature, with which to measure customer perceptions of satisfaction or service quality.

As has been true with the management literature, SERVQUAL studies have primarily been conducted at the group or organizational level. As has also been true in the employee-customer linkage models found in the management literature, the marketing literature suggests that customer perceptions about service quality and customer satisfaction may not be directly and immediately connected with organizational profitability (Anderson, Fornell, & Lehman, 1994). Zeithaml, Berry, and Parasuraman (1996) argue that evaluating service quality as a tool for customer retention—and for customers' increasing or extending their service utilization—may provide this critical link with profitability. By integrating research findings and anecdotal evidence, they developed and tested a four-factor, 13-item customer-based behavioral intentions battery. The four factors were:

1. loyalty (e.g., saying positive things, recommending the service to others),
2. propensity to switch,
3. willingness to pay more, and
4. external response to problems (e.g., complaining to other customers, complaining to external agencies such as the Better Business Bureau, etc.).

The battery was tested using SERVQUAL scores as predictors, plus an overall assessment of service quality, with customers in four types of organizations (computer manufacturer, retail chain, automobile insurer, life insurer). The findings supported the hypothesis that high perceptions of service quality were associated with strong levels of customer behavioral intentions. Review of recent marketing literature indicates that, although future customer intentions have not yet been directly linked to actual customer behavior (Mittal & Kamakura, 2001), the use of future customer intentions is preferable to assuming that satisfaction alone will directly translate into positive returns for organizations (Lemon, White, & Winer, 2002). On the basis of this, then, we would expect to find the following:

H:2.   Customer SERVQUAL scores will be significantly correlated with customer future behavioral intentions.

Our primary interest here is in replicating the previous study and seeing whether its effects generalize to a model concerning the performance of individual service workers. In addition, management research has not extended customer responses beyond quality perceptions and general satisfaction.

PERFORMANCE APPRAISAL USING CUSTOMERS AS RATERS

SERVQUAL contains no explicit dimension that measures the actual performance of the service providers themselves, despite the assumed central role of these providers in the service equation. Interestingly, in its original draft, SERVQUAL contained ten dimensions, at least four of which directly evaluated some element of the performance of contact personnel (Para-suraman, Zeithaml, & Berry, 1985).

- *Competence* was defined as possession of the required skills and knowledge to perform the service. Its facets included the knowledge and skill of both contact personnel and operational support employees.
- *Courtesy* involved the consideration, friendliness, politeness, and respect of contact personnel for customers.
- *Communication* involved the performance of the organization in effectively explaining the service and its attributes to customers using understandable language and in displaying a willingness to sincerely listen to customers.
- *Credibility* involved the believability, trustworthiness, and honesty of the organization which was hypothesized to be influenced by company name and reputation, as well as the personal characteristics of the contact personnel.

These dimensions were identified as important contributors to quality perceptions on the basis of in-depth interviews with organizational executives (3-4 interviews in each of four organizations) and twelve consumer focus groups. After testing and refining the instrument based on samples from five different industries (i.e., appliance repair and maintenance, retail banking, long distance telephone services, securities brokerage, and credit cards) only five of the original ten dimensions remained distinct. The five collapsing dimensions were communication, competence, credibility, courtesy, and security. Additional samples and testing resulted in the five dimension, 21-item scale, described earlier. Thus, the currently-used version of SERVQUAL captures some general information concerning performance of personnel, but it lacks the specificity recommended for effective appraisal programs (Bernardin et al., 1998).

As indicated earlier, multi-rater feedback systems are rapidly growing in popularity and use. Borman (1997) asserts that two assumptions underlie these programs: (1) each source of rating offers at least somewhat unique data concerning the ratee's performance; and (2) evaluations from different rating sources provide incremental validity over and above any single source.

A key element in appraisal is deciding who is qualified to rate performance. Existing theory describes a competent rater as one who:

1. is knowledgeable about the objectives of the position (Latham & Wexley, 1981);
2. has sufficient access and opportunity to observe performance (Bernardin & Beatty, 1984);
3. is able to discern satisfactory from unsatisfactory performance (Latham & Wexley, 1981); and

4.   is an individual whose opinion the organization values (Tornow, 1993).

Traditionally, the most common source of performance evaluation information was an individual's supervisor, since the supervisor was directly accountable for the work unit, its processes, efficiency and effectiveness. However, Murphy and Cleveland (1995) argue that traditional appraisal was developed in relation to a particular context:

1.   large, hierarchical organizations in which power and control flowed downward;
2.   relatively stable markets and general environments;
3.   relatively homogenous workforces;
4.   long-term employment.

As environments, markets and customers changed over these last decades, changes in organizational strategies, structures, and processes were accompanied by concern over the continued viability of traditional management practices. Thus, multi-rater appraisal may represent a better appraisal tool given today's downsized, outwardly-focused, more horizontal firms.

Even without the massive organizational changes over the past few decades, researchers documented shortcomings of traditional appraisal and utilized alternative sources of information. Borman (1991) argued that, although supervisors should have reasonably good norms for performance, they do not actually observe much of the operational performance of subordinates. In addition, supervisors often focus on achievement of end results only (Bass, 1990). For example, a manager who assesses the performance of a subordinate leader, does so inferentially, since he is not one of the led (Yammarino & Atwater, 1993). Thus, subordinates have been a popular source of behavioral descriptions and evaluations concerning their leaders. In both the Ohio State and the University of Michigan studies, subordinates were considered to be the best source of information about leader behaviors (Bass, 1990). Bernardin and Beatty (1987) found that managers themselves judged subordinates to be a more valid source of information than supervisors about several performance dimensions.

Peers have also been considered to be a credible information source regarding performance. In two West Point studies, peer opinions, rather than supervisor evaluations were the best single predictors of future success as an army officer (Baier, 1947; Haggerty, Johnson & King, 1954). Similar findings were reported in studies involving the US Marine Corps, the US Air Force, and the US Navy (Bass, 1990). Peers were more likely to differentiate effort from performance (Wohlers & London, 1989) and were more sensitive to system factors that could constrain performance (Cardy & Dobbins, 1994). Borman (1991) argued that peers were usually privy to the most performance information regarding their fellow workers because of the difficulty in trying to hide one's actual performance behaviors from immediate co-workers.

As indicated earlier, several treatments of the subject of multi-rater appraisal have advocated the inclusion of customers in this network (Bernardin et al., 1998; Cardy, 1998; Church & Bracken, 1997; London & Beatty, 1993; Paradise-Tornow, 1998). Performance appraisal researchers explicitly recommend the use of customer-generated criteria in the derivation of performance standards and performance management systems (Bernardin, 1992; Bernardin, Hagan, Kane, & Villanova, 1998; London & Beatty, 1993). Villanova (1992) articulated a four-step framework for identifying customer-based performance criteria and integrating them into performance appraisal systems. Paradise-Tornow (1998) cites four advantages related to customer appraisal:

1. to assess individual performance and its impact from a customer's perspective;
2. to monitor the degree to which employee performance is aligned with strategic objectives throughout the organization;
3. to enable an organization to evaluate and adjust its customer-oriented, value-adding processes; and
4. to monitor and discern information about long-term customer behavior, such as loyalty and retention.

Edwards and Ewen (1996) assert that customer feedback provides valuable information to an organization, especially as input to the production process, as a presence in the quality control area, as an opportunity to increase understanding about what customers value, and as information on which to base future product development efforts. Yet, as indicated earlier, we could find no published, empirical study which specifically includes external customers as a source of information concerning the performance of their service providers. Within service industries, where provider performance is so interwoven with the content and outcome of the service itself, the inclusion of external customers in the performance appraisal network would appear to constitute a critical element—perhaps, the MOST critical element—of feedback initiatives. The use of supervisors (and/or other internal raters) as "surrogate customers" suggests that supervisors are able to assume a customer's perspective and provide valid, reliable, and useful information (Bernardin, 1992). Many decades of problems with raters, performance standards, and poorly-defined rating criteria should create a healthy level of skepticism concerning these unproven assumptions.

Although this component of our study is largely exploratory, we believe that the evidence strongly suggests that customer appraisals of the performance of individual service providers will be significantly correlated with

1. the service provider's job satisfaction;

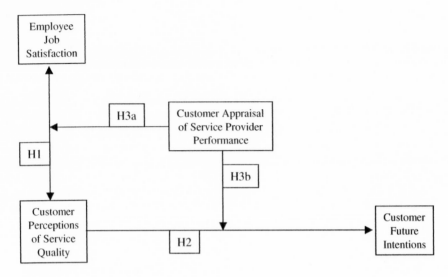

FIgure 1.   Model of Hypotheses Tested.

2. customer appraisals of service quality in general; and
3. customer behavioral intentions concerning use of the service in the future.

However, considering the focus and nature of SERVQUAL, it is expected that specific appraisal of contact worker performance by customers will account for unique variance in relationships with the outcome measures. Specifically, it is hypothesized that:

H:3. When specific customer appraisal of service providers is added to more general customer ratings of service quality (SERVQUAL), significantly more variance will be accounted for in the correlation with (a) provider job satisfaction; and (b) customer future behavioral intentions.

A model of the hypotheses being tested is illustrated in Figure 1.

METHODS

This study was conducted in a large, national organization, headquartered in the southeast US ("target organization"), which provides human resource services to "client firms" including flexible staffing, full-time placement, executive search, consulting, work force management, and outplacement. This research was conducted in the commercial staffing division which specializes in providing traditional temporary workers, predominantly in the clerical and light maintenance areas.

The level of analysis of this study was the individual temporary worker whose job-related satisfaction was measured as described below. For the purpose of this study, the "customer" was defined two ways. First, we were interested in the perceptions of the individual in the client firm who was responsible for selecting the temporary services firm that would be used when the need for contingent workers arose. This individual was asked to report his/her perceptions of the service quality provided by the target firm and their behavioral intentions concerning doing business in the future with the target firm. Second, we were interested in the assessment of the temporary worker's client firm supervisor, who was asked to provide a specific appraisal of the individual temporary worker's performance.

The 1997 version of the Job Descriptive Index (JDI) was used to gauge employee satisfaction with current work assignment (Balzer et al., 1997). The survey included the Job in General scale (Ironson, Smith, Brannick, Gibson, & Paul, 1989), as well as the following four facet scales:

1. Work on Present Job,
2. Present Pay,
3. Supervision, and
4. Co-workers.

The Opportunities for Promotion scale was excluded because it lacked meaning in this particular setting. In accordance with the authors' specifications, the JDI scales were not altered in any way and were presented on the survey in the recommended order (Balzer et al., 1997).

Customer perceptions of service quality were assessed using the 3-column version of SERVQUAL in its latest form (Parasuraman, Zeithaml, & Berry, 1994; Zeithaml, Berry, & Parasuraman, 1996). All 21 items were included in the survey and the recommended 9-point response scale was utilized (Parasuraman, Zeithaml, & Berry, 1994). Two minor modifications were made. First, all scale item references to "customers" was changed to "you", in order to eliminate confusion. For example, "Willingness to help customers" was changed to "Willingness to help you." Second, the six SERVQUAL items that referred to "employees" was each asked twice, in order to distinguish between the temporary worker and the contract representative who serviced the firm's account. For example, the item "Employees who are consistently courteous" was replaced with the following two items: "Temporary associates who are consistently courteous" and "Client Service Representatives who are consistently courteous." These alterations are consistent with those recommended by marketing services researchers when SERVQUAL is used (e.g., Carman, 1990; Parasuraman, Berry, & Zeithaml, 1991).

Customer future behavioral intentions were measured using the 13-item measure as it appeared in Zeithaml, Berry, and Parasuraman (1996).

The form to capture customer appraisal of worker performance was the only measure specifically created for this study. Designed for completion by the worker's immediate supervisor in the contracting organization, it included six performance dimensions with definitions for each. Performance was rated using a five-point scale plus a "not applicable" rating. This appraisal format was consistent with recommendations found in the general performance appraisal literature (e.g., Bernardin & Beatty, 1984; Bernardin, 2003).

Job Descriptive Index (JDI) surveys were mailed to a sample of workers that was randomly selected from the population of temporary workers who had been actively engaged in their work assignment for at least two weeks. Upon receipt of completed JDI forms, a survey package was sent to the worker's immediate supervisor at his or her current job assignment. The supervisor survey package included a performance appraisal form and a cover letter which generally explained the purpose of the study, stressed that individual confidentiality would be protected, and indicated that survey results would be provided to the temporary services firm only in aggregate form. The supervisor survey package also included the SERVQUAL instrument with an accompanying cover letter. Supervisors were asked to forward this survey package to the individual in the organization who was empowered to select the temporary services firm that would be used when such needs arose.

For hypothesis testing purposes, employee job satisfaction (Hypotheses 1, 3) was operationalized using the total score (summed) on the Job-in-General scale of the JDI. This is the recommended measure for studies focusing on overall job satisfaction (Balzer et al., 1997; Ironson et al., 1989; Smith, 1992). Due to the exploratory nature of this research, scores on each facet scale are examined in the *Results* and *Discussion* sections of this study. Customer perceptions of service quality were operationalized (Hypotheses 1, 2, 3) using the SERVQUAL "perceptions only" scores. This is the recommended approach when predictive power is the objective (Zeithaml, Berry, & Parasuraman, 1996). Scores for each dimension of service quality (Reliability, Responsiveness, Assurance, Empathy, Tangibles) were derived by averaging across the appropriate individual items. An overall service quality score was obtained by averaging (unweighted) the scores of the five dimensions. This approach conforms to the instructions of the survey's developers (Parasuraman, Zeithaml, & Berry, 1994; Zeithaml, Berry, & Parasuraman, 1996; Zeithaml, Parasuraman, & Berry, 1990). Customer future behavioral intentions (Hypotheses 2, 3) were operationalized using the summed scores on the 13-item instrument previously described. For the measure of customer appraisal of performance (Hypothesis 3), the summed scores across the six performance dimensions were utilized. This approach was supported by a factor analysis in which only one dimension emerged.

RESULTS

A total of 384 temporary workers responded to our survey by completing and returning JDI packages. In this sample, 66 percent were female and the mean age was 36.5 years. Most workers (67%) were educated beyond high school and close to half (49%) reported that they were currently working in a clerical capacity. Light industrial assignments were reported by 40 percent of the sample. The remaining work assignments (11%) involved para-professional, supervisory, or customer service positions. In terms of racial composition, most workers (62%) reported that they were white with African-Americans comprising the second largest proportion of the respondents (22%). The remaining was split among Hispanic (10%), Asian-Americans (5%), and Native Americans (1%). This sample of workers reported that they had been employed as temporary workers for an average of 13 months and had been on their current assignment for 6 months. Most (69%) indicated that they were seeking full-time employment. These returns were evaluated two ways. First, the demographic profile of the respondents was reviewed in comparison with the firm's worker population. Organization management reviewed our respondents' profile and indicated that it was very similar to the population they employed as temporary workers. Second, the demographic profile of this group was compared with the profiles reported in three other temporary worker studies recently described in the literature (Ellingson, Gruys, & Sackett, 1998; Feldman, Doerpinghaus, & Turnley, 1994; von Hippel, Greenberger, Heneman, Mangum, & Skoglind, 1997). This comparison also indicated no significant demographic differences in our sample.

Our request for SERVQUAL and performance appraisal information yielded 73 usable and complete (i.e., included both a performance appraisal and SERVQUAL) forms that were returned for analysis. Once again, we analyzed the final sample (n = 73) of survey respondents and found them to be very similar to both our larger sample of JDI respondents (n = 384), as well as to the samples described in other studies.

Hypothesis 1 predicted that employee job satisfaction, as measured by the job-in-general scale, would be correlated with positive customer perceptions of service quality. As Table 1 indicates, the correlation between a worker's satisfaction with the job-in-general and customer SERVQUAL ratings was .27 ($p \leq .01$). Thus, Hypothesis 1 was supported.

To further explore the relationships between the components of satisfaction and customer service quality perceptions, SERVQUAL scores were regressed on the four JDI facets (work, pay, supervision, and co-worker) and the global job-in-general (JIG) scale. These five worker satisfaction variables together accounted for 24 percent of the variance (R = .49; F = 4.26; $p < .01$) in customer perceptions of service quality (SERVQUAL). When the total variance was partitioned across each of the worker satisfaction variables, it is evident that significant contributions to the equation were attributable to satisfaction with co-workers (R^2 change = .12; F = 10.47; $p < .01$), followed by supervision (R^2 change = .06; F = 5.60; $p < .05$), and the job-in-general (R^2 change = .05; F = 4.63; $p < .05$).

Hypothesis 2 predicted that customer perceptions of service quality (SERVQUAL) would be correlated with customer future behavioral intentions. A regression of customer intentions on customer perceptions of service quality (SERVQUAL) indicated that the two were significantly related ($r = .71$; F = 71.26; $p < .01$), with SERVQUAL scores accounting for 50 percent of the variance in customer future intentions. Thus, Hypothesis 2 was also supported.

Hypothesis 3 posited that, when specific customer appraisal of a temporary worker's performance was added to the more general customer ratings of service quality, significantly more variance would be accounted for in the correlation with (a) temporary worker job satisfaction; and (b) customer future behavioral intentions. The first part of the hypothesis was concerned with whether specific customer performance appraisal significantly improved the correlation between customer service quality perceptions and the worker's satisfaction with the job-in-general. To test this, we converted both the customer perceptions of the service quality scores (SERVQUAL) and the specific customer performance appraisal scores into standardized (Z) scores and tested whether the sum of the two achieved significantly greater correlation with job satisfaction than was achieved by the SERVQUAL score alone. The results of this test indicated that, although the combination of SERVQUAL scores and customer performance appraisal ratings was significantly correlated with employee satisfaction with the job-in-general ($r = .32$; $p < .01$), it did not represent a statistically significant improvement over the correlation using SERVQUAL alone ($p > .05$). Thus, Hypothesis 3a was not supported.

We were also interested in the change in correlation when specific performance appraisal was added across the four JDI facet scales. The addition of customer appraisal of specific worker performance to SERVQUAL ratings improves the correlation across all the satisfaction facets, but not sufficiently to achieve statistical significance in the work ($r = .01$ for SERVQUAL alone versus $r = .11$ for SERVQUAL plus performance appraisal; $p > .05$), pay ($r = .03$ versus $r = .06$; $p > .05$) or supervision dimensions ($r = .02$ versus $r = .10$; $p > .05$). Concerning satisfaction with co-workers, the correlation improves from .39 ($p < .01$) using SERVQUAL alone to .45 ($p < .01$) when specific performance appraisal is added. Once again, however, the change is not statistically significant ($p > .05$).

To test the second part of Hypothesis 3, a multiple regression was performed using customer service quality ratings and customer specific appraisals of worker performance as the predictors, and customer future behavioral intentions as the criterion. Both predictors were entered simultaneously into a multiple regression ($R = .71$; F = 35.27; $p < .01$); together they explained 50 percent of the variance in customer future intentions.

Variance partitioning indicated that customer performance appraisal did not contribute significantly to predictive ability (R^2 change = .00; F = .14; p > .05). Thus, Hypothesis 3(b) is not supported.

DISCUSSION

This study found that individual service provider job satisfaction was significantly related to general customer perceptions of service quality, specific customer appraisal of service provider performance, and customer intentions about doing business with the firm in the future. These findings fit well with the growing body of literature which suggests that groups of customers and their service providers maintain a significant level of attitudinal congruence, or intimacy. These results extend the literature in three ways. First, both criteria (job satisfaction and customer perceptions of service quality) were measured using instruments that have been both widely used and widely researched. Second, this study extends the job satisfaction linkage beyond customer perceptions of service quality by reporting a direct, significant correlation between service provider job satisfaction and customer intentions concerning doing business with the firm in the future. Third, this study extends these findings to include the individual service encounter level involving a single service provider interacting with a single customer. These findings also fit well with previous research that meta-analytically demonstrated a satisfaction-performance linkage when performance was judged by the worker's immediate supervisor (Iaffaldano & Muchinsky, 1985; Petty, McGee, & Cavender, 1984). The results presented here extend our understanding through the use of customers, external to the organization, to whom the service was provided, as the source of evaluative information concerning performance.

We found that, although both SERVQUAL and specific customer performance appraisal were each significantly correlated with service provider satisfaction and customer future behavioral intentions, specific customer appraisal of service provider performance did not account for significant, unique variance in either relationship. SERVQUAL and the performance appraisal results were also highly intercorrelated (r = .63; p < .01). As we stated earlier, the hypothesis concerning the SERVQUAL/performance appraisal relationship was exploratory. To date, although customer performance appraisal would appear to be a key ingredient in multi-source feedback, no study has been published in the research literature concerning its value, its characteristics, or its utility. Needless to say, then, no research has focused on the overlap of such feedback with other forms of customer-generated information typically utilized within organizations.

In discussing these results, the link between employee job satisfaction and SERVQUAL/performance appraisal will be considered; then attention will be directed to the SERVQUAL/performance appraisal linkage with customer future intentions. On the basis of these findings, primary attention will be directed at explaining the overlap of the two instruments, rather than explaining their differences.

Earlier in this paper, we expressed concern that SERVQUAL contained no explicit dimension to measure quality of service provider performance as perceived and experienced by the customer. Yet, our results suggest that SERVQUAL is indeed capturing some element relating to performance. It has also been argued that as the nature of a service increases in intangibility, heterogeneity, and inseparability, the performance of the service provider would become increasingly integrated with the customer perceptions about the quality of the services that were received (Bitner, Booms, & Mohr, 1994; Gronroos, 1982; Schneider & Bowen, 1985; Zeithaml, Berry, & Parasuraman, 1988). The provision of traditional temporary services is an extremely intangible, heterogeneous, and inseparable service that is strongly contingent on personal performance. Other than the prices charged and the convenience of contacting the firm, there is little else to evaluate about the service other than the attributes and performance of the workers provided by the firm. Based on the above, it is possible that SERVQUAL successfully captures service provider performance because the performance of the individual worker (from the customer's viewpoint) is the crux of the service.

However, other explanations warrant serious consideration. The conditions under which the customers completed the surveys are unknown. Due to record-keeping problems on the part of the temporary services firm, it was necessary to transmit SERVQUAL to the work supervisor and request that it be passed on to the individual within the organization who was empowered to make the decision about which temporary services firm would be used. This introduced the possibility that the same individual might have completed both the SERVQUAL instrument and the performance appraisal. In order to learn the answer to this, the surveys were re-examined to ascertain the degree of respondent overlap. This analysis revealed that, of the 73 cases included in this study, both surveys were completed by the same individual in 19 cases (26% of the sample). Surveys were completed by different individuals in 45 cases (62% of sample). In 9 cases (12%), we were not able to tell due to lack of signature on at least one of the two surveys. Thus, the fact that both surveys were completed by the same individual in some cases could explain why performance appraisal did not uniquely contribute.

Similarly, in those cases in which the surveys were completed by different individuals, the two customers (i.e., the "work supervisor" and the "decision-maker") might have completed them together discussing their responses in some detail. This explanation suggests that the SERVQUAL/performance appraisal overlap was influenced by the limitations of our research design or by the dynamics present in the research setting, rather than by the characteristics of either instrument on its own.

Why didn't specific customer appraisal explain unique variance concerning customer future intentions? Some of the above may also apply to this relationship. Two additional explanations are offered. First, the customer behavioral intentions battery was part of the SERVQUAL survey. Even though Table 1 indicates that customer future intentions are significantly correlated with the customer performance appraisal ($r = .59$; $p < .01$), the fact that the intentions survey was completed right after an individual responded to the SERVQUAL items may have left little opportunity for the performance appraisal to contribute significantly to predictive power. Second, previous researchers have argued that the relationship between quality perceptions and future customer behavioral intentions will become stronger as services become more intangible, heterogeneous, and inseparable (Parasuraman, Zeithaml, & Berry, 1994; Zeithaml, Berry, & Parasuraman, 1996). In this case, due to the nature of the service workers under study, there may have been a "crowding out" effect such that the performance appraisal instrument had relatively little opportunity to significantly influence predictive power.

The fact that customer appraisal of specific service provider performance did not add significant predictive or explanatory power beyond that provided by SERVQUAL does not mean that customer performance appraisal lacks value. If the purpose of feedback is to inform future planning and decision-making, then the question: "*Which* of these tools provides *better* information for those purposes?" must be considered. In this particular sample, customer performance appraisal and customer perceptions of service quality were each significantly associated with employee job satisfaction and with customer future intentions. If an organization achieves competitive advantage on the basis of its workforce competencies, performance appraisal might more specifically identify individual developmental gaps and might more efficiently steer an organization's investment in programs targeted at training or upgrading worker skills. Similarly, organizations that wish to structure reward programs to specifically recognize individuals for providing service excellence to customers would probably find the individual specificity of performance appraisal more valuable than the more generic SERVQUAL.

In this particular setting, it is believed that both instruments were valuable. SERVQUAL was aimed at the individual in the organization who was empowered to make the choice of the temporary services firm that would be used when such needs arose. As such, the instrument probably captured a cumulative effect. This individual's assessment of service quality is important to the organization that is interested in repeat business, positive word of mouth communications, and customers' extending service utilization. By contrast, performance appraisal requested the specific experience of a particular supervisor with regard to an individual worker. As such, it was more transaction-specific. If individual performance is the major part of the service offered in this industry, one might hope that these two users (the "work supervisor" and the "decision-maker") would communicate regularly with one another, and that the choices made by a decision-maker would be strongly influenced by the reports of direct work supervisors about individual performance quality.

Future research efforts should be directed at exploring and determining under what conditions these relationships occur as they do here. We have noted the lack of management research that is focused on customer issues in general. We have also suggested that greater degrees of intangibility, heterogeneity, and inseparability in the nature of a service could increase the degree of integration of service provider performance with performance content from the customer's point of view. In a similar vein, Lengnick-Hall (1996) suggests that customers have varying feelings about service quality based on the fundamental importance of a particular service to the individual. She suggests that providers of customized services (e.g., health care providers and beauticians) that influence our sense of well-being or self-esteem, are "high involvement" services, as opposed to other types of services (e.g., trash collection or valet parking services). This would be an interesting avenue of inquiry, particularly as it relates to the opportunity of service providers and their behaviors to fundamentally influence the success of the firm.

Second, this study found a very strong correlation between satisfaction with co-workers, customer perceptions of service quality, customer appraisal of specific service provider performance, and customer future intentions. This finding was unexpected. Management research has focused very little on quantifying the value of the social elements involved in lateral, on-the-job relationships. This is a bit surprising given the interest among US organizations in team-oriented work processes. A better understanding of what is operating here could have implications for recruitment and selection practices, organizational entry programs, recognition, and reward programs.

Third, research needs to be directed at whether customer future behavioral intentions are, in fact, linked with their actual behavior. The lack of empirical evidence that customers actually behave as they previously reported that they intended to behave means that this entire line of inquiry continues to be unlinked to actual business results. It is difficult to believe that organizational investment in service quality or customer satisfaction initiatives would continue indefinitely on the basis of faith or anecdotal evidence alone (Mittal & Kamakura, 2001).

Fourth, the area of customer appraisal would appear to be an important, valuable avenue for research inquiry. Popular treatments of the subject typically suggest that the customer's evaluation is the ultimate criterion of performance. But little effort has been made in the human resource field to understand the interactive nature of the customer-service provider transaction and the mental models customers use to mold their expectations and to evaluate their actual experiences. Current research about multi-rater appraisal appears to be much more concerned with internal stakeholders than it is with external customers. Perhaps it is more convenient to conduct research within an organization. Perhaps firm managers are reluctant to permit access to customers for research purposes. Whatever the reason, when individual performance forms a critical component of service content, ignoring customer evaluation creates a sizable gap in our understanding of the nature and scope of the actual contribution made by individual workers to the success of the organization.

REFERENCES

Anderson, E. W., Fornell, C. & Lehmann, D. R. (1994). Customer satisfaction, market share, and profitability: Findings from Sweden. *Journal of Marketing, 8*(7), 53–66.

Baier, D. E. (1947). Note on "A review of leadership studies with particular reference to military problems. *Psychological Bulletin, 44,* 466–467.

Balzer, W. K., Kihm, J. A., Smith, P.C., Irwin, J. L., Bachiochi, P. D., Robie, C., Sinar, E. F., & Parra, L. F. (1997). *Users' manual for the Job Descriptive Index (JDI; 1997 revision) and the Job-in-General scales.* Bowling Green, OH: Bowling Green State University.

Bass, B. M. (1990). *Bass & Stodgill's handbook of leadership: Theory, research and managerial applications,* (3rd Ed.). New York: Free Press.

Bateman, T. S., & Organ, D. W. (1983). Job satisfaction and the good soldier: The relationship between affect and employee "citizenship". *Academy of Management Journal, 26,* 587–595.

Bernardin, H. J. (1992). An 'analytic' framework for customer-based performance content development and appraisal. *Human Resource Management Review, 2,* 81-102.

Bernardin, H. J., (2003). *Human resource management: An experiential approach.* New York: Irwin McGraw-Hill.

Bernardin, H. J., & Beatty, R. W. (1984). *Performance appraisal: Assessing human behavior at work.* Boston: Kent.

Bernardin, H. J., & Beatty, R. W. (1987). Can subordinate appraisals enhance managerial productivity? *Sloan Management Review, 28*(4), 63-73.

Bernardin, H. J., Hagan, C. M., Kane, J. S., & Villanova, P. (1998). Effective performance management: A focus on precision, customers and situational constraints. In J. W. Smither (Ed.), *Performance appraisal: State of the art in practice.* (pp. 3-48). San Francisco: Jossey-Bass.

Berry, L. L., & Parasuraman, A. (1991). *Marketing services: Competing through quality.* New York: The Free Press.

Bitner, M. J. (1990). Evaluating service encounters: The effects of physical surroundings and employee responses. *Journal of Marketing, 54*(4), 69-82.

Bitner, M. J. (1992). Servicescapes: The impact of physical surroundings on customers and employees. *Journal of Marketing, 56*(4), 57-71.

Bitner, M. J., Booms, B. H, & Mohr, L. A. (1994). Critical service encounters: The employee's point of view. *Journal of Marketing, 58*(10), 95-106.

Bitner, M. J., & Hubbert, A. R. (1994). Encounter satisfaction versus overall satisfaction versus quality: The customer's voice. In R. T. Rust & R. L. Oliver (Eds.), *Service quality: New directions in theory and practice* (pp. 72-94). Thousand Oaks, CA: Sage.

Borman, W. C. (1991). Job behavior, performance, and effectiveness. In M.D. Dunnette & I. Hough (Eds.), *Handbook of industrial and organizational psychology* (2nd Ed,. Vol. 2, pp. 271-326). Paolo Alto, CA: Consulting Psychologists Press.

Borman, W. C. (1997). 360 degree ratings: An analysis of assumptions and a research agenda for evaluating their validity. *Human Resource Management Review, 7*, 299-316.

Boulding, W., Kalra, A., Staelin, R., & Zeithaml, V. A. (1993). A dynamic process of service quality: From expectations to behavioral intentions. *Journal of Marketing Research, 30*, 7-27.

Bowen, D. E., & Hallowell, R. (2002). Suppose we took service seriously? An introduction to the special issue. *Academy of Management Executive, 16*(4), 69-72.

Burke, M. J., Borucki, C. C., & Hurley, A. E. (1992). Reconceptualizing psychological climate in a retail service environment: A multiple-stakeholder perspective. *Journal of Applied Psychology, 77*, 717-729.

Cardy, R.L. (1998). Performance appraisal in a quality context: A new look at an old problem. In J. W. Smither (Ed.), *Performance appraisal: State of the art in practice.* (pp. 132-162). San Francisco: Jossey-Bass.

Cardy, R. L., & Dobbins, G. H. (1994). *Performance appraisal: Alternate perspectives.* Cincinnati, OH: South-Western.

Carman, J. W. (1990). Consumer perceptions of service quality: An assessment of the SERVQUAL dimensions. *Journal of Retailing, 66*, 33-55.

Church, A. H., & Bracken, D. W. (1997). Advancing the state of the art of 360-degree feedback. *Group & Organization Management, 22*, 149-161.

Cronin, J. J., & Taylor, S. A. (1992). Measuring service quality: A reexamination and extension. *Journal of Marketing, 56*(7), 55-68.

Dalessio, A. T. (1998). Using multisource feedback for employee development and personnel decisions. In J. W. Smither (Ed.), *Performance appraisal: State of the art in practice.* (pp. 278-331). San Francisco: Jossey-Bass.

Edwards, M. R., & Ewen, A. J. (1996). *360-degree feedback: The powerful new model for employee assessment and performance improvement.* New York: AMACOM.

Ellingson, J. E., Gruys, M. L., & Sackett, P. R. (1998). Factors related to the satisfaction and performance of temporary employees. *Journal of Applied Psychology, 83*, 913-921.

Facteau, J. D., & Graig, S. B. (2001). Are performance appraisal ratings from different rating sources comparable? *Journal of Applied Psychology, 86*, 215-277.

Feldman, D. C., Doerpinghaus, H. I., & Turnley, W. H. (1994). Managing temporary workers: A permanent HRM challenge. *Organizational Dynamics, 23*, 49-63.

Gronroos, C. (1982). *Strategic management and marketing in the service sector.* Cambridge, MA: Marketing Science Institute.

Gutek, B. A., Groth, M., & Cherry, B. (2002). Achieving service success through relationships and enhanced encounters. *Academy of Management Executive, 16*(4), 132-144.

Haggerty, H. R., Johnson, C. C., & King, S. H. (1954). Evaluation of ratings on combat performance of officers, obtained by mail. *American Psychologist, 9*, 388 (abstract).

Iaffaldano, M. T., & Muchinsky, P. M. (1985). Job satisfaction and job performance: A meta-analysis. *Psychological Bulletin, 97,* 251-273.

Ironson, G. H., Smith, P. C., Brannick, M. T., Gibson, W. M., & Paul, K. B. (1989). Construction of a "Job in General" scale: A comparison of global, composite, and specific measures. *Journal of Applied Psychology, 78,* 753-762.

Johnson, J. W. (1996). Linking employee perceptions of service climate to customer satisfaction. *Personnel Psychology, 49,* 831-851.

Katzell, R. A., & Guzzo, R. A., (1983). Psychological approaches to productivity improvement. *American Psychologist, 38,* 468-472.

Katzell, R. A., Thompson, D. E., & Guzzo, R. E. (1992). How job satisfaction and job performance are and are not linked. In C. J. Cranny, P. C. Smith, & E. F. Stone (Eds.), *Job satisfaction: How people feel about their jobs and how it affects their performance* (pp. 195-218). New York: Lexington.

Kohli, A. K., & Jaworski, B. J. (1990). Market orientation: The construct, research propositions, and managerial implications. *Journal of Marketing, 54*(4), 1-18.

Latham, G. P., & Wexley, K. N. (1981). *Increasing productivity through performance appraisal.* Reading, MA: Addison-Wesley.

Lawler, E. E., & Porter, L. W. (1967). The effects of performance on job satisfaction. *Industrial Relations, 7,* 20-28.

Lemon, K. N., White, T. B., & Winer, R. S. (2002). Dynamic customer relationship management: Incorporating future considerations into the service retention decision. *Journal of Marketing, 66,* 1-14.

Lengnick-Hall, C. A. (1996). Customer contributions to quality: A different view of the customer-oriented firm. *Academy of Management Review, 21,* 791-824.

Leong, F. T. L., & Vaux, A. (1992). Job Descriptive Index. In Daniel J. Keyser & Richard C. Sweetland (Eds.), *Test critiques* (vol. 9, pp 319-334). Austin, TX: Pro-Ed.

London, M. & Beatty, R. W. (1993). 360-degree feedback as a competitive advantage. *Human Resource Management, 32,* 353-372.

Malos, S. B. (1998). Current legal issues in performance appraisal. In J. W. Smither (Ed.), *Performance appraisal: State of the art in practice.* (pp. 49-94). San Francisco: Jossey-Bass.

McChrystal, E. L., Steelman, L. S. (2003). *An exploratory customer rating study.* Paper presented at the annual meeting of the Society for industrial-Organizational Psychologists (SIOP), Orlando, FL.

Mittal, V., & Kamakura, W. A. (2001). Satisfaction, repurchase intent, and repurchase behavior: Investigating the moderating effect of customer characteristics. *Journal of Marketing, 38,* 131-142.

Murphy, K. R., & Cleveland, J. (1995). *Understanding performance appraisal: Social, organizational, and goal-based perspectives.* Thousand Oaks, CA: Sage.

Organ, D. W. (1977). A reappraisal and reinterpretation of the satisfaction-causes-performance hypothesis. *Academy of Management Review, 2,* 46–53.

Paradise-Tornow, C. A., (1998). The competitive advantage of customer involvement in 360-degree feedback. In W. W. Tornow & M. London, *Maximizing the value of 360-degree feedback: A process for successful individual and organizational development* (pp. 101-119). San Francisco: Jossey-Bass.

Parasuraman, A., Berry, L. L., & Zeithaml, V. A. (1991). Refinement and reassessment of the SERVQUAL scale. *Journal of retailing, 67,* 420-450.

Parasuraman, A., Zeithaml, V. A., & Berry, L. L. (1985). A conceptual model of service quality and its implications for future research. *Journal of Marketing, 49*(9). 41-50.

Parasuraman, A., Zeithaml, V. A., & Berry, L. L. (1988). SERVQUAL: A multiple-item scale for measuring consumer perceptions of service quality. *Journal of Retailing, 64*, 12-39.

Parasuraman, A., Zeithaml, V. A., & Berry, L. L. (1994). Alternative scales for measuring service quality: A comparative assessment based on psychometric and diagnostic criteria. *Journal of Retailing, 70*, 201-230.

Parkington, J. J., & Schneider, B. (1979). Some correlates of experienced job stress: A boundary role study. *Academy of Management Journal, 22*, 270-281.

Petty, M. M., McGee, G. W., & Cavender, J. W. (1984). A meta-analysis of the relationships between individual job satisfaction and individual performance. *Academy of Management Review, 9*, 712-721.

Pugh, S. D. (2001). Service with a smile: Emotional contagion in the service encounter. *Academy of Management Journal, 55*, 1018-1027.

Pugh, S. D., Dietz, J., Wiley, J. W., & Brooks, S. M. (2002). Driving service effectiveness through employee-customer linkages. *Academy of Management Executive, 16*(4), 73-84.

Rucci, A. J., Kim, S. P., & Quinn, R. T. (1998). The employee-customer profit chain at Sears. *Harvard Business Review, 76*(1), 82-97.

Rust, R. T., & Oliver, R. L. (1994). Service quality: Insights and managerial implications from the frontier. In R. T. Rust & R. L. Oliver (Eds.), *Service quality: New directions in theory and practice* (pp. 1-20). Thousand Oaks, CA: Sage.

Ryan, A. M., Schmit, M. J., & Johnson, R. (1996). Attitudes and effectiveness: Examining relations at an organizational level. *Personnel Psychology, 49*, 853 –882.

Schmit, M. J., & Allscheid, S. P. (1995). Employee attitudes and customer satisfaction: Making theoretical and empirical connections. *Personnel Psychology, 48*, 521-536.

Schneider, B., & Bowen, D. E. (1985). Employee and customer perceptions of service in banks: Relication and extension, *Journal of Applied Psychology, 70*, 423-433.

Schneider, B., & Bowen, D. E. (1995). *Winning the service game.* Boston: Harvard.

Schneider, B., Parkington, J. J., & Buxton, V. M. (1980). Employee and customer perceptions of service in banks. *Administrative Science Quarterly, 24*, 252-267.

Schneider, B., Wheeler, J. K., & Cox, J. F. (1992). A passion for service: Using content analysis to explicate service climate themes. *Journal of Applied Psychology, 77*, 705-516.

Schwab, D. P. & Cummings, L. L. (1970). Theories of performance and satisfaction: A review. *Industrial Relations, 9*, 408-430.

Singh, J. (2000). Performance productivity and quality of frontline employees in service organizations. *Journal of Marketing, 64*(2). 15-34.

Smith, P. C. (1992). In pursuit of happiness. Why study general job satisfaction? In C. J. Cranny, P. C. Smith, & E. F. Stone (Eds.), *Job satisfaction: How people feel about their jobs and how it affects their performance* (pp. 5-20). New York: Lexington.

Susskind, A. M., Kacmar, K. M, & Borchgrevink, C. P. (2003). Customer service providers' attitudes relating to customer service and customer satisfaction in the customer-server exchange. *Journal of Applied Psychology, 88*, 179-187.

Taylor, S. A., & Baker, T. L., (1994). An assessment of the relationship between service quality and customer satisfaction in the formation of consumers' purchase intentions. *Journal of Retailing, 70,* 163-178.

Tornow, W. W. (1993). Perceptions or reality: Is multi-perspective measurement a means or an end? *Human Resource Management, 32,* 249-263.

Treacy, M. & Wiersema, F. (1993). Customer intimacy and other value disciplines. *Harvard Business Review, 71,* 84-93.

Triandis, H. C. (1959). A critique and experimental design for the study of the relationship between productivity and job satisfaction. *Psychological Bulletin, 56,* 309-312.

Ulrich, D. (1992). Strategic and human resource planning: Linking customers and employees. *Human Resource Planning , 15*(2), 47-62.

Villanova, P. (1992). A customer-based model for developing job performance criteria. *Human Resource Management Review, 2,* 103-114.

Von Hippel, C., Mangum, S. L., Greenberger, D. B., Heneman, R. L., & Skoglind, J. D. (1997). Temporary employment: Can organizations and employees both win? *Academy of Management Executive, 11,* 93-104.

Vroom, V. H. (1964). *Work and Motivation.* New York: Wiley.

Waldman, D. A. (1994). The contributions of total quality management to a theory of work performance. *Academy of Management Review, 19,* 510-536.

Waldman, D. A., Atwater, L. E., & Antonioni, D. (1998). Has 360 degree feedback gone amok? *Academy of Management Executive, 12,* 86-94.

Wohlers, A. J., & London, M. (1989). Ratings of managerial characteristics: Evaluation difficulty, co-worker agreement, and self-awareness. *Personnel Psychology, 42,* 235-261.

Yammarino, F. J., & Atwater, L. E. (1993). Understanding self perception accuracy: Implications for human resource management. *Human Resource Management, 32,* 231-247.

Zeithaml, V. A. (1988). Consumer perceptions of price, quality , and value: A means-end model and synthesis of evidence. *Journal of Marketing, 52*(7), 2-22.

Zeithaml, V. A., Berry, L. L., & Parasuraman, A. (1988). Communication and control processes in the delivery of service quality. *Journal of Marketing, 52*(4), 35-48.

Zeithaml, V. A., Berry, L. L., & Parasuraman, A. (1996). The behavioral consequences of service quality. *Journal of Marketing, 60*(4), 31-46.

Zeithaml, V. A., Parasuraman, A., & Berry, L. L. (1990). *Delivering quality service: Balancing customer perceptions and expectations.* New York: Free Press.

CHAPTER 2

ACCOUNTABILITY IN HUMAN RESOURCES MANAGEMENT

Angela T. Hall
Florida State University
Dwight D. Frink
University of Mississippi
Gerald R. Ferris, Wayne A. Hochwarter, Charles J. Kacmar
Florida State University
Michael G. Bowen
University of South Florida

ABSTRACT

Accountability is an inherent characteristic of organizations, yet it only seems to be of interest when it is abused or when lapses in accountability occur. Interestingly, significant aspects of accountability manifest themselves in key human resources management systems, but there have been few attempts to systematically model and discuss the implications of accountability for the reactions of employees operating within these domains. The present chapter presents a theoretical model of accountability in human resources systems, and then reports empirical results demonstrating support for antecedents and consequences of accountability. Implications of these conceptual and empirical findings, directions for future research, and suggestions for practice are proposed.

New Directions in Human Resource Management
A Volume in: Research in Management, pages 29–63.
Copyright © 2003 by Information Age Publishing, Inc.
All rights of reproduction in any form reserved.
ISBN: 1-59311-099-5 (hardcover), 1-59311-098-7 (pbk.)

BACKGROUND

Accountability, as a mechanism for establishing mutual obligation, represents the foundation for virtually all employer-employee relationships. Employers are accountable to employees in that they have an obligation for providing a safe work environment, resources to maximize performance, and most importantly, compensation. On the other hand, employee accountability is calculated in terms of positive behaviors that contribute to the success of the organization. The popular press has paid considerable attention to organizational accountability. In general, this discussion centered on the indiscretions of those who have intentionally manipulated or disregarded the obligations that surface when one is held accountable to others. Conversely, academic research investigating accountability processes in organizations (i.e., its antecedents and consequences) is vastly underrepresented in the scholarly literature despite its obvious importance. Because much of what constitutes accountability is manifested through important human resources management systems (HRMS), it is incumbent upon scholars to develop a more informed understanding of precisely how accountability is influenced by these systems and, in turn, how accountability affects critical work outcomes.

This chapter attempts to contribute to the existing body of knowledge by examining the importance of accountability in human resources management systems. This chapter unfolds in the following way. First, relevant theory is examined as a precursor to the introduction of a comprehensive definition of individual-level accountability in organizations. Second, the importance of accountability in HRMS is discussed. Third, a process model is presented that explores the relationship between accountability antecedents and consequences, and traditional human resource management activities (i.e., performance appraisal, compensation, etc.). Fourth, the results of an empirical study that examined many of the linkages in the proposed model are provided, as well as implications of these findings for theoretical development. Fifth, avenues for subsequent inquiry are offered, as well as implications for practice.

Individual-Level Accountability in Organizations: Toward Definitional Clarity

Individual-Level Accountability

Accountability is an important phenomenon. Specifically, accountability is the basic principle upon which societies, and the organizations within them, rests. Social systems, regardless of their size, are fundamentally comprised of sets of shared expectations for behavior. Often these behavioral norms are codified. More often, however, such norms for behavior are socially understood. Accountability has been described as "the adhesive that binds social systems together" (Frink & Klimoski, 1998, p. 3). That is, if individuals were not answerable for their behavior, there would be neither shared expectations nor a basis for them, and it would be impossible to maintain any form of social system (Frink & Klimoski, 1998; Tetlock, 1985).

Despite its importance to understanding individual behavior, theory and empirical research on accountability at the individual level is still in its nascent development. Moreover, the majority of the body of accountability research resides mainly in the social psychology literature, and is based largely on the work of only a few scholars, chief among them is Tetlock (1985, 1992), who proposed the social contingency model of accountability. Specifically, Tetlock (1985, 1992) argued that accountability is the fundamental social contingency driving individuals' behaviors and decisions. Because individuals are concerned about their image and status, accountability represents an expectation of a potential evaluation. Consequently, individuals position themselves to defend their decisions or actions, should they be subjected to an evaluation.

Furthermore, Tetlock (1985, 1992) was a proponent of what has been labeled the phenomenological view of accountability (Frink & Klimoski, 1998). Under this view, accountability is seen as a state of mind, rather than as a state of affairs. The phenomenological approach acknowledges that objective, external conditions are important because individuals use these objective conditions to form their subjective assessments of accountability. Nevertheless, one's subjective interpretations of these objective conditions typically are more important than the actual conditions themselves, because these subjective interpretations of reality are what drive individual behavior and attitudes (Lewin, 1936).

Other important work on accountability at the individual level has been developed by Schlenker and colleagues (e.g., Schlenker, Britt, Pennington, Murphy, & Doherty, 1994), who proposed the pyramid model of accountability. An important contribution of the pyramid model of accountability is the distinction made between accountability and responsibility. Specifically, responsibility, which can connote causality or a sense of duty, is conceptualized as being distinct from accountability, yet a "necessary component of the process of holding people accountable for their conduct" (Schlenker et al., 1994, p. 634).

Individual-Level Accountability in Organizations

If research on individual-level accountability in general is in its infancy, research on individual-level accountability in organizations is in its embryonic stage. To date, only a few conceptualizations of individual accountability in organizations have been offered. Arguably, the most influential model of accountability in organizations to date is that of Cummings and

Anton (1990), who offered a model of the accountability process that included key elements, such as rewards (or punishment) and individual expectancies. However, it is important to note although this conceptualization has been labeled to be a model of accountability in organizations, its components are general (e.g., "rewards" and "punishments"), and do not really tap into key constructs that are unique to organizations, such as human resources management systems.

Ferris, Mitchell, Canavan, Frink, and Hopper (1995) set out a general framework that serves to outline accountability in HRM. They proposed notable HRM functions that are especially relevant as accountability mechanisms, including staffing, performance evaluations, compensation, and outflow management. They also related specific theories to accountability, including agency theory (Eisenhardt, 1985) and control theory (Ouchi & Macguire, 1975). In addition, they proposed a series of ambiguities embedded in accountability perceptions and systems. Their model outlined causes, cognitive processing, attributions, and consequences related to perceptions of accountability in HRM systems.

Another very limited model of accountability in organizations was offered by Ferris, Dulebohn, Frink, George-Falvy, Mitchell, and Matthews (1997) in which four variables were explored:

1.   job characteristics (operationalized as job ambiguity),
2.   organizational characteristics (operationalized as hierarchical level),
3.   accountability, and
3.   influence tactics.

Apart from the work of the above scholars, there have been few attempts to understand the accountability process in organizations.

Defining Accountability

There are two distinct vantage points to viewing or understanding accountability. One is the common notion of accountability as an objective set of reporting rules or protocols that are imposed on some individual or entity. The second is that, because individuals respond to their subjective perceptions rather than "objective" realities, it is these individualized perceptions of accountability, or *felt accountability* that, in the end, drive decisions and actions. This duality compels using a framework that accommodates the development of both these objective and subjective factors.

Definitions of Accountability.

Definitions of accountability permeate the literature. For example, Lerner and Tetlock (1999) defined accountability as "the implicit or explicit expectation that one may be called on to justify one's beliefs, feelings, and actions to others" (p. 255). This definition is similar to others that have been offered in the social psychology field in that it emphasizes the centrality of the evaluation expectation to the construct of accountability.

Ferris et al. (1995) defined accountability as "the extent to which a person's behaviors are observed and evaluated by others, with important rewards and punishments contingent upon those evaluations" (p. 187). This definition was one of the first that addressed accountability in the organizational context, and it provided a framework for future research (e.g., Ferris et al., 1997). Nevertheless, this definition does not tap into the underlying psychological mechanisms associated with accountability.

More recently, as an attempt to address individual-level accountability within the organizational context, Frink and Klimoski (1998) offered another definition of accountability:

> the perceived need to justify or defend a decision or action to some audience which has potential reward and sanction power, and where such rewards and sanctions are perceived as contingent on accountability conditions (p. 9).

This definition captures several distinct aspects of individual-level accountability in organizations, including: the perceptual nature of accountability (however, perception is based on an "objective" reality), internal and external rewards and sanctions, multiple audiences, including self, and the social context of accountability. To date, this definition has been the only one to capture these major factors of individual accountability in the workplace.

Building on the work of Tetlock (1985, 1992), Ferris et al. (1995), and Lerner and Tetlock (1999), this chapter proposes the following definition of felt accountability in organizations:

> Felt accountability refers to an implicit or explicit expectation that one's decisions or actions will be subject to evaluation by some salient audience(s) with the belief that there exists the potential for one to receive either rewards or sanctions based on this expected evaluation.

IMPORTANCE OF ACCOUNTABILITY IN HUMAN RESOURCES MANAGEMENT SYSTEMS

Formal Accountability Mechanisms

Through the use of human resources management systems (HRMS), an organization manages and monitors the behaviors of its employees. As such, HRMS are an important control mechanism (Eisenhardt, 1985;

Ouchi & Macguire, 1975) for organizations that ultimately can have a significant effect on effectiveness and performance (Ferris et al., 1995). Traditionally, accountability in HRM has connoted formal accountability mechanisms, such as staffing, performance evaluation, and compensation. The importance of "formal accountability" mechanisms for these functions is outlined below.

Staffing Systems

Staffing systems are important to organizations, as they are the means by which organizations recruit, select, and promote employees. Scholars have emphasized the importance for organizational fit (Schneider, 1987) when making staffing decisions, and this is the perspective that is taken by most organizations. Although organizational fit should be a consideration in hiring decisions, hiring for this basis alone can result in dysfunctional outcomes when the decision makers are not held accountable to justify their decisions on the basis of job requisite criteria for selection or promotion decisions (Frink & Ferris, 1996).

Specifically, making staffing decisions largely on the basis of fit subjects the hiring process to the effects of the political behaviors of both decision makers and job incumbents/applicants. For example, using an argument that they are hiring based on fit, managers might hire certain individuals for the purpose of coalition building (Ferris & King, 1991). Additionally, staffing decisions can be influenced by job incumbents who use influence tactics to shape the impressions decision makers form of them and their job qualifications (Howard & Ferris, 1996). Thus, job incumbents who are highly politically skilled (Ferris, Perrewé, Anthony, & Gilmore, 2000) might attempt to convince decision makers that they have skills they actually do not possess or they might engage in ingratiation or other impression management tactics in order for the decision maker to hire them based on liking or perceived similarity, rather than on credentials.

The presence of formal accountability mechanisms within HRMS, such as objective job qualifications and evaluations of the hiring decisions made by decision makers, should decrease the influence of the above-described political behaviors on the staffing process. Moreover, such formal accountability mechanisms should help neutralize the dysfunctional effects of other biases (such as a personal bias against a member of a certain demographic group).

Performance Evaluation Systems

Performance appraisal systems consist of two key elements: defining and evaluating performance. A third, and often overlooked, element that is necessary for effective performance evaluation systems is providing feedback. Accountability can be seen as a mechanism for linking all three of these elements. Specifically, by articulating the standards by which individuals will be judged, evaluating individuals by those standards, and providing information to employees regarding their achievement of these standards, organizations can direct and monitor the behaviors of employees. Given the essential nature of employee performance to firm effectiveness, performance evaluation is a fundamental aspect of any human resources management system.

Specificity is an important criterion for a performance evaluation system. For example, a performance evaluation system should provide information on to whom one is accountable and for what one is accountable. Generally, formal accountability mechanisms can be examined in terms of *process accountability* and *outcome accountability* (Siegel-Jacobs & Yates, 1996). Briefly, process accountability refers to being held accountable for the procedures and processes an individual follows when attempting to complete a task. It also refers to the behaviors that are displayed. Alternatively, outcome accountability refers to being held accountable for the quantity and/or quality of outcomes, without regard to the procedures followed. In general, whereas a focus on outcome accountability has been found to be associated with dysfunctional decisions, an emphasis on process accountability has been linked to more positive decision behavior (Lerner & Tetlock, 1999). That is, when individuals focus on the "means" rather than on the "ends," often the quality and/or quantity of their outcomes is better than when "ends" are emphasized over "means."

An example of how outcome accountability is ordinarily associated with poor management can be extrapolated from the escalation of commitment literature (Drummond, 1996; Staw, 1976), where hiring supervisors might tend, and then continue, to give overly positive evaluations to the individuals they have hired despite their poor performance outcomes. Furthermore, although process accountability generally has been linked to positive decision making, it also can have dysfunctional outcomes. To this point, Pfeffer (1981) has suggested that individuals often are not held accountable for the outcomes of their actions, but rather for the behaviors that they display (e.g., *appearing* as though one is working hard, or, cleverly covering up the fact that sound, organizationally required, decision-making processes have been disregarded). Evaluating employees solely on such behaviors can lead to dysfunctional results if evaluators do not consider the quality (and in production-related situations, the quantity) of those outcomes, particularly over the longer term.

To help avoid such potentially dysfunctional situations, we thus argue that holding employees accountable for *both* processes and outcomes should be a key consideration as organizations attempt to develop a useful performance evaluation system (cf. Bowen, 1987).

Compensation

Compensation is considered to be one of the essential HRM functions, and it is has been the subject of considerable research attention (Gerhart

& Milkovich, 1992). Additionally, compensation can have important relevance for accountability. Indeed, it is likely that no area of accountability in HRM has received more scholarly and media attention than executive compensation (Mero & Frink, 2002). Individuals who are believed to have high levels of formal accountability often are compensated for the additional duties and responsibilities they are assumed to have. Both expectancy theory (Vroom, 1964) and equity theory (Adams, 1965) would suggest that individuals should be compensated based on their level of accountability, and that those at higher levels of the organizations should be compensated more generously than those individuals occupying lower positions. Also, these theories would suggest that CEOs should be compensated based on their performances (i.e., the performances of their firms). However, this is not always the case.

First, there are those who argue that a CEO does not have a significant impact on organizational effectiveness (Thomas, 1988). Specifically, the argument is made that industry and economic constraints limit a CEO's ability to effect significant change within an organization (Meindl, Ehrlich, & Dukerich, 1985). This is the classic strategic choice (Child, 1977) versus environmental determinism (Hannan & Freeman, 1977) argument (Hrebiniak & Joyce, 1985). However, given the fact that that CEOs are given "film star" status by the popular business press (Elliott, 2002) and the significant body of scholarly research that has examined the means through which managers can increase organizational performance, it would seem that the prevailing view is that CEOs *do* matter when it comes to firm performance, at least on the surface.

As indicated above, most scholarly discussions of accountability in organizations have centered around the issue of compensation, especially executive compensation (Mero & Frink, 2002). Nevertheless, given its impact on such factors as intent to turnover, productivity, and job satisfaction (Miceli & Lane, 1991), compensation is an issue that is pertinent to employees at all levels of the organization. Consequently, in this study, perceptions of pay and compensation practices of the organization are examined as a representative operationalization of the HRM systems variable in the model to be tested.

Informal Accountability Mechanisms

Only recently have researchers begun to pay attention to the "informal" accountability mechanisms in an organization. These are the mechanisms not found in an employee handbook, but that nevertheless influence individual behavior. Role theory (Katz & Kahn, 1978) provides an excellent conceptual framework in which to understand these informal accountability mechanisms. Specifically, role theory has suggested that individuals (role takers) can be attuned to expectations that are informally communicated to them by salient others (role senders). Under this theory, it is further hypothesized that individuals will use these perceived role expectations to shape their attitudes and guide their behavior.

CONCEPTUALIZATION OF ACCOUNTABILITY IN HUMAN RESOURCES MANAGEMENT SYSTEMS

Most HRM functions (e.g., performance evaluations, compensation, and disciplinary procedures) are mechanisms by which accountability is enacted, at least in theory, in typical organizations. Moreover, we contend that the entire domain of HRM research is well-served by an accountability framework, especially as set forth within a role theory framework (Katz & Kahn, 1978).

A model of accountability in human resources management systems is presented in Figure 1. The model examines factors (organizational, environmental, and job) that lead to the formation of HRMS, focusing specifically here on staffing, performance evaluation, and compensation systems. The model then considers how human resources systems and personal characteristics of employees affect felt accountability, which, in turn, lead to a number of important work outcomes: illegal behaviors, job tension, job satisfaction, job performance, citizenship behavior, political behavior, and job involvement. A brief explanation of the linkages in Figure 1 follows.

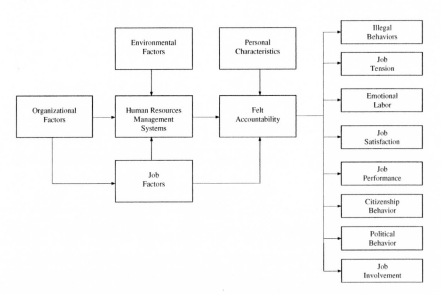

Figure 1.   Model of Accountability in Human Resource Management

Contextual Factors as Inputs to Human Resources System Development

Although sometimes overlooked in discussions of accountability in HRM, contextual concerns, such as:

1.   organizational factors (e.g., centralization),
2.   environmental factors (e.g., the legal system), and
3.   job factors (such as task significance)

have important implications for HRMS, and ultimately, the experienced or felt accountability of employees. Below, these three important contextual factors are discussed in greater detail and their importance to human resources management systems is explained.

Environmental Factors

Human resources management systems are not created in a vacuum. Rather, these systems are developed, in large part, as a result of the organization's attempt to control or respond to its external environment. Frink and Klimoski (1998) suggested that environmental factors such as industry factors and standards, professional and certifying organizations, and the legal system affect human resource management systems. For example, an organization might create a requirement for monthly safety inspections in an attempt to maintain compliance with the external factor of Occupational Safety and Health Administration (OSHA) requirements. Organizations take cues from their environment, which ultimately affect the policies and procedures they employ. Thus, these policies and procedures are argued to have an indirect influence on the level of felt accountability experienced by employees.

Organizational Factors

Organizational factors also are conceptualized to have a direct effect on the HRMS developed and utilized by the organization (Frink & Klimoski, 1998). Organizational factors that affect HRMS can be "objective" factors, such as the extent to which an organization is centralized (Ferris et al., 1997). However, organizational factors that affect human resources management systems also can be "informal" ones, in the sense that they are not found in, or dictated by, an employee handbook or other formal organizational policy or procedure. Examples of informal organizational factors include the culture and climate of the organization (Frink & Klimoski, 1998). Informal norms, for example, can affect the nature and extent to which formal human resource management systems are developed, applied, or understood.

Job Factors

In the current model, job characteristics are shown to influence felt accountability through their effects on HRMS. In job design theory (Hackman & Oldham, 1975), certain job characteristics have been delineated, including task identity, skill variety, and task significance. For example, jobs that have a high task significance, because they are critical to the core functions of the organizations, most likely will be associated with HR systems and practices that have increased formal accountability requirements. These formal accountability requirements should, in turn, influence the extent of an employee's felt accountability.

Personal Characteristics

Historically, personality research has played an important role in the organizational sciences. Moreover, within the past decade, there has been a resurgence of interest and activity in personality research (Perrewé & Spector, 2002). Some researchers (e.g., Yarnold, Mueser, & Lyons, 1988) focused on the effects of personality differences on accountability outcomes, but the research investigating any type of individual differences has been limited in the accountability area. Moreover, in the few studies that have been conducted, personality differences typically have been treated as moderators of the accountability-outcomes relationships, rather than as antecedents.

For example, Yarnold et al. (1988) found a significant Type A × accountability interaction on performance such that Type A individuals who were accountable outperformed every other group. However, it has been argued that individual differences should be conceptualized as antecedents to felt accountability (Frink & Klimoski, 1998). For example, personal characteristics such as Agreeableness (Mount & Barrick, 1995) and Conscientiousness (Frink & Ferris, 1999) have been theorized to have a significant influence on felt accountability.

Consequences of Felt Accountability

Scholars have examined only a limited number of accountability outcomes. There has been little research that has examined task performance (Motowidlo & Van Scotter, 1994) as an outcome of accountability within organizational contexts (Frink & Klimoski, 1998). Still fewer studies have examined contextual performance (Borman & Motowidlo, 1993), or citizenship, as an accountability outcome (Frink & Klimoski, 1998). In the model of accountability in HRM that is shown in Figure 1, the following accountability outcomes are addressed: illegal behaviors, job tension, emotional labor, job satisfaction, job performance, citizenship behavior, political behavior, and job involvement.

EMPIRICAL EXAMINATION OF ANTECEDENTS AND CONSEQUENCES OF FELT ACCOUNTABILITY

In the current study, several key linkages in the model proposed in Figure 1 are empirically tested. Specifically, it is contended that job competency, human resources practices, negative affect, and positive affect predict the onset of felt accountability. Furthermore, it is then hypothesized that accountability affects the outcomes of job involvement, citizenship behavior, emotional labor, and job tension. Theoretical justification for each of these relationships, found in Figure 2, is provided below. We should briefly mention that the relationship between human resource systems and felt accountability is shown in Figure 2 as negative because our measure of human resource systems is essentially reverse-scored (see below).

Antecedents of Felt Accountability

Human Resources Management Systems
Formal HR policies are essentially organizational control mechanisms that are designed to monitor employees and shape their behavior (Eisenhardt, 1985; Ouchi & Macguire, 1975). As such, HRMS systems are formal accountability mechanisms put in place by organizations ostensibly with the ultimate goal of maximizing organizational effectiveness. Role theory (Katz & Kahn, 1978) suggests that individuals are attuned to cues in the environment regarding their expected behaviors. It is argued here that these norms of behavior will be based, at least in part, on the formal, objective mechanisms that are communicated to employees by the organization.

One of the essential HRM functions is compensation. At the most basic level, compensation is the key reason that induces employees to enter into an employment relationship with an organization. Moreover, compensation has important implications for employee motivation, intent to turnover, and job satisfaction (Gerhart & Milkovich, 1992; Miceli & Lane 1991). For these reasons, compensation will be the proxy variable for HRMS in the empirical study.

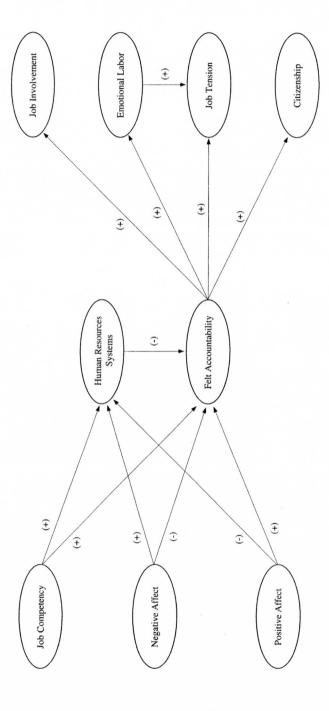

Figure 2.   Hypothesized Relationship of Antecedents and Consequences

H: 1.   There will be a significant positive relationship between human resources systems and felt accountability.

Personal Characteristics

Negative Affectivity

Negative affectivity (NA) reflects the tendency to experience a wide array of negative emotions across time and situation (George, 1992; Spector & O'Connell, 1994). Research indicates that possessing high levels of NA heightens an individual's susceptibility to adverse events at work, including an increase in perceived stressors and strains (Burke, Brief, & George, 1993; Ganster & Schaubroeck, 1991). On the basis of previous studies, researchers have concluded that NA leads to the inception of negative emotions via two mechanisms, each of which is posited to lead to avoiding responsibility at work, thus being subjected to lower levels of accountability. As such, it is argued that those individuals who are high in NA should experience lower levels of felt accountability.

H: 2.   There will be a significant negative relationship between negative affectivity and felt accountability.

Positive Affectivity

Positive affectivity (PA) refers to "the extent to which a person feels enthusiastic, active, and alert" (Watson, Clark, & Tellegen, 1988, p. 1063). Further, high PA individuals possess personality traits that are likely to be viewed positively by external constituents. For example, Judge, Thoresen, Pucik, & Welbourne (1999) suggested that high PAs possess gregariousness and affiliation, both of which should aid in the development of social relationships at work. As evidence, previous research has shown PA to correlate positively with organizational, supervisor, and co-worker support (Iverson, Olekalns, & Erwin, 1998).

Consequently, if it is perceived that individuals could call on others to help facilitate the successful completion of work tasks, they are more likely to take on additional responsibility. Watson and Clark (1984) asserted that high PAs covet change and variety, and tend to become uninterested and frustrated if change is lacking. High PAs have been shown to be more apt to seek out environments that are stimulating and challenging (Watson & Clark, 1984). Consequently, opting to take on additional responsibility fits high PAs' cognitive schema that focuses on the development of stimulating work activities. Thus, it is posited that those possessing high levels of positive affect will be more likely to perceive that they have become accountable at work.

H: 3.   There will be a significant positive relationship between positive affectivity and felt accountability.

Job Competency

White (1959) based the sense of competence (SOC) dimension of performance on the idea that individuals are psychologically predisposed to influence and control their immediate work setting. Like the key elements in job design theory (task significance, task identity, skill variety, autonomy, and feedback) (Hackman & Oldham, 1975), sense of competence taps into the subjective, perceptual nature of one's feelings regarding one's job. Sense of competence has been defined as "the set of psychological feelings of confidence an individual has about his abilities to master his external environment" (Morse, 1976, p. 1195). In addition, because an important component of accountability is the evaluation of one's efforts by external constituencies for the purpose of reward or sanction, it is reasonable to assume that individuals who feel that their efforts would receive positive appraisals would be more likely to accept greater responsibility at work, and hence feel more accountable. Conversely, if it is perceived that attributes of the job have yet to be adequately mastered, it is unlikely that judgments regarding work performance would be sought from external evaluators.

H: 4.   There will be a significant positive relationship between job competency and felt accountability.

Consequences of Felt Accountability

Job Tension

As suggested above, felt accountability involves an expectation that one will be evaluated by relevant others. Implicit in these feelings of an expected evaluation is the belief that one will be required to defend one's actions or decisions (Lerner & Tetlock, 1999). A potential evaluation of one's performance might be a cause of concern, especially for employees who believe that their performance does not meet perceived standards. Additionally, every employee is accountable to someone, either formally or informally. Moreover, every individual must balance multiple accountabilities to multiple individuals (Carnevale, 1985; Frink & Klimoski, 1998). In line with role theory (Katz & Kahn, 1978), attempts to navigate this "web of accountabilities" (Frink & Klimoski, 1998) could potentially cause role stress, role conflict, and role overload. Viewing felt accountability in this manner, it is possible to conceptualize how felt accountability could be a work environment stressor with potentially harmful strain responses, such as job anxiety.

Furthermore, those who feel more accountable are likely to take on more responsibilities at work. Previous research has suggested that additional responsibility at work can predict the development of work stress (Goldenhar, Swanson, Hurrell, Ruder, & Deddens, 1998; Lu, Kao, Cooper, & Spector, 2002; Williams & Cooper, 1998). For example, Lu et al. (2002) found that responsibility at work predicted strains for managers in the United Kingdom. Goldenhar et al. (1998) found that increased responsibility was associated with psychological symptoms of stress. Consequently, by choosing to do more at work, high accountability individuals are more likely to subject themselves to work overload.

H:5.   There will be a positive relationship between felt accountability and job tension.

Emotional Labor

Employees engage in emotional labor when they display organizationally appropriate emotions, without regard to the actual emotion they might be experiencing (Hochschild, 1979, 1983). In the proposed model, felt accountability is positively related to emotional labor. Individuals who feel accountable expect to receive an evaluation of their performance (Tetlock, 1985, 1992). Because individuals generally want to receive a positive evaluation, it is likely that they will modify their behavior in ways they believe will be acceptable to the relevant audiences (Tetlock, 1985, 1992). To receive favorable evaluations, employees are expected to employ appropriate emotional demonstrations (Schaubroeck & Jones, 2000).

Previous research has suggested that the manner in which emotions are displayed in organizations can have a strong influence on the effectiveness of interpersonal transactions, as well as the favorability of the interpersonal climate at work (Rafaeli & Sutton, 1987; Sutton, 1991; Van Maanen & Kunda, 1989). Ashforth and Humphrey (1993) suggested that the effective execution of emotions at work has the capacity to increase self-efficacy. Moreover, increased levels of efficacy can enhance the belief that individuals can execute successfully the requirements of a job. With regard to the current study, it is unlikely that the constituents with which interactions occur will view individuals favorably if their emotions are displayed ineptly.

H: 6.   There will be a positive relationship between felt accountability and emotional labor.

Citizenship Behavior

Organizational citizenship behaviors (OCBs) describe extrarole behaviors that facilitate organizational performance (Van Dyne, Graham, & Dienesch, 1994). Although such behaviors typically are not found in a formal description of job duties, they are still vital for the successful performance of a job and for the effective operation of the organization.

Despite their apparent importance with respect to the accountability construct (Frink & Klimoski, 1998), there have been surprisingly few empirical studies that have examined the relationship between contextual performance or OCBs and accountability. Moreover, this small body of research has produced seemingly conflicting arguments. It has been suggested that increased accountability is related to decreased OCBs (Frink & Klimoski, 1998; Frink, Klimoski, Hopper, Mitchell, Mera, & Motowidlo, 1995). This argument appears to be at odds with studies that have found a positive relationship between accountability and the related, yet separate, construct of prosocial behavior (Mitchell, Hopper, Daniels, George-Falvy, & Ferris, 1998). We argue that felt accountability will be positively associated with OCBs. Because employees who feel accountable expect a potential evaluation, it is conceivable that they will take steps to appear in the most positive light. Although OCBs are not formally part of an employee's formal job duties, they are still important to the operation of the organization and are often used in evaluating the performance of the employee (Borman & Motowidlo, 1993).

Thus, it seems likely that employees will use OCBs as a way to manage impressions of their performance, when they deem that an important evaluation is likely (Bolino, 1999; Ferris, Bhawuk, Fedor, & Judge, 1995). High accountability individuals are likely to participate in OCBs because doing so is likely to increase the positive opinions of important constituents.

H: 7.   There will be a positive relationship between felt accountability and organizational citizenship behaviors.

Job Involvement

Job involvement has been described as a psychological identification with one's job (Kanungo, 1982; Lodahl & Kejner, 1965). Research has suggested that job involvement reflects a level of engagement with one's present job including a focus on the successful completion of specific work tasks (Keller, 1997). Because those held accountable assume their job activities will be closely scrutinized and potentially questioned (Ferris et al., 1995), it is presumable that they would make an attempt to maximize their contribution at work.

Past research has suggested that high involvement individuals are committed employees who are highly devoted to their work and sensitive to the changes that occur on the job (Kahn, 1990). These attributes provide clear evidence that job involvement should have the capacity to predict performance, a result that has been substantiated in previous research (Diefendorff, Brown, Kamin, & Lord, 2002; Keller, 1997). In sum, because involved individuals are likely to exert more time commitment and work intensity on the job (Brown & Leigh, 1996), they are more likely to assume that their work-related activities will be viewed favorably by those responsible for making such judgments.

H:8.   There will be a positive relationship between felt accountability and job involvement.

Alternative Relations Contained in the Model

To gain the most accurate depiction of relationships among study variables, additional linkages were examined. These relationships are shown in Figure 3. Each of these additional linkages is briefly described.

We expect a positive association between NA and emotional labor. Research has suggested that high NAs possess an overall negative view of themselves (Watson & Clark, 1984). Furthermore, high NAs tend to be more nervous and interpersonally incompetent (Watson & Tellegen, 1985), relative to their low NA counterparts. For these reasons, it is unlikely that high NAs would possess the skill or confidence needed to display the appropriate emotions at work.

Previous research has substantiated relationships between affective disposition and job tension (George, 1992; Watson & Pennebaker, 1989). It has been suggested that high NAs possess the dispositional underpinnings to experience negative affective states, whereas high PAs experience positive ones. Building on this theoretical work, research has shown NA to directly predict distress (Brief, Burke, George, Robinson, & Webster, 1988; Watson & Clark, 1984). Additionally, we expect there to be a negative association between NA and job involvement and citizenship.

As discussed below, the variable used to measure HRMS actually assesses the lack (or disregard) of formal accountability mechanisms in the workplace. Because those who are high in NA tend to view the world negatively, it is expected that there will be a positive association between NA and HRMS. Additionally, because those high in job competency might be more attuned to the performance standards and attendant rewards in the workplace, it is expected that there will be a positive relationship between job competency and the HRMS variable.

We also expect that PA will exhibit direct associations with job involvement, emotional labor, job tension, citizenship behaviors, and HRMS. Because past research has shown those with high positive affect to be more dedicated to the job (Allen, Freeman, Russell, Reizenstein, & Rentz, 2001; Cropanzano, James, & Konovsky, 1993), it is expected that PA will be associated with increased levels of involvement at work. High PAs have been described as interpersonally efficacious (George, 1992), and those in a positive mood are often viewed as socially active and enthusiastic (Watson & Clark, 1984). We also expect high PAs to express more emotional labor at

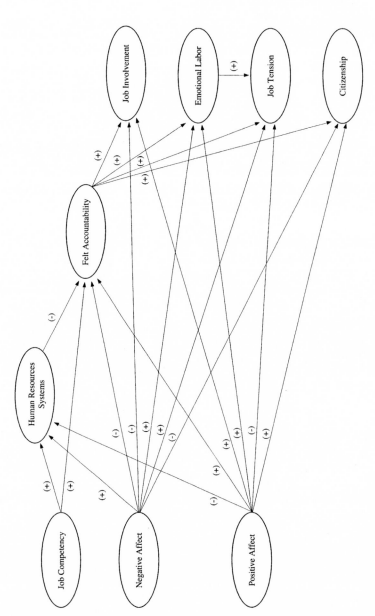

Figure 3.   Revised Model

work because they are confident that they possess the interpersonal skills needed to be successful in this domain. PA has been found to indirectly predict job tension (Iverson et al., 1998). Consequently, it is predicted that there will be a negative association between PA and job tension.

Finally, it has been suggested that high PAs are efficacious with respect to achievement, and are more prone to develop plans that lead to positive outcomes (George, 1992). Hence, in addition to being more committed at work (Cropanzano et al., 1993), we posit that high PA individuals will opt to participate in extrarole behaviors as a mechanism for securing positive outcomes. As evidence, Organ and Konovsky (1989) found that PA was associated with altruism and compliance dimensions of organizational citizenship behaviors. Furthermore, given the nature of the operationalization of HRMS as a negative phenomenon (i.e., the lack of formal accountability), it is also hypothesized that there will be a negative association between PA and the HRMS variable.

METHOD

Participants and Procedures

For class credit, students at a large university in the Southeastern United States were each given three surveys to have completed by full-time employees. Of the 330 surveys distributed to employees, a total of 311 completed surveys were returned. A wide range of occupations was included in the sample such as accountant, marketing representative, human resource manager, and chief executive officer. The sample consisted of both blue-collar and white-collar employees, although most of the respondents were professionals.

The sample consisted of 148 males (48%) and 163 females (52%), and the average age of respondents was 42 years ($SD = 11.40$). Education ranged from a high school degree to a graduate degree with 77 percent of respondents earning at least a bachelor's degree. Tenure in one's current position was approximately seven years ($SD = 7.26$) and organizational tenure was roughly 10 years ($SD = 9.27$).

Measures

Human Resources Systems

As a proxy for the human resources systems variable, which should reflect aspects of formal accountability systems, we used the "Pay and Promotions" subscale of the Kacmar and Carlson (1997) Perceptions of Politics Scale (POPS). Sample items include: "When it comes to pay raise and promotion decisions, policies are irrelevant"; "Promotions around here are not valued much because how they are determined is so political"; "The stated pay and promotion policies have nothing to do with how pay raises and promotions are determined." Because the tone of these questions is negative, and thus reflects a lack of formal accountability, we have hypothesized that this variable is related inversely to felt accountability. The coefficient alpha internal consistency reliability estimate for this scale .67.

Negative and Positive Affect

Negative (NA; α = .82) and positive (PA; α = .90) affect were measured using a scale developed by Watson et al. (1988).

Job Competency

Job competency was measured using the problem-solving dimension of Wagner and Morse's (1975; α = .70) index.

Felt Accountability

Because of the lack of perceptual accountability measures in the literature, eight items that measured an employee's level of accountability were developed for this study (α = .84). Representative items included, "I am held very accountable for my actions at work" and "To a great extent, the success of my immediate work group rests on my shoulders."

Job Involvement

Job involvement (α = .70) was measured using a 3-item scale (Camman, Fichman, Jenkins, & Klesch, 1979).

Emotional Labor

Emotional labor (α = .70) was measured with a 10-item scale (Schaubroeck & Jones, 2000).

Job Tension

Job tension (α = .82) was measured with House and Rizzo's (1972) 6-item subscale of the Anxiety-Stress Questionnaire.

Organizational Citizenship Behaviors

Organizational citizenship behaviors were measured using a 6-item scale from Podsakoff, MacKenzie, Moorman, and Fetter (1990; α = .78).

Data Analyses

The model presented in Figure 2 was tested using maximum likelihood structural equation modeling. The following fit indices and standards were used to assess model fit: goodness-of-fit index (GFI) greater than 0.90 (Jaccard & Wan, 1996), adjusted goodness-of-fit index (AGFI) greater than 0.80 (Gefen, Straub, & Boudreau, 2000), normed fit index (NFI) greater than 0.90 (Kelloway, 1998), comparative fit index (CFI) greater than .90 (Jiang & Klein, 1999/2000), root mean square of approximation (RMSEA) lower than 0.08 for a good fit and lower than 0.05 for an excellent fit (Browne & Cudeck, 1992), and standardized root mean squared residual (RMR) below 0.05 (Kelloway, 1998).

Input to the analysis consisted of a scale-level covariance matrix with each element of the matrix representing a latent construct. Measurement error was factored into the analysis by setting each path from the latent variable to indicator variable equal to the square root of the reliability (Wayne & Liden, 1995). Error variance was computed as one minus alpha multiplied by the scale variance (Wayne & Liden, 1995).

RESULTS

Zero-Order Correlations

Table 1 reports means, standard deviations, and intercorrelations among study variables. As shown, job competency ($r = .21$, $p < .01$) and positive affectivity ($r = .31$, $p < .01$) were associated with accountability, whereas negative affectivity ($r = .08$, $p = .16$) was not. Moreover, felt accountability was positively correlated with job involvement ($r = .31$, $p < .01$), emotional labor ($r = .35$, $p < .01$), job-induced tension ($r = .31$, $p < .01$), and citizenship behaviors ($r = .29$, $p < .01$).

Table 1 also reports a positive relationship between HRMS and NA ($r = .22$, $p < .001$), emotional labor ($r = .15$, $p < .01$), and job tension ($r = .13$, $p < .05$). Additionally, a negative relationship was found between HRMS and PA ($r = -.20$, $p < .091$), job involvement, ($r = .18$, $p < .01$), and organizational citizenship ($r = -.11$, $p < .05$). A negative ($r = -.05$, $p < .16$), albeit insignificant relationship, was found between HRMS and felt accountability.

Items were subjected to a confirmatory factor analysis using maximum likelihood estimation for the purpose of demonstrating construct reliability (Anderson & Gerbing, 1988). LISREL reported, via t-values, that all items loaded significantly on their intended constructs except for the item "Generally, I keep my emotions to myself—its better that way" in the emotional labor scale. LISREL reported a t-value of 1.86 for this item. Because the alpha for the emotional labor scale was reported as .68, and since eliminating this item would have only improved the reliability to just over .70, we decided to retain this item in order to maintain the integrity of the emotional labor scale.

Structural Equation Modeling Results

Maximum likelihood estimation was performed on the model shown in Figure 2. The model did not exhibit adequate fit: $\chi^2 = 144.45$, $df = 21$, $p =$

Table 1

Correlations, Means, and Standard Deviations

Variable	Mean	Std. Dev.	1	2	3	4	5	6	7	8	9	10	11
1. Job Competency	4.13	0.50											
2. Human Resources Systems	3.50	1.04	-0.02										
3. Negative Affect	1.66	0.52	-0.23***	0.22***									
4. Positive Affect	3.69	0.71	0.31***	-0.20***	-0.18**								
5. Felt Accountability	4.90	1.05	0.22***	-0.05	0.08	0.33***							
6. Job Involvement	3.81	1.22	0.13*	-0.18**	-0.07	0.38***	0.31***						
7. Emotional Labor	2.89	0.42	0.01	0.15**	0.40***	0.16**	0.35***	0.12*					
8. Job Tension	2.74	0.77	-0.03	0.13*	0.37***	-0.07	0.31***	0.09	0.50***				
9. Organizational Citizenship	5.81	0.66	0.15**	-0.11*	-0.07	0.30***	0.29***	0.12*	0.20***	-0.02			
10. Age	42.08	11.41	-0.02	-0.07	-0.15**	0.05	-0.02	0.09	-0.07	0.03	0.06		
11. Gender	0.52	0.50	-0.02	0.08	-0.06	0.01	-0.16**	-0.08	0.05	-0.05	0.08	0.06	
12. Education	3.08	1.45	0.03	-0.04	-0.08	0.07	-0.05	0.09	0.04	0.09	0.13*	-0.09	-0.04

Notes: *$p < .05$; **$p < .01$; ***$p < .001$

0.00, GFI = .91, AGFI = .80, NFI = .69, CFI = .71, RMSEA = .14, and standardized RMR = .11. To improve model fit, the model was revised (see Figure 3) and re-estimated.

The fit for the revised model was strong: χ^2 = 21.70, df = 13, p = .06, GFI = .98, AGFI = .95, NFI = .95, CFI = .98, RMSEA = .05, and standardized RMR = .03. A chi-square difference test between the two models was performed; the results were significant. Because the revised model (Figure 3) had better fit, a lower chi-square value, and lower chi-square to degrees of freedom ratio over the model in Figure 2, the model shown in Figure 3 was accepted. Path loadings and overall contributions to explained variance (i.e., R^2) for the revised model are shown in Figure 4.

To investigate alternative theoretical models, which might have similar or better fit than the model shown in Figure 3, nested model testing was performed. For each model investigated, a chi-square difference test was performed to determine if the model differed significantly from the revised model.

Nested Model 1 removed all paths from accountability to the outcome variables in order to position accountability as a dependent variable. Results indicated unacceptable fit for this model (χ^2 = 85.02, df = 17, p = .00, GFI = .94, AGFI = .85, NFI = .83, CFI = .85, RMSEA = .11, and standardized RMR = .07). The chi-square difference test was significant indicating the superiority of the accepted model.

Nested Model 2 added paths from the human resources systems variable to each of the outcome variables (job involvement, emotional labor, tension, and citizenship). The rationale here was to mirror the same set of paths from each of the antecedents (negative and positive affectivity) to the outcome variables, but more importantly, to investigate possible effects of the human resources systems variable directly on the outcomes. Not surprisingly, the virtually saturated model had acceptable fit (χ^2 = 14.65, df = 9, p = .10, GFI = .99, AGFI = .95, NFI = .97, CFI = .99, RMSEA = .05, and standardized RMR = .02). The chi-square difference test was not significant. However, none of the added paths were significant; thus, this model provided no additional insight or evidence concerning human resources systems as a predictor of job involvement, emotional labor, tension, or organizational citizenship. Furthermore, this model was almost fully saturated; therefore in the interest of parsimony, this model was dropped in favor of the revised model (Figure 3).

DISCUSSION

Accountability has important implications for HRM systems. Adopting the phenomenological approach advocated by Tetlock (1985, 1992) and others (e.g., Frink & Klimoski, 1998), felt accountability is conceptualized both as a state of mind and as a state of affairs. Precisely, it is the case that,

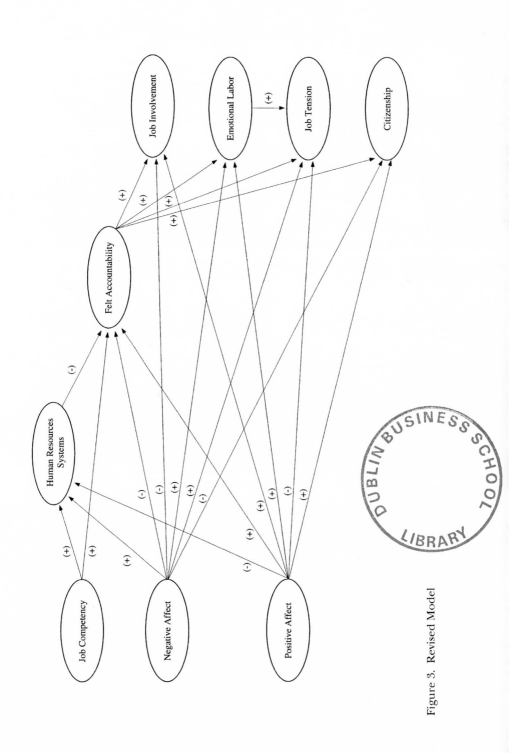

Figure 3. Revised Model

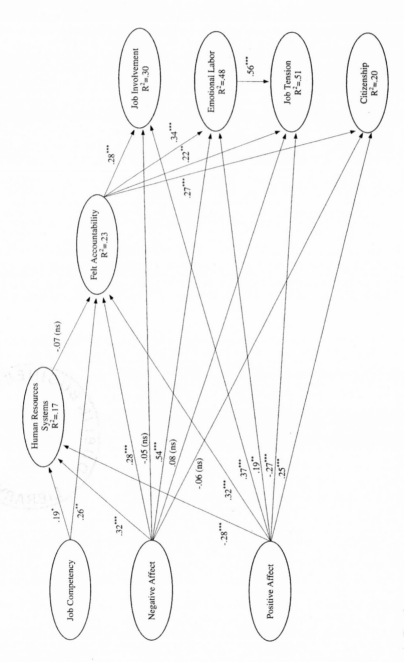

Figure 4. Results
Notes: * p < .05; **p < .01; ***p < .001

even though formal accountability mechanisms might be present, this does not automatically imply that employees will perceive these mechanisms (or perceive them accurately) or use them as a means to guide their behavior. However, without a sense of felt accountability, an organization's HRM systems will have a diminished (or contrary) effect on desired organizational outcomes.

This is not to say that accountability is a panacea for all the ills facing organizations. Although research generally has suggested that accountability leads to positive outcomes for both individuals and organizations, assuming that this is always the case seems overly optimistic. Previous work has suggested that accountability can lead to adverse consequences including reduced cognitive complexity (Tetlock, Skitka, & Boettger, 1989), increased stereotyping (Gordon, Rozelle, & Baxter, 1988), and inaccurate performance evaluations (Klimoski & Inks, 1990).

Role theory (Katz & Kahn, 1978) suggests that operating in the work environment constitutes an emergent and socially defined understanding. Consequently, there are a host of personal and contextual variables that serve to individualize this understanding for each person. Accountability is at the heart of this understanding because it drives performance expectancies and is a salient source of information about behavioral norms. Furthermore, it is appropriate to assess perceptions about accountability (Cummings & Anton, 1990; Frink & Ferris, 1998; Frink & Klimoski, 1998). It then follows that variables such as job competency, human resources systems, negative affectivity, and positive affectivity should correlate with accountability, and should further correlate with such variables as job involvement, emotional labor, job tension, and organizational citizenship behaviors.

The findings that positive affectivity and job competency predicted felt accountability were expected. However, we did not anticipate finding a *positive* (albeit not significant) association between negative affect and accountability. Perhaps the relationship with their coworkers and supervisor dictates the form of the relationship between NA and accountability. For example, George (1992) suggested that high NAs tend to have substandard relationships with supervisors, and are often seen as less likeable by coworkers. Confirming this point, research corroborates an inverse relationship between negative affectivity and peer cohesion (Dollard, Winefield, Winefield, & Jonge, 2000).

Results from this investigation also suggested that those held accountable were more involved in work, exerted more emotional labor, experienced more job tension, and were prone to greater participation in citizenship behaviors. We are unaware of any previous investigation that has examined job involvement and emotional labor as outcomes of accountability. However, previous research has investigated the association between accountability and job tension and citizenship behaviors (Frink, et al., 1995). Our results provide additional support for the contention that taking on additional responsibility at work leads to increased stress.

Conversely, our findings are inconsistent with those reported by Frink et al. (1995), who indicated that accountability leads to reduced OCBs. What accounts for these disparate findings? Individuals have at their disposal a number of ways to ensure that their efforts will be viewed favorably. As was the case in this study, employees might opt to employ citizenship behaviors to ensure that their work efforts are viewed auspiciously.

Alternatively, employees might pursue other methods of impression management if it is thought that citizenship behaviors would fail to have their desired effect. For example, previous research indicates that one reaction to accountability is the increased use of influence tactics (Fandt & Ferris, 1990; Ferris et al., 1997). Perhaps the use of influence tactics comes at the expense of more organizationally appropriate behaviors, such as OCBs. However, the influence tactics—OCB distinction is far from clear-cut and, indeed, might reflect behavior labeling based merely on perceived intent (Bolino, 1999; Fandt & Ferris, 1990; Ferris et al., 1995; Ferris, Judge, Rowland, & Fitzgibbons, 1994). Research building on these results will need to simultaneously examine the full spectrum of accountability reactions, which include (but are not limited to) influence, citizenship, manipulation, and aggressive behaviors.

Contrary to Hypothesis 1, HRM systems did not show a significant path to felt accountability. There are two possible reasons why a non-significant path was found. First, the measure used for the HRM systems variable was the "Pay and Promotions" subscale of the perceptions of politics measure developed by Kacmar and Carlson (1997). This measure taps into the negative or dysfunctional aspects of a pay and promotion system, rather than its motivational or other positive benefits.

Another plausible cause of a non-significant path might be that other factors overshadow the importance of formal accountability systems. For example, dispositional differences, such as NA and PA played a prominent role in felt accountability. If this were the case, this would be further support of the phenomenological approach, which emphasizes the importance of the subjective nature of felt accountability. Furthermore, role theory (Katz & Kahn, 1978) would suggest that informal norms and expectations might be more at the root of individual behavior and attitudes, such as felt accountability, than formal organizational accountability mechanisms, which might be unknown or perceived differently than intended.

Directions for Future Research

Despite its apparent importance, theoretical and empirical research on felt accountability is still in its nascent development. Frink and Klimoski (1998) argued that scholars were aware of certain aspects of the phenomenon, but lacked a complete understanding of felt accountability processes. This research expands the accountability research by theorizing and testing portions of one of the few models of felt accountability in organizations. Nevertheless, there is still much work to be done in this developing line of human resource management research.

For example, future researchers should explore other antecedents to felt accountability. Specifically, given their apparent theoretical connection to accountability, researchers should consider looking at factors such as reputation (Tsui, 1984), political skill (Ahearn, Ferris, Hochwarter, Douglas, & Ammeter, in press), Agreeableness (Mount & Barrick, 1995), Conscientiousness (Mount & Barrick, 1995), and informal workplace norms (Frink & Klimoski, 1998) as antecedents to felt accountability.

Although the model of felt accountability offered in this chapter provides a foundation for future research, it is by no means comprehensive. For example, no potential moderators or mediators were explored. However, this might provide a fruitful line of inquiry for future researchers. For example, in this chapter, felt accountability is argued to be a potential work stressor (Siegel-Jacobs & Yates, 1996). However, there is a long line of research in the stress literature that has examined potential moderators of the stress-strain relationship (Danna & Griffin, 1999). For example, control has been found to ameliorate the negative relationship between stressors and attendant strain reactions (Danna & Griffin, 1999). Future research should examine potential moderators, such as control, of the accountability-outcomes relationship.

Implications for Practice

An important implication for practice is that accountability is a necessary component of an effective human resource management system. However, accountability has been linked with negative outcomes. As such, accountability is not "universally positive" (Frink & Klimoski, 1998). Given both the "dark side" of accountability and the costs of operating elaborate employee monitoring systems, organizations would be well-served if they could determine the "right" amount of accountability; that is, the highest level of accountability that is possible before negative outcomes occur. Furthermore, organizations should examine substitutes to accountability, such as encouraging trusting relationships with employees (Ammeter, Douglas, Ferris, & Goka, in press.)

CONCLUSION

Accountability is critical to organizations and human resources systems. Indeed, it forms the very essence of effective individual and organizational functioning. Unfortunately, to date, we have had little knowledge of the nature, antecedents, and consequences of accountability in organizations. Furthermore, because accountability mechanisms overlap with key human resources management systems, we need to know more about how accountability, as it plays out in HRMS, affects important individual reactions and behavior. The proper balance of accountability is critical whereby enough accountability is in place to ensure that appropriate behaviors be demonstrated, but not too much so as to produce excessive control and possible reactance (Ferris et al., 1995; Lerner & Tetlock, 1999).

REFERENCES

Adams, J. S. (1965). Inequity in social exchange. In L. Berkowitz (Ed.), *Advances in experimental social psychology* (Vol. 2, pp. 267-296). New York: Academic Press.

Ahearn, K. K., Ferris, G. R., Hochwarter, W. A., Douglas, C., & Ammeter, A. P. (in press). Leader political skill and team performance. *Journal of Management*.

Allen, T., Freeman, D., Russell, J., Reizenstein, R., & Rentz, J. (2001). Survivor reactions to organizational downsizing: Does time ease the pain? *Journal of Occupational and Organizational Psychology, 74*, 145-164.

Ammeter, A.P., Douglas, C., Ferris, G. R., Goka, H. (in press). A social relationship conceptualization of trust and accountability in organizations. *Human Resource Management Review.*

Anderson, J. C., & Gerbing, D. W. (1988). Structural equation modeling in practice: A review and recommended two-step approach. *Psychological Bulletin, 103*, 411-423.

Ashforth, B., & Humphrey, R. (1993). Emotional labor in service roles: The influence of identity. *Academy of Management Review, 18*, 88-115.

Bolino, M. (1999). Citizenship and impression management: Good soldiers or good actors? *Academy of Management Review, 1*, 82-98.

Borman, W. C., & Motowidlo, S. J. (1993). Expanding the criterion domain to include elements of contextual performance. In N. Schmitt & W. C. Borman (Eds.), *Personnel selection in organizations* (pp. 71-98). San Francisco: Jossey-Bass.

Bowen, M. G. (1987). The escalation phenomenon reconsidered: Decision dilemmas or decision errors? *Academy of Management Review, 12*, 52-66.

Browne, M., & Cudeck, R. (1992). Alternative ways of assessing model fit. In K. A. Bollen & J. S. Long (Eds.), *Testing structural equation models* (pp. 136-162). Beverly Hills, CA: Sage.

Brief, A., Burke, R., George, J., Robinson, B., & Webster, J. (1988). Should negative affectivity remain an unmeasured variable in the study of job stress? *Journal of Applied Psychology, 73*, 193-198.

Brown, S., & Leigh, T. (1996). A new look at psychological climate and its relationship to job involvement, effort and performance. *Journal of Applied Psychology, 81*, 358-368.

Burke, M., Brief, A., & George, J. (1993). The role of negative affectivity in understanding relations between self-reports of stressors and strains: A comment on the applied psychology literature. *Journal of Applied Psychology, 78*, 402-412.

Cammann, C., Fichman, M., Jenkins, D., & Klesh, J. (1979). *Michigan organizational assessment questionnaire.* Unpublished manuscript, University of Michigan, Ann Arbor.

Carnevale, P. J. D. (1985). Accountability of group representatives and intergroup relations. In E. J. Lawler (Ed.), *Advances in group processes* (Vol. 2, pp. 227-248). Greenwich, CT: JAI Press.

Child, J. (1977). Strategic choice in the analysis of action, structure, organizations and environment: Retrospect and prospect. *Organization Studies, 18,* 43-76.

Cropanzano, R., James, K., & Konovsky, M. (1993). Dispositional affectivity as a predictor of work attitudes and job performance. *Journal of Organizational Behavior, 14,* 595-607.

Cummings, L. L., & Anton, R. J. (1990). The logical and appreciative dimensions of accountability. In S. Srivastva, D. Cooperrider, & Associates (Eds.), *Appreciative management and leadership* (pp.257-286). San Francisco: Jossey-Bass.

Danna, K. & Griffin, R. W. (1999). Health and well being in the workplace: A review and synthesis of the litrature. *Journal of Management, 25,* 357-384.

Diefendorff, M., Brown, D., Kamin, M., & Lord, R. (2002). Examining the roles of job involvement and work centrality in predicting organizational citizenship behaviors and job performance. *Journal of Organizational Behavior, 23,* 93-108.

Dollard, M., Winefield, H., Winefield, A., & Jonge, J. (2000). Psychosocial job strain and productivity in human service workers: A test of the demand-control-support model. *Journal of Occupational and Organizational Psychology, 73,* 501-510.

Drummond, H (1996). *Escalation in Decision-Making: The tragedy of Taurus.* NY: Oxford University Press.

Elliott, M. (February 4, 2002). The incredible shrinking business. *Time,* 26

Eisehardt, K. M. (1985). Control: Organizational and economic approaches. *Management Science, 31,* 134-149.

Fandt, P. M., & Ferris, G. R. (1990). The management of information and impressions: When employees behave opportunistically. *Organizational Behavior and Human Decision Processes, 45,* 140-158.

Ferris, G. R., Bhawuk, D. P. S., Fedor, D. B., & Judge, T. A. (1995). Organizational politics and citizenship: Attributions of intentionality and construct definition. In M. J. Martinko (Ed.), *Advances in attribution theory: An organizational perspective* (pp. 231-252). Delray Beach, FL: St. Lucie Press.

Ferris, G. R., Dulebohn, J. H., Frink, D. D., George-Falvy, J., Mitchell, T. R., & Matthews, L. M. (1997). Job and organizational characteristics, accountability, and employee influence. *Journal of Managerial Issues, 9,* 162-175.

Ferris, G. R., & King, T. R. (1991). Politics in human resources decisions: A walk on the dark side. *Organizational Dynamics, 20,* 59-71.

Ferris, G., Judge, T., Rowland, K., & Fitzgibbons, D. (1994). Subordinate influence and the performance evaluation process: Test of a model. *Organizational Behavior and Human Decision Processes, 58,* 101-135.

Ferris, G. R., Mitchell, T. R., Canavan, P. J., Frink, D. D., & Hopper, H. (1995). Accountability in human resource systems. In G.R. Ferris, S.D. Rosen, & D.T. Barnum (Eds.), *Handbook of human resource management* (pp.175-196). Oxford, UK: Blackwell Publishers.

Ferris, G. R., Perrewé, P. L., Anthony, W. P., & Gilmore, D. C. (2000). Political skill at work. *Organizational Dynamics, 28,* 25-37.

Frink, D. D., & Ferris, G. R. (1996). Accountability in the management of human resources. In G. R. Ferris & M. R. Buckley (Eds.), *Human resources management: Perspectives, context, functions, and outcomes* (3rd Ed., pp. 422-446). Englewood Cliffs, NJ: Prentice-Hall.

Frink, D. D., & Ferris, G. R. (1998). Accountability, impression management, and goal setting in the performance evaluation process. *Human Relations, 51,* 1259-1283.

Frink, D. D., Ferris, G. R. (1999). The moderating effects of accountability on the conscientiousness-performance relationship. *Journal of Business and Psychology, 13,* 515-524.

Frink, D. D., & Klimoski, R. J. (1998). Toward a theory of accountability in organizations and human resource management. In G. R. Ferris (Ed.), *Research in personnel and human resources management* (Vol. 16, pp. 1-51). Stamford, CT: JAI Press.

Frink, D. D., (chair), Klimoski, R. J., Hopper, H., Mitchell, T. R., Mero, N. P., & Motowidlo, S. J. (1995). *Dramaticus personae in organizations: Two faces of accountability effects.* Symposium presented at the Academy of Management, 55th Annual Meeting, Vancouver, British Columbia, Canada.

Ganster, D., & Schaubroeck, J. (1991). Work stress and employee health. *Journal of Management, 17,* 235-271.

Gefen, D., Straub, D., & Boudreau, M. (2000). Structural equation modeling and regression: Guidelines for research practice. *Communications of AIS, 7,* 1-78.

George, J. (1992). The role of personality in organizational life: Issues and evidence. *Journal of Management, 18,* 185-213.

Gerhart, B., & Milkovich, G. T. (1992). Employee compensation: Research and practice. In M. D. Dunnette & L. M. Hough (Eds.), *Handbook of industrial and organizational psychology* (2nd Ed., Vol. 3, pp. 481-569). Palo Alto, CA: Consulting Psychologists Press.

Goldenhar, L., Swanson, N., Hurrell, J., Ruder, A., & Deddens, J. (1998). Stressors and adverse outcomes for female construction workers. *Journal of Occupational Health Psychology, 3,* 19-32.

Gordon, R. A., Rozelle, R. M., & Baxter, J. C. (1988). The effect of applicant age, job level and accountability on the evaluation of job applicants. *Organizational Behavior and Human Decision Processes, 41,* 20-33.

Hackman, J. R., & Oldham, G. R. (1975). Development of the job diagnostic survey. *Journal of Applied Psychology, 60,* 159-170.

Hannan, M. T., & Freeman, J. H. (1977). The population ecology of organizations. *American Journal of Sociology, 91,* 481-510.

Hochschild, A. R. (1983). *The managed heart: Commercialization of human feeling.* Berkeley, CA: University of California Press.

Hochschild, A. (1979). Emotional work, feeling rules, and social structure. *American Journal of Sociology, 85,* 551-575.

House, R. J., & Rizzo, J. R. (1972). Role conflict and ambiguity as critical variables in a model of organizational behavior. *Organizational Behavior and Human Performance, 7,* 467-505.

Howard, J., & Ferris, G. (1996). The employment interview context: Social and situational influences on interviewer decisions. *Journal of Applied Social Psychology, 26,* 112-136.

Hrebiniak, L., & Joyce, W. (1985). Organizational adaptation: Strategic choice and environmental determinism. *Administrative Science Quarterly, 30,* 336-349.

Iverson, R., Olekalns, M., & Erwin, P. (1998). Affectivity, organizational stressors, and absenteeism: A causal model of burnout and its consequences. *Journal of Vocational Behavior, 52,* 1-23.

Jaccard, J., & Wan, C. (1996). *LISREL approaches to interaction effects in multiple regression.* Thousand Oaks, CA: Sage.

Jiang, J. J., & Klein, G. (1999/2000). Supervisor support and career anchor impact on the career satisfaction of the entry-level information systems professional. *Journal of Management Information Systems, 16,* 219-240.

Judge, T., Thoresen, C., Pucik, V., & Welbourne, T. (1999). Managerial coping with organizational change: A dispositional perspective. *Journal of Applied Psychology, 84,* 107-122.

Kacmar, K. M., & Carlson, D. S. (1997). Further validation of the perceptions of politics scale (POPS): A multiple sample investigation. *Journal of Management, 23,* 627-658.

Kahn, W. (1990). Psychological conditions of personal engagement and disengagement in work. *Academy of Management Journal, 33,* 692-724.

Kanungo, R. (1982). Measurement of job and work involvement. *Journal of Applied Psychology, 67,* 341-349.

Katz, D., & Kahn, R. (1978). *The social psychology of organizations* (2nd Ed.). New York: Wiley.

Keller, R. (1997). Job involvement and organizational commitment as longitudinal predictors of job performance: A study of scientist and engineer. *Journal of Applied Psychology, 82,* 539-545.

Kelloway, K. (1998). Using *LISREL for structural equation modeling: A researcher's guide.* Thousand Oaks, CA: Sage.

Klimoski, R., & Inks, L. (1990). Accountability forces in performance appraisal. *Organizational Behavior and Human Decision Processes, 45,* 194-208.

Lerner, J. S., & Tetlock, P. E. (1999). Accounting for the effects of accountability. *Psychological Bulletin, 125,* 255-275.

Lewin, K. (1936). *Principles of topological psychology.* New York: McGraw-Hill.

Lodahl, T., & Kejner, M. (1965). The definition and measurement of job involvement. *Journal of Applied Psychology, 49,* 24-33.

Lu, L., Kao, S., Cooper, C., & Spector, P. (2002). Managerial stress, locus of control, and job strain in Taiwan and UK: A comparative study. *International Journal of Stress Management, 7,* 209-226.

Meindl, J., Ehrlich, S., & Dukerich, J. (1985). The romance of leadership. *Administrative Science Quarterly, 30,* 78-102.

Mero, N.P., & Frink, D.D. (2002). Accountability in organizations and human resources management. In G. R. Ferris, M. R. Buckley, & D. B. Fedor (Eds.), *Human resources management: Perspectives, context, functions, and outcomes* (4th Ed., pp. 422-439). Upper Saddle River, NJ: Prentice-Hall.

Miceli, M. P., & Lane, M. C. (1991). Antecedents of pay satisfaction: A review and extension. In G. R. Ferris & K. M. Rowland (Eds.), *Research in personnel and human resources management* (Vol. 9, pp. 235-309). Greenwich, CT: JAI Press.

Mitchell, T. R., Hopper, H., Daniels, D., George-Falvy, J., & Ferris, G. R. (1998). Power, accountability, and inappropriate actions. *Applied psychology: An International Review, 47,* 497-517.

Morse, J. J. (1976). Sense of competence and individual managerial performance. *Psychological Reports, 38,* 1195-1198.

Motowidlo, S., & Van Scotter, J. (1994). Evidence that task performance should be distinguished from extrarole performance. *Journal of Applied Psychology, 79,* 475-480.

Mount, M. K. & Barrick, M. R. (1995). The big five personality dimensions: Implications for research and practice in human resources management. In Gerald R. Ferris (Ed.). *Research in Personnel and Human Resources Management,* (Vol. 13, pp. 153-201). Oxford, UK: JAI Press/Elsevier Science.

Organ, D., & Konovsky, M. (1989). Cognitive versus affective determinants of organizational citizenship behaviors. *Journal of Applied Psychology, 74,* 157-164.

Ouchi, W. G., & Macguire, M. A. (1975). Organizational control: Two functions: *Administrative Science Quarterly, 20,* 559-569.

Perrewé, P. L., & Spector, P. E. (2002). Personality research in organizational sciences. In G. R. Ferris & J. J. Martocchio (Eds.), *Research in personnel and human resources management* (Vol. 21, pp. 1-64). Oxford, UK: JAI Press/Elsevier Science.

Pfeffer, J. (1981). Management as symbolic action: The creation and maintenance of organizational paradigms. In L. L. Cummings & B. M. Staw (Eds.), *Research in organizational behavior* (Vol. 3, pp. 1-52). Greenwich, CT: JAI Press.

Podsakoff, P., MacKenzie, P., Moorman, R., & Fetter, R. (1990). Transactional leader behaviors and their effects on followers' trust in leader, satisfaction, and organizational citizenship behaviors. *Leadership Quarterly, 2,* 107-142.

Rafaeli, A., & Sutton, R. (1987). Expression of emotion as part of the work role. *Academy of Management Review, 12,* 23-37.

Schlenker, B.R., Britt, T.W., Pennington, J., Murphy, R., & Doherty, K. (1994). The triangle model of responsibility. *Psychological Review, 101,* 632-652.

Schneider, B. (1987). The people make the place. *Personnel Psychology, 40,* 437-453.

Schaubroeck, J., & Jones, J. (2000). Antecedents of workplace emotional labor dimensions and moderators of their effects on physical symptoms. *Journal of Organizational Behavior, 21,* 163-183.

Siegel-Jacobs, K., & Yates, J. F. (1996). Effects of procedural and outcome accountability on judgment quality. *Organizational Behavior and Human Decision Processes, 65,* 1-17.

Spector, P., & O'Connell, B. (1994). The contribution of personality traits, negative affectivity, locus of control, and Type A to the subsequent reports of job stressors and job strains. *Journal of Occupational and Organizational Psychology, 67,* 1-21.

Staw, B. M. (1976) Knee-deep in the big muddy: A study of escalating commitment to a course of action. *Organization and Human Performance, 16,* 27-44.

Sutton, R. (1991). Maintaining norms about expressed emotions: The case of bill collectors. *Administrative Science Quarterly, 36,* 245-268.

Tetlock, P.E. (1985). Accountability: The neglected social context of judgment and choice. In L.L. Cummings & B.M. Staw (Eds.), *Research in organizational behavior* (Vol. 7, pp. 297-332). Greenwich, CT: JAI Press.

Tetlock, P. (1992). The impact of accountability on judgment and choice. Toward a social contingency model. In M. Zanna (Ed.), *Advances in experimental social psychology* (pp. 331-377). New York: Academic Press.

Tetlock, P. E., Skitka, L., & Boettger, R. (1989). Social and cognitive strategies for coping with accountability: Conformity, complexity, and bolstering. *Journal of Personality and Social Psychology, 57,* 632-640.

Thomas, A. (1988). Does leadership make a difference to organizational performance? *Administrative Science Quarterly, 33,* 388-400.

Tsui, A. S. (1984). A role set analysis of managerial reputation. *Organizational Behavior and Human Performance, 34,* 64-96.

Van Dyne, L., Graham, J. W., & Dienesch, R. M. (1994). Organizational citizenship behavior: Construct redefinition, measurement, and validation. *Academy of Management Journal, 37,* 765-802.

Van Maanen, J., & Kunda, G. (1989). "Real feelings": Emotional expression and organizational culture. *Research in Organizational Behavior, 11,* 43-103.

Vroom, V. H. (1964). *Work and motivation.* New York: Wiley.

Wagner, F. R., & Morse, J. J. (1975). A measure of individual sense of competence. *Psychological Reports, 36,* 451-459.

Watson, D., & Clark, L. (1984). Negative affectivity: The disposition to experience aversive emotional states. *Psychological Bulletin, 96,* 465-490.

Watson, D., Clark, L., & Tellegen, A. (1988). Development and validation of brief measures of positive and negative affect: The PANAS scale. *Journal of Personality and Social Psychology, 54,* 1063-1070.

Watson, D., & Pennebaker, J. (1989). Health complaints, stress, and distress: Exploring the central role of negative affectivity. *Psychological Review, 96,* 234-254.

Watson, D., & Tellegen, A. (1985). Toward a consensual structure of mood. *Psychological Bulletin, 98,* 219-235

Wayne, S., & Liden, R. (1995). Effects of impression management on performance ratings: A longitudinal study. *Academy of Management Journal, 38,* 232-260.

White, R. W. (1959). Motivation reconsidered: The concept of competence. *Psychological Review, 5,* 297-333.

Williams, S., & Cooper, C. (1998). Measuring occupational stress: Development of the Pressure Management Indicator. *Journal of Occupational Health Psychology, 3,* 306-321.

Yarnold, P. R., Mueser, K. T., & Lyons J. S. (1988). Type A behavior, accountability, and work rate in small groups *Journal of Research in Personality, 22,* 353-360.

CHAPTER 3

ERGONOMIC TRAINING AND ORGANIZATIONAL STRESS

Implications for Human Resource Professionals

Angela K. Miles
North Carolina A&T University
Pamela L. Perrewé
Florida State University

ABSTRACT

Ergonomic programs are becoming increasingly recognized in the work-place. This trend may be due, in part, to the economic implications of ergonomics as well as a genuine concern for employees. The effects of ergonomic design and training on personal and work outcomes have not been extensively researched. This chapter offers one of the first attempts at empirically linking ergonomic training concepts with experienced stress. We argue that understanding the ergonomic design of one's workstation and satisfaction with the ergonomic training, play a critical role in the experienced work stress of employees. A conceptual model of ergonomic training, person-envi-

New Directions in Human Resource Management
A Volume in: Research in Management, pages 65–89.
Copyright © 2003 by Information Age Publishing, Inc.
All rights of reproduction in any form reserved.
ISBN: 1-59311-099-5 (hardcover), 1-59311-098-7 (pbk.)

ronment fit, and experienced stress is developed. The proposed model is empirically examined in office settings across a variety of organizations. Findings indicate that perceptions of person-environment fit fully mediate the relationship between ergonomic training satisfaction and organizational strain (i.e., job-induced tension and somatic complaints).

Now actively involved in the strategic planning process, HR managers are continuously tasked with cost reduction. In attempts to streamline overhead costs, boost company image, and increase stock prices, companies continue to appraise methods that promote organizational profitability while protecting organizational assets. Considering employees an essential asset, employers are consistently examining opportunities to reduce costs by evaluating areas that affect the productivity and well-being of their employees. Organizational stress has been empirically linked to employee well-being due to its association with employee illness. Furthermore, experienced stress or strain contributes to lost time at work and lowers productivity. Interestingly, ergonomics, the science of fitting the environment to people, is an area of responsibility for HR professionals that has the opposite affect on organizational strain. There is evidence that ergonomics can reduce medical costs, lower absenteeism, and improve worker satisfaction and productivity (OSHA, 2003; Ramsey, 1995). However, these two concepts have not been often empirically linked. This chapter outlines the practical implications of stress as an HR issue. In addition, it offers a linkage to ergonomics as a theoretical and practical solution to strain prevention. Examining the conceptual and empirical linkages between aspects of ergonomic training and strain extends the work on both ergonomics and organizational stress.

STRESS IN ORGANIZATIONS

Job stress continues to be a major problem today, costing organizations billions of dollars in employee disability claims, employee absenteeism, and lost productivity (e.g., Xie & Schaubroeck, 2001). McGrath (1976) indicated that stress occurs when an environmental situation is perceived by an individual as presenting a demand that threatens to exceed the individual's capabilities and resources for meeting that demand. Organizational stress is defined as a problematic level of environmental demand that interacts with the individual to change his or her psychological or physiological condition such that the person (mind/body) is forced to deviate from normal functioning (Bhagat, Allie, & Ford, 1995). Organizational stress has been viewed as dysfunctional for organizations and its members. The costs of stress to organizations are apparent in the outcomes of physical debilitation, turnover, and illness. The costs can become considerable, particularly for companies operating in states where stress is considered an occupational injury under workers' compensation law.

A simplistic stress process suggests that environmental demands influence one's perceptions of stress that, in turn, manifests into the experience of stress and a subsequent outcome. Furthermore, perceived stress is influenced by a host of variables that change one's perception of a demand. Samplings of these variables include: coping strategies, individual characteristics, cognitive assessments, and situational contexts. Accordingly, research on organizational stress can be classified into studies on stressors, moderating and intervening strategies, strains and stress management, and prevention. A stressor is defined as objective and perceived environmental demands. Outcomes are denoted as strain. Strain is defined as psychological, physiological (Perrewé & Ganster, 1989), and behavioral responses made by individuals to environmental demands.

Studies on stressors have most often encompassed the role demands of work overload, role ambiguity, and role conflict in which workers have too much to do, have uncertainty regarding task requirements and discord between life and work responsibilities (Frone, 1990; Kaldenberg & Becker, 1992; O'Driscoll & Beehr, 1994; Parasuraman, Greenhous, & Granrose, 1992). Another area of concentration has been on organizational stressors such as politics (Cropanzano, Howes, Grandey, & Toth, 1997; Ferris, Frink, Gilmore, & Kacmar, 1994). These stressors are often subjective. Studies on moderation and intervening techniques have focused on individual coping strategies, perceptions of control, attribution, and personality. Studies on strains have concentrated on the psychological responses of job dissatisfaction, depression, tension and burnout (Burke & Greenglas, 1995; Buunk, Schaufeli, & Ybema, 1994; Cherniss, 1992; Cordes & Dougherty, 1993; Lee & Ashforth, 1996; Zellars & Perrewé, 2001), the behavioral responses of performance and absenteeism (Xie & Schaubroeck, 2001), and physiological responses of heart rate (Perrewé & Ganster, 1989), blood pressure (Perrewé, Zellars, Ferris, Rossi, Kacmar, & Ralston, in press), and cholesterol level. Stress management techniques most often target the individual for intervention as opposed to the organization (Kahn & Byosiere, 1992) and encompass activities such as exercise and cognitive reappraisal. The majority of research has primarily focused on reducing strain affecting the organization—not preventing it. Thus, "Preventive stress management is an organization philosophy and set of principles which employs specific methods for promoting individual and organizational health while preventing individual and organizational distress" (Quick, Quick, & Nelson, 2001, p. 247).

CONCEPTUAL BACKGROUND

According to Lazarus (1994) stress is best viewed as a relationship between an individual and a specific environment and its occurrence depends upon how an individual appraises the situation. Although Lazarus acknowledges physical stressors, he emphasizes that individual characteristics have a primary relationship to stress. Stress only occurs when an individual makes an appraisal that demands exceed his or her resources. Brief and George (1995) agree that experienced stress fundamentally occurs at the individual level, but they argue that it is necessary to discover working conditions that are likely to adversely affect most workers exposed to them. Evidence suggests that poorly designed equipment or workstations can create demands that are of significance to experienced stress because they influence fatigue and also influence worker attitude and behavior; factors that affect workers' response to stressors (Braganza, 1994; Smith, 1987).

It has been determined that the environment can operate as a stressor, as evidenced by the emotional stress and physical debilitation resulting from exposure to uncontrollable environmental demands (Karasek, 1979; Dwyer & Ganster, 1991). Interestingly, the environment can also act to alleviate strain and promote physical and emotional well being when one is exposed to natural and aesthetic conditions (Stokols, 1992).

Prior management research on organizational stress has concentrated on the consequences of stressful situations and has often neglected the antecedents to perceived stress, (Quick, Quick, & Nelson, 2001; Kahn & Byosiere, 1992), particularly objective antecedents. Theoretically, it has been noted that perceived stress is an individual phenomenon and most suitable to subjective measures (Lazarus, 1994; Perrewé & Zellars, 1999). There have been few studies that examine organizational interventions designed to reduce or eliminate stressful conditions in the workplace. In support of this finding, Kahn and Byosiere (1992) contend that stress management techniques most often target the individual for intervention as opposed to the organization. For instance, employee assistance programs, relaxation techniques, exercise, and work/lifestyle modification skills designed to extend individual psychological resources are methods targeted toward individual intervention (Cartwright, Cooper, & Murphy, 1995).

These techniques address the consequences of organizational stress— not the sources of organizational stress. In addition, the positive influence of stress management programs on individuals is likely to become eroded if an employee returns to an unchanged work environment (Cartwright et al., 1995). The value to the organization of targeting objective stressors is that the organization can have control of the process and voluntarily implement changes in the environment to reduce, minimize, and perhaps eliminate problematic environmental demands that lead to employee strain in the workplace.

THE SIGNIFICANCE OF ERGONOMICS TO ORGANIZATIONS

The Occupational Safety and Health Administration (OSHA) defines ergonomics as adapting jobs and workplaces to the worker by designing tasks, workstations, tools, and equipment that are within the worker's physical capabilities and limitations (Schwind, 1995). The practice and benefits of ergonomics, which traditionally focused on the physical aspects and outcomes of work, now incorporates the procedures of job design and human factors engineering. A traditional HR activity, job design analysis is the thorough examination of job task requirements. Job design is a management tool expanded ergonomically to identify workplace hazards and tasks and to compare task demands to worker capabilities (Grant, 1996). Ergonomic practices should be integrated into the design of jobs and work areas to eliminate hazards and to match task demands with worker capabilities (Miles & Perrewé, 2001).

Ergonomics embodies appropriate workspace design. Well-designed jobs improve efficiency, safety, and satisfaction of employees (Grant, 1996). The elements of one's job include management interfacing relationships, as well as task responsibilities and characteristics (Grant, 1996). Hackman and Oldham (1980) offer a classic model outlining important job characteristics relative to positive work outcomes. The model suggests that jobs designed with high skill variety, task identity, task significance, autonomy, and feedback will positively affect the employee's critical psychological states of meaningfulness of the work, responsibility, and knowledge of work; which in turn affect selected job outcomes. However, Hackman and Oldham (1980) also suggest that the relationship between job characteristics and psychological states and the relationship between psychological states and outcomes is moderated by knowledge and skills, growth need strength and contextual satisfaction. From an ergonomic perspective, work area design often incorporates immediate feedback and contextual reaction. For instance, if a piece of equipment is not suitable to an individual, the individual experiences immediate discomfort. This ignored reaction, due to cognitive processing, may later lead to medical conditions. Likewise, contextual factors encompass aesthetics and physical conditions that can be pleasing or not. For instance, small physical space in the environment can lead to perceived instances of overcrowding and lack of privacy. Clark (1996) suggests that the work area is a personal process where workers have a sense of ownership for the workstation, and the morale, health and safety, and productivity of workers can be affected both positively and negatively by the success and failure of design efforts.

HUMAN FACTORS ENGINEERING

Human factors engineering concentrates on the psychophysical interference between the worker and the task (Clark, 1996). Psychophysical methods are often used to assess physical over-exertion of the body. However, these tests have a psychological genesis. Psychophysical law states that psychological magnitude is related to physical magnitude. Modern psychophysical theory provides that the strength of a sensation, or psychological magnitude, is related by a power function to the intensity of its physical stimulus (Krawczyk, 1996). This power function may itself be subjective. This means that one's experience depends on the physical environment and perhaps their perceptions of the physical environment. Accordingly, psychological methodologies utilize an individual's perception of physical exertion on the body and are used to identify physical demands (Krawczyk, 1996). This exertion incorporates feelings of tension, fatigue, and discomfort (Krawczyk, 1996). Thus, the physical impact of psychological outcomes has become a growing concern of human factor engineering and, moreover, the field of ergonomics. Since it has been noted that an improper environment can have an effect on a worker's psychological health, ergonomics now involves all proactive measures designed to prevent injury and to reduce the effect of repetitive wear and tear on workers' minds and bodies (Ramsey, 1995).

Individual physical and psychological characteristics (work environment) contribute to ergonomic injury. The surge of musculoskeletal disorders (MSD) or cumulative trauma injuries, such as carpal tunnel and tension neck syndromes especially with the increase in computer usage, has escalated workers' compensation claims (Hurrell, 2001). OSHA reports that ergonomic injuries impose significant cost to employers. According to OSHA, each year, approximately 1.8 million workers report work related MSDs each year, while 600,000 workers miss work due to MSDs (OSHA, 2000). Other MSDs due to computer usage are eyestrain, back, shoulder and neck pain (Brophy & Grant, 1996; Lindsey, 1999; OSHA, 2003).

The increased incidence of MSDs emphasized the impact that an improper environment can have on workers' physical and psychological health; and thereby strain (Mansfield & Armstrong, 1997; Smith, 1987; Updegrove & Updegrove, 1991). The prevalence of MSDs has prompted OSHA to implement a four-pronged approach to reduce the occurrence of these ergonomic injuries in the workplace. The four-pronged approach encompasses the use of ergonomic guidelines, enforcement, outreach, and assistance (training) plus a national advisory committee to reduce workplace MSDs. OSHA's actions demonstrate the seriousness and importance of ergonomics.

ERGONOMIC PROGRAMS

The implementation of ergonomic programs has grown among corporations as they have sought to address rising medical expenses, higher workers' compensation claims, and lower productivity due to worker physical injury and pain (Mansfield & Armstrong, 1997; Nickerson, 2001; Sheley, 1995). Studies on the ergonomic programs reported that ergonomic programs have resulted in fewer injuries, and better physical and psychological health. In addition, the studies reported that workers felt more productive, satisfied, and comfortable following ergonomic implementation. A study conducted by Williamson, Gower, and Clarke (1994) on implementing ergonomic modifications through job design by changing the hours of shift work from 8 to 12 hour shifts (from 5 to 4 days) for computer operators, reported improvements in health, primarily psychological stress. They report that the improvements are likely due to the increased leisure time and better sleep patterns experienced by the workers after job stressors had been modified.

Although the latter studies indicate that ergonomics can affect other outcomes besides workers' compensation costs, ergonomic literature has primarily focused on cost reduction and the physical benefits of ergonomics. Nevertheless, the examination of the physical environment to improve psychological, as well as physical conditions, is suggested by human factors engineers (Clark, 1996) and management scholars (Frese & Zapf, 1999; Quick, Quick, & Nelson, 2001; Schaubroeck, 1999). Although OSHA reports that ergonomic injuries have been declining since 1994 (OSHA, 2003), the biggest problem faced now with ergonomic implementation is the lack of training. Workers continue to lack the knowledge on causation and, surprisingly, there is a lack of cost-effective solutions (Elliott, 2002; OSHA, 2003).

THE SIGNIFICANCE OF ERGONOMIC TRAINING TO ORGANIZATIONS

Training is the acquisition of knowledge, skills, and abilities (KSA) to perform more effectively (Blanchard & Thacker, 1999). According to Wright and McMahan (1992), training and skill development help sustain a competitive advantage based upon the resource-based view of the firm (Barney, 1991). The resource-based view advocates added value, no substitutes, and scarcity for a competitive advantage. Interestingly, Delery and Doty (1996) note that Pfeffer (1994) included training and skill development as one of sixteen management practices that result in higher productivity and profit across organizations. In concurrence with the importance of training, Delaney and Huselid (1996) reported a positive relationship between perceived financial performance and the use of formal training systems. Research further indicates that management support of training (Cohen, 1990; Wright & McMahan, 1992) and other environmental factors, such as climate (Bennett, Lehman, & Forst, 1999; Tracey, Tannenbaum, & Kavanagh, 1995) relates to effective training transfer. Training transfer involves applying the KSAs acquired during training to one's job for the enhancement of job performance. Training transfer is an acceptable measure of training effectiveness (Kirkpatrick, 1967; Tracey et al., 1995).

Training objectives are necessary to realize the desired benefits of training. Training objective categories based upon Kirkpatrick's (1967) level of training criteria include: trainee reactions to training, learning objectives, training transfer, and training outcomes. Trainee reactions encompass trainee attitudes (affective) and subjective evaluations of training (Blanchard & Thacker, 1999). Learning objectives focus on behaviors that demonstrate learning. Transfer objectives describe the job behaviors that will be affected and maintained by training. Outcomes are the organizational effects that one wants to observe from training such as higher productivity and profitability. Although ergonomically designed workstations have been found to improve working conditions, the absence of training minimizes benefits.

TRAINING AND EMPLOYEE ATTITUDES

While historically considered a prelude to training effectiveness, employee reactions had until recently fallen out of favor as a significant criterion of training effectiveness due solely to negative reactions to the use of attitudinal measures (Haccoun & Saks, 1998). Attitudinal measures were concluded to explain little variance in objective outcomes (Haccoun & Saks, 1998). However, Blanchard and Thacker (1999) recommend that training for attitudinal changes should focus on activities that provide information that contradicts inappropriate attitudes and supports the desired attitude. Therefore, training for attitudinal adjustment must concentrate on the acquisition of knowledge, not changing the attitude (Blanchard & Thacker, 1999). Haccoun and Saks (1998) advocate the use of affective measures in conjunction with other trainee reaction measures. Ideally, ergonomic training should give employees an understanding of how to use their workstations, employees should be satisfied with the ergonomic training they receive, and employees should perceive the training as practical, applicable, and useful. These desired trainee reactions, or attitudes, from an ergonomic perspective promote a higher likelihood for training transfer and a reduction in injury, tension, and fatigue (Cohen, 1996). OSHA advocates training in safe work practices and promotes ergonomic training to ensure that employees are sufficiently informed about the ergonomic hazards to which they may be exposed and thus are able to participate actively for their own protection (Waters & Putz-Anderson, 1996; OSHA 2003).

However, training is one of the most neglected aspects of organizations (OSHA 2003; Smith, 1987) and often one of the first programs to be reduced or omitted during periods of organizational decline (Wright & McMahan, 1992). Most often, training only encompasses on-the-job training, which in itself can be stressful. Therefore, comprehensive procedures that develop skills and enhance worker confidence and self-esteem should be offered.

Ergonomic training begins with an explanation of how the equipment works and how it benefits the company and the employee (productivity and well-being). Alternative maneuverings of the equipment are also explained, as well as the detriments of improper equipment use. Training benefits are accentuated with proper equipment use (Waters & Putz-Anderson, 1996). Accordingly, the detriment segment of training offers information on injury potential, type, and prevention (Waters & Putz-Anderson, 1996). The identification and elimination of discomfort sources improves loss frequency and severity (negative outcomes). To maximize training transfer, training must be associated with employee experiences (Cohen, 1996). For instance, real workplace examples should be given. At Mitshibishi, training courses explain "What causes MSD injuries, What can be done to prevent them, What a good posture is, and What a poor posture is" (Tyler, 1998). Training manuals offer documentation for workers to refer to for guidance on how to alter workstations for comfort.

THE RELATIONSHIP BETWEEN ERGONOMIC TRAINING AND STRAIN

Various stress reduction and stress management techniques are often directed at increasing individual resistance to stressors at work (prevention). Such programs include training, counseling, and exercise. According to Kahn and Byosiere (1992), programs can be classified into four groups:

a. "those that attempt to alter the stressors as perceived by the individual,
b. those that concentrate directly on reducing the strains evoked by perceived stressors,
c. those that aim to alter the stress-resistant properties of the person more generally, and
d. those that are intended to improve the stress-moderating properties of the interpersonal situation (p. 632)."

Stress management programs are intended to train individuals in techniques for reducing their physiological and psychological responses to stressors. Stress reduction programs are few and primarily deal with aspects of control such as increased participation in decision making, autonomy on the job itself, and control over one's work schedule (Kahn & Byosiere, 1992). The examination of other environmental interventions such as ergonomic training offers promise for reducing and preventing experienced workplace strain.

Lazarus (1994) offered three main strategies for reducing stress in the workplace. First, alter the conditions of work so that they are either less stressful or less counterproductive for those attempting to use effective coping. This method is primarily used for reducing stress for large groups when there is a widespread or common reaction to the environment. Ergonomic design is applicable to this method. For instance, change the physical environment to reduce demands and to allow employee participation and decision making in regard to that environment (Houtman & Kompier, 1995). Second, help those who are having difficulty adapting to conditions that are impossible or difficult to change to cope more effectively. Ergonomic training answers this call for stress reduction (management) techniques. For instance, ergonomic training encourages participation to influence change over one's physical environment; thereby, reducing stress-related illness (Schurman & Israel, 1995). Third, identify the individual or group relationships within the work setting that are stressful, and try to change them for the individual or group on the basis of relational findings. This approach does not treat everyone alike and assumes that work environments may not have the same effect on everyone. Ergonomics recognizes that individuals have different needs and ergonomic implementation through practice and training addresses individual differences. Thus, the examination of environmental interventions such as ergonomic design offer promise for reducing and preventing experienced workplace strain.

MODEL DEVELOPMENT

Experienced stress in the work environment stems from a mismatch in the combination of the following sources:

- the social and physical environments at work and at leisure,
- the task, organizational factors, and
- the personality attributes of the individual (Smith, 1987).

Figure 1 depicts the predicted relationships between understanding ergonomic training, ergonomic training satisfaction, and organizational stress. In the following hypothesis, the results of ergonomic training include two components, understanding ergonomic training and ergonomic training satisfaction. Person-environment fit theory is utilized as the conceptual foundation linking ergonomic training understanding and satisfaction with experienced strain.

PERSON-ENVIRONMENT FIT:
THE ENVIRONMENT AS A STRESSOR

The central hypothesis of Person-Environment Fit (P-E) theory is that misfit between the person and the environment leads to psychological, physiological, and behavior strains (Caplan, 1987). P-E fit can take either of two forms. The first form, Supplies-Values fit (S-V), is the extent to which the rewards and supplies provided by the environment match the needs and

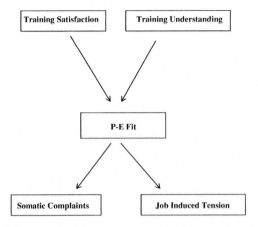

Figure 1.   Ergonomic Training and Stress Model

preferences of the person (values). Supplies may include extrinsic rewards like pay, as well as intrinsic rewards like self-praise. The second form, Demand-Ability fit (D-A), is the extent to which the demands and require- ments of the environment match the skills and abilities of the person (Edwards & Harrison, 1993). Fundamentally, ergonomic practices are a natural fit with this theory as it applies more to the D-A form of P-E Fit. Ergonomically designed workstations are associated with demands, while individual worker characteristics represent abilities.

Ergonomic implementation embraces the idea that work environments should fit people, not the reverse. The OSHA definition of ergonomics emphasizes ergonomic redesign—providing working environments that minimize physical demands on the worker. When a process is implemented in which workers do not exceed their physical capabilities, they can work without fatigue and do their jobs better, thereby increasing productivity and improving quality (Rose, 1995). If workers are required to perform tasks beyond their capabilities, damage to the worker may result and pro- duction and quality may suffer from improper tool use and from tasks that are not designed to fit the worker (Champion, 1995). The ergonomic workstation should be designed to minimize reach, offer enough clearance without interference to body segments, encompass the available strength of the operator, and reduce biomedical stress. Accordingly, it is important to analyze the physical needs, preferences, and job demands of workers to identify work postures and positions that may be contributing to fatigue and discomfort (Napoli, 1994).

Although ergonomically designed workstations have been found to improve working conditions, less is known about the results of ergonomic *training* on employee outcomes. Accordingly, OSHA (2003) has suggested training as a complementary tool to ergonomic implementation to maximize health benefits. Ergonomic training facilitates the manipulation of the physical work environment to achieve proper fit (Miles & Perrewé, 2001). Ideally, ergonomic training should give employees an understanding of how to use their workstations and employees should be satisfied with the ergonomic training they receive. Provided that understanding and satisfaction of ergonomic training is achieved, it is suggested that individuals will perceive a fit with their environments and, subsequently experience less strain. Thus, the following exploratory hypothesis linking these relationships is offered:

H.1: Perceptions of person-environment fit will mediate the relationship between ergonomic training (i.e., understanding and satisfaction) and strain (i.e., job tension and somatic complaints).

SAMPLE AND PROCEDURE

A questionnaire was distributed to office workers by the researchers and assistants. The surveys were completed at the point of distribution for a 90 percent response rate. The sample comprised 89 office workers from various industries including education, technology, banking, and the military. The location of the respondents included the mid-Atlantic and southern states. Demographically, the sample was 47 percent male and 53 percent female. The most prevalent age group ranged from 31 to 40, having 15 average years of work experience. Job responsibilities comprised clerical to executive management assignments. Sixty-six percent of the respondents were married, 20 percent were single, and the balance had other personal arrangements. Forty-eight percent of the respondents had children living at home. Seven questionnaires had missing data and were omitted from the study.

MEASURES

The variables were measured using 5- and 7-point Likert-type scales. Unless indicated otherwise, higher scores indicated greater levels of the variable measured. The items were averaged for each construct. Construct assessment incorporated scales used in previous research and scales designed specifically for the study.

Ergonomic training includes all methods and policies used to help workers fully comprehend the features and importance of ergonomic tools and practices. Training encompasses formal programs, equipment use demonstrations, safety policies and manuals. It is comprised of two constructs.

Training Satisfaction

Satisfaction with the training received on workstation usage is an indicator of successful ergonomic training, since training satisfaction promotes practice. Three items were specifically designed to assess this construct. The corresponding Cronbach reliability estimate was .94. (A sample item is "I am satisfied with the training I have received regarding the use of my work area"—scale from "strongly disagree" to "strongly agree").

Training Understanding

Understanding how to adjust the workstation suggests that the ergonomic training was effective. Two items were specifically designed to assess this construct. The corresponding Cronbach reliability coefficient of .69 is near the .70 threshold suggested by Nunnally (1978). (A sample item is "I understand how to use my workstation"—scale from "strongly disagree" to "strongly agree").

Perceptions of Person-Environment Fit (P-E Fit).

Person-environment fit requires demands and conditions of the environment to match the skills and abilities of the person. Postural comfort and environmental comfort provide evidence of P-E Fit. If employees experience physical discomfort in the environment there is inadequate person-environment fit. The eight items used for postural comfort were adapted from previous research (Cakir, 1995) and reverse coded. (A sample item is "I feel strain in my wrists while I am working at my workstation"—scale from "strongly disagree" to "strongly agree"). Environmental comfort likewise provides evidence of P-E Fit. Environments free from physical distraction are conducive to worker comfort and productivity. Nine items measure this construct. Two items were adopted from previous research (Perrewé & Ganster, 1989). The balance of these items was specifically designed to assess this construct. The corresponding Cronbach reliability estimate was .90. (A sample adopted item is "The temperature in my work area during the summer is:" A sample designed item is "Viewing my monitor is:—scale from "very uncomfortable" to "very comfortable").

Strain

Two measures of strain were examined. Somatic complaints was measured by a five-item scale developed by House and Rizzo (1972). This is a component of their Anxiety-Stress Questionnaire. The corresponding Cronbach reliability estimate was .72. Job-induced tension was measured by a seven-item scale developed by House and Rizzo (1972), also a part of their Anxiety-Stress Questionnaire. The corresponding Cronbach reliability estimate was .82.

Negative Affectivity

Negative affectivity was used as a control variable, as suggested by previous research (Brief, Burke, George, Robinson, & Webster, 1988; Schaubroeck, Ganster, & Fox, 1992) when utilizing self-report measures in stress studies to minimize dispositional bias. Negative affectivity was measured by ten negative emotions using the PANAS Scale (Watson, Clark, & Tellegen, 1988). The corresponding Cronbach reliability estimate was .84.

ANALYSIS

Following Baron and Kenny (1986), a series of three regression equations were estimated to test whether there is a mediating effect of person-environment fit between ergonomic training and job tension and somatic complaints. First, the mediator (i.e., person-environment fit) is regressed on the independent variable (i.e., training understanding and training satisfaction). Second, the dependent variables (i.e., job tension and somatic complaints) are regressed on the independent variable (i.e., training understanding and training satisfaction). Third, the dependent variables are regressed on both the independent variable and the mediator. In order for mediation to be established, the effect of the independent variable on the dependent variable must be less in the third equation than in the second. If the beta is less in the third equation, but significant, partial mediation has been established. If the beta is no longer significant in the third equation, full mediation has been established.

RESULTS

Means, standard deviations, reliability estimates, and intercorrelations among the study variables are reported in Table 1. As shown, training satisfaction was positively correlated with PE-Fit and negatively correlated with somatic complaints and job-induced tension. Conversely, training understanding was only negatively related to the strain variable of job-induced tension.

To test the mediations, we used hierarchical regression analysis (Cohen & Cohen, 1975) commencing with the control variable, negative affectivity, followed by the regression equations as previously described. As can be seen in Table 2, training understanding did not have a statistically signifi-

TABLE 1

Means, Standard Deviation, Reliability Estimates and Intercorrelations Among Study Variables

Variable	M	SD	1	2	3	4	5	6
1. Negative Affectivity	1.70	.56	(.84)					
2. Training Satisfaction	3.17	1.06	.03	(.94)				
3. Training Understanding	4.09	.73	-.13	.29**	(.69)			
4. PE-Fit	3.38	.65	-.16	.46**	.16	(.90)		
5. Somatic Complaints	2.24	.80	.39**	-.24*	-.15	-.45**	(.72)	
6. Job Induced Tension	2.68	.83	.30**	-.24*	-.28*	-.46**	.67**	(.82)

Notes: $N = 82$; *$p < .05$; **$p < .01$

TABLE 2

Regression Results: Test of Mediating Effects of Person-Environment Fit on the Relationship between Ergonomic Training and Job Induced Tension

Variables	Mediator Person-Environment Fit				Dependent Job Induced Tension			
	β	R^2	F	df	β	R^2	F	df
Negative Affectivity	-.16	.01	2.16	1, 81	.30**	.09	8.01**	1, 8
Negative Affectivity	-.17	.21	8.30***	3, 79				
Training Understanding	.01							
Training Satisfaction	.46***							
Negative Affectivity					.31**	.15	7.21***	2, 79
Training Satisfaction					-.25*			
Negative Affectivity					.33***	.27	9.45***	2.78
Training Satisfaction					-.07			
Person-Environment Fit					-.39***			

Notes: * $p < .05$; ** $p < .01$; ; *** $p < .001$

TABLE 3

Regression Results: Test of Mediating Effects of Person-Environment Fit on the Relationship between Ergonomic Training and Somatic Complaints

| | Mediator | | | | Dependent | | | |
| | *Person-Environment Fit* | | | | *Somatic Complaints* | | | |
Variables	β	R^2	F	df	β	R^2	F	df
Negative Affectivity	-.16	.01	2.16	1, 81	.39***	.15	14.46***	1, 81
Negative Affectivity	-.17	.21	8.30***	3, 79				
Training Understanding	.01							
Training Satisfaction	.46***							
Negative Affectivity					.40***	.21	10.90***	2, 80
Training Satisfaction					-.25*			
Negative Affectivity					.33***	.31	11.94***	3, 79
Training Satisfaction					-.08			
Person-Environment Fit					-.36***			

Notes: $*p < .05$; $**p < .01$; $***p < .001$

cant relationship with perceptions of person-environment fit. Thus, Hypothesis 1 was not supported. Given that understanding was not related to the proposed mediating variable, further mediation analysis did not include training understanding.

Training satisfaction, however, had a positive relationship with perceptions of person-environment fit (β =.46, $p < .01$), supporting Hypothesis 2. The final hypothesis proposed that perceptions of person-environment fit would mediate the relationship between ergonomic training and strain. As can be seen in Tables 2 and 3, training satisfaction had a negative relationship with job-induced tension (β = -.25, $p < .05$) and somatic complaints (β = -.25, $p < .05$). Further, perceptions of person-environment fit had negative associations with job-induced tension (β = -.39, $p < .01$) and somatic complaints (β = -.36, $p < .01$). In regard to mediation, when perceptions of person-environment fit are entered into the equation, the betas for training satisfaction on both job-induced tension and somatic complaints are no longer statistically significant. Thus, according to Baron and Kenny (1986), perceptions of person-environment fit fully mediate the relationship between training satisfaction and the outcomes of job-induced tension and somatic complaints.

Study results suggest ergonomic training as a means to lessen perceived stress; thereby supporting the value of the organization's focus on minimizing objective stressors. Ergonomics has become an important practice in the workplace as it lowers health costs and affects absenteeism, job satisfaction, and productivity through its role as a stress prevention mechanism. The results from this study suggest that receiving satisfying ergonomic training reduces both job-induced tension and somatic complaints through improved perceptions of person-environment fit.

DISCUSSION AND IMPLICATIONS
FOR MANAGEMENT

This chapter offers further well-being considerations to human resources professionals by revealing the impact that ergonomics via ergonomic training can have on organizational stress in the workplace. The role of ergonomic training has been identified as a means to prevent or reduce stressors. Both ergonomic training and organizational stress have economic implications to the corporation in the areas of medical costs, absenteeism, and productivity. Organizational stress at its worse can be debilitating to an employee such that it manifests itself in physical conditions (high blood pressure), psychological conditions (job dissatisfaction), or organizational conditions (absenteeism). By implementing satisfying ergonomic training programs corporations can intervene in the stress process by preventing or reducing the magnitude of physical stressors. Evidence provided by our study indicates that satisfaction with ergonomic training can reduce the strains of somatic complaints and job-induced tension. Training satisfaction appears to be more important than training understanding in affecting perceptions of person-environment fit and stress reduction. Understanding the use of workstations does not necessarily imply that the environment fits well with one's needs. Training satisfaction, on the other hand, supports the person-environment fit perspective and, subsequently, has a negative association with organizational strain.

Accordingly, this work encourages the intervention of ergonomics and ergonomic training as means of reducing employee strain through its effect on the person-environment fit. Given previous research, cost reductions may be achieved through lower medical costs and fewer worker compensation claims as debilitating aspects of stress are limited for the worker. In addition, the implementation of programs may have a lasting impact on workers' physical and mental health. The physical impact would be in the form of fewer physical problems such as eyestrain, back strain, neck strain, and carpal tunnel syndrome, while the psychological side would realize fewer strains such as tension, depression, and job dissatisfaction. Although the scope of the study was limited to workers in an office environment, ergonomic design and programs are presumed to be applicable to a variety of jobs in different industries. It is applicable to those who work in production, construction and service. It is applicable to those that sit, stand, twist, turn, think, walk, run, and work with heavy equipment. In other words, ergonomics is applicable to every worker who uses a tool.

STUDY LIMITATIONS

First, the sample size was small and may have constrained some of the findings. For example, the effects of ergonomic training understanding on perceptions of person-environment fit and experienced strain may not have been detected due to low statistical power. Further, all measures were cross-sectional and self-reported. Self-report data has the potential to inflate the observed relationships spuriously, thus, introducing common method variance as an alternative explanation for the findings. However, according to James, Gent, Hatter, and Corey (1979), common method variance should be considered seriously when there appears to be a general and pervasive influence that operates in a systematic fashion to inflate the observed relationships. By examining the correlation matrix in Table 1, it can be seen that the correlations are not uncharacteristically high. Third, the ergonomic training measures were not well established. Other limitations include our minimal attention to how individual differences moderate stress and subsequent outcomes, and our concentration primarily on physical stressors and job demands. However, these limitations offer numerous considerations for future research in the ergonomic-stress area.

FUTURE RESEARCH

The areas for future research are broad. First, by extending the study to encompass ergonomic design of workstations, the study could provide additional evidence of the importance of ergonomic design to preventing stress. Likewise, by extending the study to encompass groups other than office workers, such as factory workers, the study could again provide further evidence of the importance of ergonomic design at a group level. Furthermore, incorporating the effects of organizational factors such as corporate culture and health and safety policies into the relationships between ergonomics, person-environment fit and organizational strain may offer additional insight into the complexities of these relationships. Other considerations include the individual differences moderation of stress and subsequent outcomes.

CONCLUSION

Experienced stress remains a critical concern to HR professionals. Due to the rising costs associated with workplace stress the search for continued practices and methods to intervene and reduce experienced stress continues. Identifying and minimizing workplace stressors are strategies that organizations can embrace to combat unfavorable strains. The implementation of ergonomic practices and training are methods to assist in attaining these goals. Ergonomics has become an important practice in the workplace as it lowers health costs and affects absenteeism, job satisfaction, and productivity through its role as a stress prevention mechanism. The results from our study suggest that receiving satisfying ergonomic training reduces both job-induced tension and somatic complaints through improved perceptions of person-environment fit.

REFERENCES

Barney, J. (1991). Firm resources and sustained competitive advantage. *Journal of Management, 17,* 99-120.

Baron, R. M., & Kenny, D. A. (1986). The moderator-mediator variable distinction in social psychological research: Conceptual, strategic, and statistical considerations. *Journal of Personality and Social Psychology, 5,* 1173-1184.

Bennett, J. B., Lehman, W. E. K., & Forst, J. K. (1999). Change, transfer, and customer orientation: A contextual model and analysis of change-driven training. *Group & Organization Management, 24*(2), 188-216.

Bhagat, R. S., Allie, S. M., & Ford, D. L. (1995). Coping with stressful life events: An empirical analysis. In R. Crandall & P. L. Perrewé (Eds.), *Occupational Stress: A Handbook* (pp. 93-112). New York: Taylor and Francis Publishing.

Blanchard, P. N., & Thacker, J. W. (1999). *Effective Training: Systems, Strategies and Practices.* Englewood Cliffs, NJ: Prentice Hall.

Braganza, B. J. (1994). Ergonomics in the office. *Professional Safety, 39,* 22-27.

Brief, A. P., Burke, M. J., George, J. M., Robinson, B. S., & Webster, J. (1988). Should negative affectivity remain an unmeasured variable in the study of job stress? *Journal of Applied Psychology, 73,* 193-198.

Brief, A. P. & George, J. M. (1995). Psychological stress and the workplace: A brief comment on Lazarus' outlook. In P. L. Perrewé & R. Crandall (Eds.), *Occupational Stress: A Handbook* (pp. 15-20). New York: Taylor and Francis Publishing.

Brophy, M. & Grant, C. (1996). Office ergonomics. In A. Bhattacharya & J. D. McGlothlin (Eds.), *Occupational Ergonomics: Theory and Applications* (pp. 387-401). New York: Marcel Dekker.

Burke, R. J. & Greenglas, E. (1995). A longitudinal study of psychological burnout in teachers. *Human Relations, 48,* 187-202.

Buunk, B. P., Schaufeli, W. B., & Ybema, J. F. (1994). Burnout, uncertainty, and the desire for social comparison among nurses. *Journal of Applied Social Psychology, 24,* 1701-1718.

Cakir, A. (1995). Acceptance of the adjustable keyboard. *Ergonomics, 38,* 1728-1744.

Caplan, R. D. (1987). Person-environment fit theory and organizations: Commensurate dimensions, time perspectives, and mechanisms. *Journal of Vocational Behavior, 31,* 248-267.

Cartwright, S., Cooper, C. L., & Murphy, L. R. (1995). Diagnosing a healthy organization: A proactive approach to stress in the workplace. In L. R. Murphy, J. J. Hurrell, Jr., S. L. Sauter, & G. P. Keita, (Eds.), *Job Stress Interventions,* 217-233. Washington, DC, American Psychological Association.

Champion, F. M. (1995). Ergonomic design options for call centers. *Telemarketing, 63,* 38-42.

Cherniss C. (1992). Long-term consequences of burnout: An exploratory study. *Journal of Organizational Behavior, 13,* 1-11.

Clark, D. R. (1996). Workstation evaluation and design. In A. Bhattacharya & J. D. McGlothlin (Eds.), *Occupational Ergonomics: Theory and Applications* (pp. 279-301). New York: Marcel Dekker.

Cohen, A. L. (1996). Worker participation: Approaches and issues. In A. Bhattacharya & J. D. McGlothlin (Eds.), *Occupational Ergonomics: Theory and Applications* (pp. 259-277). New York: Marcel Dekker.

Cohen, D. J. (1990). What motivates trainees? *Training and Development Journal, 44*(11), 91-94.

Cohen J., & Cohen P. (1975). *Applied Multiple Regression/Correlation Analysis for the Behavioral Sciences,* Hillsdale, NJ: Lawrence Erlbaum Associates.

Cordes, C. L., & Dougherty, T. W. (1993). A review and an integration of research on job burnout. *Academy of Management Review, 18*(4), 621-656.

Cropanzano, R., Howes, J. D., Grandey, A. A., & Toth, P. (1997). The relationships of organizational politics and support to work behaviors, attitudes and stress. *Journal of Organizational Behavior, 18,* 159-180.

Delaney, J. T., & Huselid, M. A. (1996). The impact of human resource management practices on perceptions of organizational performance. *Academy of Management Journal, 39,* 949-969.

Delery, J. E., & Doty, D. H. (1996). Modes of theorizing in strategic human resource management: Test of universalistic, contingency and, configurational performance predictions. *Academy of Management Journal, 39,* 802-835.

Dwyer, D. J., & Ganster, D. C. (1991). The effects of job demands and control on employee attendance and satisfaction. *Journal of Organizational Behavior, 12,* 595-608.

Edwards, J. R., & Harrison, R.V. (1993). Job demands and worker health: Three dimensional reexamination of the relationship between person-environment fit and strain. *Journal of Applied Psychology, 78,* 628-648.

Elliot, F. (2002). Employees it's up to you. *Occupational Health and Safety, 71*(9), 82-85.

Ferris, G. R., Frink, D. D., Gilmore, D. C., & Kacmar, K. M. (1994). Understanding as an antidote for the dysfunctional consequences of organizational politics as a stressor. *Journal of Applied Social Psychology, 24,* 1201-1220.

Frese, M., & Zapf, D. (1999). On the importance of the objective environment in stress and attribution theory. Counter point to Perrewé and Zellars. *Journal of Organization Behavior, 20*(5), 761-765.

Frone, M. R. (1990). Intolerance of ambiguity as a moderator of the occupational role stress-strain relationship: A meta-analysis. *Journal of Organizational Behavior, 11,* 309-320.

Grant, K. A. (1996). Job analysis. In A. Bhattacharya & J. D. McGlothlin (Eds.), *Occupational Ergonomics: Theory and Applications* (pp. 259-277). New York: Marcel Dekker.

Haccoun, R. R., & Saks, A. M. (1998). Training in the 21st century: Some lessons from the last one. *Canadian Psychology, 39,* 1-2, 33-51.

Hackman, J. R., & Oldham, G. R. (1980). *Work Redesign.* Reading, MA: Addison-Wesley.

House, R. J., & Rizzo, J. (1972). Role conflict and ambiguity as critical variables in a model of organizational behavior. *Organizational Behavior and Human Performance, 7,* 467-505.

Houtman, I. L. D., & Kompier, M. A. J. (1995). Courses on workstress: A growing market, but what about their quality? In L. R. Murphy, J. J. Hurrell, Jr., S. L. Sauter, & G. P. Keita (Eds.), *Job Stress Interventions* (pp. 337-349). Washington, DC, American Psychological Association.

Hurrell, J. J. (2001). Psychosocial factors and musculoskeletal disorders. In P. L. Perrewé & D. C. Ganster (Eds.), *Research in Occupational Stress and Well Being: Exploring Theoretical Mechanisms and Perspectives* (Vol. 1, pp. 233-256). Oxford, UK, JAI Press/Elsevier Science.

James, L. R., Gent, M. J., Hater, J. J., & Corey, K. E. (1979). Correlates of psychological influence: An illustration of the psychological climate approach to work environment perceptions, *Personnel Psychology, 32,* 563-588.

Kahn, R. L., & Byosiere, P. (1992). Stress in organizations. In M. Dunnette, & L. Hough, (Eds.), *Handbook of Industrial and Organizational Psychology* (3rd Ed., pp. 571-650). Palo Alto, CA: Consulting Psychology Press.

Kaldenberg, D. O., & Becker, B. W. (1992). Workload and psychological strain: A test of the French, Rodgers, and Cobb hypothesis. *Journal of Organizational Behavior, 13*, 617-624.

Karasek, R. A., Jr. (1979). Job demands, job decision latitude and mental strain: implications for job redesign. *Administrative Science Quarterly, 24*, 285-306.

Kirkpatrick, D. L. (1967). Evaluation of training. In R. L. Craig & L. R. Bittel (Eds.), *Training and Development Handbook* (pp. 87-112). New York: McGraw-Hill.

Krawczyk, S. (1996). Psychophysical methodology and the evaluation of manual material handling and upper extremity intensive work. In A. Bhattacharya & J. D. McGlothlin (Eds.), *Occupational Ergonomics: Theory and Applications* (pp. 137-163). New York: Marcel Dekker.

Lazarus, R. S. (1994). Psychological stress in the workplace. In R. Crandall & P. L. Perrewé (Eds.), *Occupational Stress: A Handbook* (pp. 3-14). New York: Taylor and Francis Publishing.

Lee, R. T., & Ashforth, B. E. (1996). A meta-analytic examination of the correlates of the three dimensions of job burnout. *Journal of Applied Psychology, 81*, 123-133.

Lindsey, E. (1999). Keying in on computer problem. *Business Insurance, 33*(37), 3, 10.

McGrath, J. E. (1976). Stress and behavior in organizations. In M. Dunnette (Ed.), *Handbook of Industrial and Organizational Psychology* (pp. 1353-1395). Chicago: Rand McNally.

Mansfield, J. A., & Armstrong, T. J. (1997). Library of Congress workplace ergonomic program. *American Industrial Association Journal, 58*(2), 138-144.

Miles, A. K., & Perrewé, P.L. (2001). Can I get a chair that fits? An examination of the ergonomic design and training association with person-environment fit, control, and strain. Presentation at Academy of Management Meetings, Washington, DC.

Napoli, L. (1994). Office product guide. *Government Executive, 26*, SS1-SS16.

Nickerson, S. (2001). Ergonomics Back to Basics, *Risk Management, 48*(12), 30-33.

Nunnally, J. (1978). *Psychometric Theory* (2nd Ed.). New York, McGraw-Hill.

O'Driscoll, M. P., & Beehr, T. A. (1994). Supervisor behaviors, role stressors and uncertainty as predictors of personal outcomes for subordinates. *Journal of Organizational Behavior, 15*, 141-155.

OSHA, Occupational Safety and Health Administration, U.S. Department of Labor. (2003). Ergonomics. *OSHA.* [Online] Accessed May 30, 2003 at http://www.osha.gov.

OSHA, Occupational Safety and Health Administration, U.S. Department of Labor. (2000). Ergonomics. *OSHA.* [Online] Accessed May 30, 2003 at http://www.osha.gov.

Quick, J. D., Quick, J. C., & Nelson, D. L. (2001). The theory of preventative stress management in organizations, In C. L. Cooper (Ed.), *Theories of Organizational Stress* (pp. 246-268). New York: Oxford University Press.

Parasuraman, S., Greenhaus, J. H., & Granrose, C. S. (1992). Role stressors, social support & well-being among two-career couples. *Journal of Organizational Behavior, 13*, 339-356.

Perrewé, P. L., & Ganster, D. C. (1989). The effects of demands and behavioral control on experienced job stress. *Journal of Organization Behavior, 10,* 213-229.

Perrewé, P. L., & Zellars, K. L. (1999). An examination of attributions and emotions in the transactional approach to the organizational stress process. *Journal of Organization Behavior, 20*(5), 739-752.

Perrewé, P. L., Zellars, K. L., Ferris, G. R., Rossi, A. M., Kacmar, C. J., & Ralston, D. (in press). Neutralizing job stressors: Political skill as an antidote to the dysfunctional consequences of role conflict stressors. *Academy of Management Journal.*

Pfeffer, J. (1994). *Competitive Advantage through People: Unleashing the Power of the Work force.* Boston: Harvard Business School Press.

Ramsey, R. D. (1995). What supervisors should know about ergonomics. *Supervision, 56,*10-12.

Rose, J. (1995). It's time to launch a win-win program. *Occupational Health & Safety, 64,* 55-60.

Schaubroeck, J. (1999). Should the subjective be the objective? On studying mental processes, coping behavior, and actual exposures in organizational stress research. *Journal of Organizational Behavior, 20*(5), 753-760.

Schaubroeck, J., Ganster, D. C., & Fox, M. L. (1992). Dispositional affect and work related stress. *Journal of Applied Psychology, 77,* 322-335.

Schwind, G. F. (1995). Ergonomics: Expanding toward 2000. *Material Handling Engineering, 50,* 141-146.

Schurman, S. J., & Israel, B. A. (1995). Redesigning work systems to reduce stress: A participatory action research approach to creating change. In L. R. Murphy, J. J. Hurrell, Jr., S. L. Sauter, & G. P. Keita, (Eds.), *Job Stress Interventions* (pp. 235-264). Washington, DC: American Psychological Association.

Sheley, E. (1995). Preventing repetitive motion injuries. *HRMagazine, 40,* 57-59.

Smith, M. J. (1987). Occupational Stress. In G. Salvendz (Ed.), *Handbook of Human Factors* (pp. 844-860). New York: Wiley-Intersection.

Stokols, D. (1992). Establishing and maintaining healthy environments: Toward a social ecology of health promotion. *American Psychologist, 47,* 6-22.

Tracey, J. B., Tannenbaum, S. I., & Kavanagh, M. J. (1995). Applying trained skills on the job: The importance of the work environment. *Journal of Applied Psychology, 80*(2), 239-252.

Tyler, K. (1998). Sit up straight. *HRMagazine, 43*(10), 122-128.

Updegrove, D. A., & Updegrove, K. H. (1991). Computers and health-individual and institutional protective measures. *Cause/Effect, 14,* 40-45.

Waters, T. R., & Putz-Anderson, V. (1996). Manual materials handling. In A. Bhattacharya & J. D. McGlothlin (Eds.), *Occupational Ergonomics: Theory and Applications* (pp. 329-349). New York: Marcel Dekker.

Watson, D., Clark, L. A., & Tellegen, A. (1988). Development and validation of brief measures of positive and negative affect: The PANAS scales. *Journal of Personality and Social Psychology, 54,* 1063-1070.

Williamson, A. M., Gower, C. G. I., & Clarke, B. C. (1994). Changing the hours of Shiftwork: A comparison of 8- and 12-hour shift rosters in a group of computer operators. *Ergonomics, 37*(2), 287-298.

Wright, P. M., & McMahan, G.,C. (1992). Theoretical perspectives for strategic human resource management. *Journal of Management, 18,* 295-320.

Xie, J. L., & Schaubroeck, J. (2001). Bridging approaches and findings across diverse disciplines to improve job stress research. In P. L. Perrewé & D. C. Ganster (Eds.), *Research in occupational stress and well being* (Vol. 1, pp. 1-53). Oxford, UK: Elsevier Science.

Zellars, K. L., & Perrewé, P. L. (2001). Affective personality and the content of emotional social support: Coping in organizations. *Journal of Applied Psychology, 86,* 459-467.

CHAPTER 4

NEW DIRECTIONS FOR RESEARCH ON POLITICAL PERCEPTIONS

Suggestions and an Illustrative Example

Ken Harris and K. Michele Kacmar
Florida State University

ABSTRACT

Previous research on perceptions of politics is briefly reviewed, highlighting five needed new directions for future research: (1) expanding and clarifying the variables that have been shown to predict, moderate, or are predicted by perceptions of politics; more critically examining the (2) measurement, (3) dimensionality, and (4) discriminant validity of perceptions of politics; and (5) exploring the value of alternative statistical analyses when examining perceptions of politics. An example of an alternative statistical analysis (testing for a 3-way interaction effect) is presented, using data from two different large samples. The results support the hypothesis tested and demonstrate the potential usefulness of at least one of the authors' recommendations.

New Directions in Human Resource Management
A Volume in: Research in Management, pages 91–109.
Copyright © 2003 by Information Age Publishing, Inc.
All rights of reproduction in any form reserved.
ISBN: 1-59311-099-5 (hardcover), 1-59311-098-7 (pbk.)

For years researchers have noted that people perceive the existence of organizational politics in virtually every organization. Although this is the case, few empirical research efforts attempted to confirm this assumption until recently. Gandz and Murray (1980) conducted one of the earliest empirical investigations and a year later Porter, Allen, and Angle (1981) wrote a conceptual piece in *Research in Organizational Behavior* on organizational politics. While both of these efforts were extremely insightful, research in this area really did not take off until Ferris, Russ, and Fandt (1989) proposed a conceptual model of perceptions of organizational politics. Since the introduction of the Ferris et al. model, numerous research investigations have tested and even extended their initial hypotheses. In fact, there have been enough recent studies in the area of perceptions of politics to warrant two reviews (Ferris, Adams, Kolodinsky, Hochwarter, & Ammeter, 2003; Kacmar & Baron, 1999).

Thus, the purpose of this chapter is not to exhaustively review, yet again, all of the literature on politics perceptions, but rather to present areas for future research that may help to advance our knowledge in this area. To accomplish this, we begin by selectively reviewing existing research on politics perceptions and offering conclusions that can be drawn from this research. After this, we suggest five different areas for future research and then actually implement one to demonstrate the plausibility and usefulness of our suggestions.

A BRIEF HISTORY OF POLITICS PERCEPTIONS RESEARCH

In an effort to secure valued rewards and to help ensure that organizational decisions produce favorable outcomes, individuals can engage in political behaviors (Kacmar & Baron, 1999). These behaviors can be covert (e.g., shoring up support for an idea prior to a meeting to discuss and vote on the idea) or overt (e.g., demeaning another's idea in a public setting). However enacted, political behaviors frequently impinge on the well-being of others and/or the organization. When this happens, those impacted recognize that political behaviors have occurred. This recognition is what researchers have referred to as perceptions of organizational politics.

A number of antecedents of politics perceptions have been suggested in the literature which can be divided into three categories: individual, job, and organizational (Ferris et al., 1989). Albeit results with respect to characteristics that predispose an individual to be more aware of political behaviors around them are mixed, some researchers have reported that employees who are older, are female, hold minority status, have longer tenure, or are more educated will have higher perceptions of politics than their counterparts (e.g., Ferris, Frink, Bhawuk, Zhou, & Gilmore, 1996; Ferris, Frink, Galang et al., 1996; Ferris & Kacmar, 1992; Parker, Dipboye, & Jackson, 1995).

More consistent results have been found with respect to the job and organizational antecedents. For instance, feedback, cooperation, formalization, and career development have been found to share a negative relationship with politics perceptions (e.g., Fedor, Ferris, Harrell-Cook, & Russ, 1998; Ferris & Kacmar, 1992; Kacmar, Bozeman, Carlson, & Anthony, 1999; Parker et al., 1995), while centralization, hierarchical level, and accountability have been found to be positively related to politics perceptions (e.g., Drory, 1993; Ferris et al., 1997; Fedor et al., 1998).

A variety of outcomes of perceptions of politics also have been investigated, the majority of which are unattractive to organizations. Specifically, the more political a work environment is viewed by those in it, the higher their intentions to turnover and levels of job anxiety and the lower their job and supervisor satisfaction, organizational citizenship behaviors, organizational commitment, and perceptions of organizational support (e.g., Anderson, 1994; Cropanzano, Howes, Grandey, & Toth, 1997; Kacmar et al., 1999; Nye & Witt, 1993; Parker et al., 1995; Randall, Cropanzano, Bormann, & Birjulin, 1999).

Finally, Ferris et al. (1989) suggested understanding and control as possible moderators of the relationship between politics perceptions and several organizational outcomes. Both of these moderators have been tested and empirically supported (Ferris, Frink, Galang et al., 1996; Kacmar et al., 1999). Other studies have investigated and found support for goal congruence (Witt, 1998), commitment (Hochwarter, Perrewé, Ferris, & Guercio, 1999), participation in decision making (Witt, Andrews, & Kacmar, 2000), and teamwork perceptions (Valle & Witt, 2001) as moderators of several perceptions of politics-outcome relationships. More recently, perceptions of politics has been found to moderate the conscientiousness-job performance relationship (Hochwarter, Witt, & Kacmar, 2000).

Although we acknowledge that what is known in the area perceptions of politics has progressed dramatically in recent years, we suggest there are still a number of unanswered questions and areas for future research. In the following sections, we offer five different areas for future research on perceptions of organizational politics that we believe, if implemented, will advance our knowledge and understanding of this area.

DIRECTIONS FOR FUTURE RESEARCH

Expand and Clarify the Antecedents, Outcomes, and Moderators of Perceptions of Politics

As the preceding review highlights, numerous investigations of antecedents, outcomes, and moderators of politics perceptions have been presented in the literature. However, because the majority of the work on politics perceptions has examined the relationships posed in the original

Ferris et al. (1989) conceptualization, there are still be a number of variables that could be examined. Several new variables were introduced in Ferris et al.'s (2003) revised model of organizational politics perceptions. New antecedents included person-organization fit, participation, and affectivity while justice, performance, and cynicism were added as new outcome variables. The revised model also introduced new moderators such as self-efficacy and political skill. Exploring the usefulness of these and other predictor variables is in the hands of future researchers.

In addition to investigating new antecedents, outcomes, and moderators of perceptions of politics, future researchers also should attempt to clarify and explain existing contradictory findings. Even a quick review of the extant literature shows that consistent results have not been reported for many of the proposed antecedents and outcomes (Ferris et al., 2003; Kacmar & Baron, 1999). It is possible that the differences across studies are a function of the sample, the job type, or some other individual or organizational characteristic. Clearly determining why the results differed across studies is an important next step because, until this is done, it will be impossible to move the field forward by comparing, contrasting, and building upon existing findings.

Consider the Measurement of Perceptions of Politics

Another area in need of attention with respect to perceptions of organizational politics is measurement. Prior to the introduction of the 12-item Perceptions of Organizational Politics Scale (POPS) developed by Kacmar and Ferris (1991), a number of different measures were used to measure politics (e.g., Biberman, 1985; Dubrin, 1978, 1988; Zahra, 1989). In essence, each set of authors developed their own measure of politics perceptions. However, since its inception, the Kacmar and Ferris (1991) measure, or variations of it (e.g., Ferris & Kacmar, 1992; Ferris, Frink, Galang, et al., 1996; Zhou & Ferris, 1995), have been used in the vast majority of investigations on politics perceptions. In 1997, Kacmar and Carlson published an article that further validated the original 12-item scale. In this article they removed a few of the original twelve items and added new ones to create a 15-item scale which was shown to have sound psychometric properties.

The variety of ways in which politics perceptions have been measured has resulted in research findings that are somewhat fragmented and lack consensus. Accordingly, it is difficult to know if the results using different measures are "true" replications or potentially just a function of the different measures used in each study. As with other fields that are accumulating considerable amounts of research in a short time frame, there is a need to determine if similar results are found when different measures are used. Thus, future research should attempt to bridge the gap across studies that used different scales as well as assess perceptions of politics using multiple measures in the same study.

The Dimensionality of Perceptions of Politics

The majority of the definitions of perceptions of organizational politics clearly indicate that it is a multi-dimensional construct (Ferris et al., 1989; Kacmar & Baron, 1999). For instance, individuals can perceive that their coworkers are acting politically, their bosses are acting politically, those in higher management are acting politically, or that the policies and procedures were designed to favor only a few.

Both versions of POPS (Kacmar & Carlson, 1997; Kacmar & Ferris, 1991) were designed to be multi-dimensional in an effort to closely map to existing definitions of politics perceptions and to cover as much of the content domain as possible. Although designed as multidimensional, POPS is frequently used as a unidimensional scale (e.g., Cropanzano et al., 1999; Ferris, Frink, Galang et al., 1996, Kacmar et al., 1999; Parker et al., 1995).

Concerns over the treatment of the dimensionality of perceptions of politics are closely related to the measurement problems noted above. That is, if researchers continue to measure only one dimension of perceptions of politics, but refer to it as perceptions of politics rather than a more specific title (e.g., perceptions of co-workers politics), comparing results across studies will not be fruitful. Further it is possible that each dimension of politics perceptions will predict and be predicted by different variables (Fedor et al., 1998). Extending this notion further, suspected moderators also differentially impact various components of perceptions of politics. Thus, to produce comparable results and so that more specific relationships with politics perceptions and other variables can be teased out, it will be important in the future to determine which aspect of perceptions of politics is the focus of the study and to select a scale or subscale that measures that dimension.

Discriminant Validity

Another important area for politics scholars to research is to further explicate and discriminate between perceptions of politics and related constructs. This is an important step as some researchers have suggested that perceptions of politics is actually the same construct as perceived organizational support, just at the opposite end of the spectrum (Nye & Witt, 1993). Thus, before researchers can feel confident that perceptions of politics is a construct worthy of research attention, it will be necessary for studies to empirically demonstrate the unique content domain of politics perceptions.

Cropanzano and Kacmar (1995) made an initial attempt to isolate the differences and similarities among three constructs often described as polar opposites on the same continuum—politics perceptions, organizational support, and justice. Several of the chapters in their book outlined theoretical arguments designed to distinguish among these constructs (e.g., Shore & Shore, 1995), providing the impetus for much of the empirical work that followed. For instance, Cropanzano et al. (1997) and Randall et al. (1999) included perceptions of politics and support in the same studies to examine their relationships with different outcome variables. Andrews and Kacmar (2001a) extended this line of work by isolating different predictors of politics perceptions, support, and justice. The results from all of these investigations provided additional support for the distinctions between these three constructs. However, more work is necessary on these and other constructs that have been found to be similar either theoretically or empirically to politics perceptions (e.g., ethics, impression management, and social influence tactics). Specifically, researchers should continue to incorporate these three constructs in studies to further elucidate the differences between their predictors, moderators, and outcomes as well as include other key variables that have been found to correlate highly with politics perceptions.

Explore Alternative Statistical Analyses

Based on the models of perceptions of politics that have been tested, we suggest that the majority of politics researchers have assumed that the relationships between politics perceptions and outcome variables are linear in nature. Whereas researchers have mentioned that curvilinear effects exist in many aspects of organizational research, these relationships often are not examined (Ganzach, 1998; MacCallum & Mar, 1995). Thus, one way to advance research in the politics perception area would be to examine curvilinear effects. Possible non-linear relationships that could be explored include perceptions of politics with job anxiety or intent to turnover. In both of these cases the linear relationship between these variables are positive—as perceptions of politics increase, so do anxiety levels and intentions to turnover. However, it is possible that at some point an increase in perceptions of politics no longer continues to increase one's level of anxiety or turnover intentions. Support for this notion can be found in the unfolding model of voluntary turnover which describes an individual's wanting to leave an organization being precipitated by something that shocks him or her (Lee & Mitchell, 1994). It may be that while the tricks of the political players initially shock those impacted by them increasing their anxiety level and intentions to turnover, at some point the victims have seen it all and are no longer shocked by the political behavior. This results in a leveling off of their anxiety level and intentions to turnover, producing a non-linear relationship.

In 1998 Maslyn and Fedor posed the following question: Does measuring different foci of perceptions of politics matter? The answer to their question was yes. Specifically, if researchers match the level of the outcome (e.g., individual, work-group, organization) with the level of the politics perceptions, additional information about the political process results. Essentially what these authors recognized is the multidimensionality of politics perceptions. Because perceptions of politics can occur at multiple levels, analysis techniques used to analyze politics data need to take this into consideration. One such technique, hierarchical linear modeling (HLM), is gaining favor in the literature. In essence, HLM allows one to model effects at multiple levels in the same equation. Thus, political activities enacted by supervisors which influence individual outcomes can be modeled as such using HLM. We believe incorporating HLM into the perceptions of politics arena will allow researchers to more accurately model the process.

A final area in which additional analyses might shed a different light on perceptions of politics research is with respect to interaction effects. While a variety of moderators of politics perceptions-outcome relationships have been proposed and tested, few investigations have examined higher order interactions (i.e., three or more independent variables). Whereas examining the moderating effect of a single variable is interesting, it may not be reflective of reality as there are a host of variables present in the workplace that are likely to exhibit interactive effects in some combination. Thus, a more complex analysis (e.g., testing for 3-way interactions) may more accurately depict the relationships found in the workplace. To our knowledge no studies in the area of politics perceptions have explored higher order interactions. This is unfortunate as previous research in a number of different organizational areas have shown the advantages and insights gained from examining three-way interactions (e.g., Duffy, Ganster, & Shaw, 1998; Gilliland, Groth, Baker, Dew, Polly, & Langdon, 2001; Jex, Bliese, Buzzell, & Primeau, 2001; Parker & Sprigg, 1999).

To demonstrate the importance of exploring higher order interactions as a means of extending research on perceptions of politics, we analyzed data that included two moderatoring variables (quality of leader-member exchange, [LMX] relationship and information received from the organization) of the politics-job satisfaction relationship. Specifically, we propose a three-way interaction between perceptions of politics, quality of LMX relationship, and information received from the organization on individuals' levels of job satisfaction. What follows describes the proposed relationships, data, and results of our illustrative example.

A HIGHER ORDER INTERACTION EXAMPLE

The quality of the relationship between a supervisor and subordinate can be described in terms of the LMX model, which is based on role theory (Dienesch & Liden, 1986; Graen & Scandura, 1987; Liden, Sparrowe, & Wayne, 1997) and social exchange theory (Blau, 1964; Homans, 1958). This model posits that subordinates enact various work roles, which are largely determined by their supervisors. More significant organizational roles are filled by those individuals that supervisors like and view as strong performers, while lesser roles are assigned to those less liked or who are viewed as less capable. Subordinates selected for the more important roles establish close, high quality LMX relationships with their supervisors and receive several advantages such as higher levels of trust and increased emotional support (Dansereau, Graen, & Haga, 1975; Dienesch & Liden, 1986; Graen & Scandura, 1987). Subordinates who do not enjoy high quality LMX relationships with their supervisors are not awarded the same privileges as those who do. Instead, the exchanges supervisors have with subordinates in low quality LMX relationships are limited to only those aspects of the job that would be expected under the normal employment contract (Liden et al., 1997). From those high quality LMX relationships, subordinates receive outcomes such as more favors, formal and informal rewards, and higher levels of communication (Wayne, Shore, & Liden, 1997).

Given all of the information and attention that subordinates in high-quality LMX relationships receive, their level of understanding of the work environment, even politically charged ones, should be high. Having a high level of understanding about the organization, its processes, and/or individuals' actions, makes perceptions of politics less of a threat (Ferris et al., 1989). When the threat from perceptions of politics is decreased, the negative outcomes associated with them should be minimized. Thus, the negative relationship between perceptions of politics and job satisfaction should be minimized by the benefits high quality LMX subordinates receive.

Although the supervisor is an important source of information, not all supervisors provide information equally to their employees. This is one of the fundamental aspects of LMX theory (Dienesch & Liden, 1986), as supervisors form differential relationships with subordinates, and primarily give the additional benefits (such as emotional support or communication) to only those individuals with whom they have high quality relationships. Thus, individuals in lower quality LMX relationships would seem to be left out or not experience a minimization of the negative relationship between politics and job satisfaction.

Upon recognizing that the supervisor is not an adequate source of information, subordinates in lower quality LMX relationships will seek information from alternative sources. One source they may turn to is the organization (Andrews & Kacmar, 2001b; Herold, Liden, & Leatherwood,

1987). Organizations are able to communicate and share information with their employees in a variety of ways including newsletters, the organization's intranet, and posted memos. When individuals believe they are receiving adequate organizational information, they are likely to experience greater feelings of understanding (Ferris et al., 1989). Their increased understanding should result in the negative relationship between politics and job satisfaction being less strong.

As has been previously discussed, we believe that the quality of LMX relationship or the amount of information received from the organization can each help to minimize the negative effects of politics on job satisfaction. However, it also is possible that these two variables will work in tandem to intensify the politics perceptions-job satisfaction relationship. In particular, when an individual is in a high quality LMX relationship and receives a high level of information from the organization, the negative effects of political perceptions on job satisfaction will be minimal. Conversely, the strongest negative effects should be found when the quality of the LMX relationship is low and individuals receive low amounts of information from the organization. Finally, when one or the other condition is positive, that is individuals in high quality LMX relationships or those who receive higher levels of information from the organization, but not both, the negative relationship between perceptions of politics and job satisfaction will be moderate. Thus, we predict:

H: 1.   The quality of LMX relationship and the amount of information received from the organization will interactively effect the negative relationship between perceptions of politics and job satisfaction. More specifically, either high quality LMX relationships or increased amounts of information will minimize the impact of politics; when the two variables are both high the negative relationship will be the weakest, whereas when the two variables are both low, the negative relationship will be the strongest.

METHOD

Sample and Procedure

A paper survey was administered to two different samples in the southeastern part of the United States. The first sample was a large division in a state government agency, from which 787 usable responses were attained (response rate of 67%). Surveys were sent via the internal mail service to each employee in the Division. The survey was accompanied by a letter from the Director of the Division requesting participation and a self-addressed stamped envelope that was to be used to return the survey directly to the researchers.

The second sample was an electric utility cooperative, from which 469 usable responses were attained (response rate of 95%). With this data site, the surveys were mailed to the HR manager. His assistant distributed the surveys to groups of 15-25 employees who were assembled in a conference room at the general office. The distributions took place over a three-day period. The respondents sealed their completed surveys in a return envelope that was provided and gave them to the assistant as they exited the room. The assistant boxed and mailed the completed surveys to the researchers.

Because the surveys were part of a larger employee opinion survey project being conducted at the request of the organizations, we did not have complete freedom in construction of the questionnaire. In particular, data on demographics could not be attained because it was believed that the demographics could be used to identify respondents, thus violating their anonymity and compromising the candor of the responses. Nonetheless, while sample demographic data are not available, it is likely that the organizations' general demographics should be representative of the samples due to the high response rates. Within the state agency, 14% of the employees were African American, 37% were women, and the average age was 42.1 years. In the electric cooperative, 5% of the employees were African American, 22% were women, and the average age was 44.6 years.

For the purposes of exploring the three-way interaction outlined above, the samples were combined to create one data set with 1256 responses. To insure that combining the samples was appropriate, a comparison of the covariance matrices across the two samples was conducted. Results from this test produced a significant chi-square ($X^2(45) = 100.47, p < .000$). However, after the chi-square was adjusted for sample size ($X^2/\text{df} = 2.23$) (Wheaton, Muthen, Alwin, & Summers, 1977), the results indicated that the datasets were combinable. Additionally, the goodness of-fit index (GFI) was .99 and the comparative fit index (CFI) was .99, providing additional evidence that the datasets were similar enough to be combined.

Measures

All of the scales described below were responded to on a 5-point Likert scale. The anchors varied from strongly agree (1) to strongly disagree (5). All scales were coded such that higher values represent higher perceptions of the construct.

Perceptions of Politics

Kacmar and Ferris' (1991) 12-item Perceptions of Organizational Politics Scale (POPS) was used to measure the respondents' perceptions of organizational politics ($\alpha = .88$). A sample item from this scale is "I have seen changes made in policies here that only serve the purposes of a few individuals, not the whole work unit or department."

Relationship Quality

Scandura, Graen, and Novak's (1986) 7-item (e.g., I feel that my immediate supervisor understands my problems and needs) Exchange Quality (LMX) scale was used to measure the quality of the relationship between respondents and their supervisors ($\alpha = .93$).

Information from the Organization

Information from the organization was measured with a 3-item scale ($\alpha = .78$) specially developed for this study. A sample item from this scale is "This organization keeps me informed about changes in policies, procedures, and regulations."

Job Satisfaction

Job satisfaction was measured with three items from Cammann, Fichman, Jenkins, & Klesh (1979) Organizational Assessment Questionnaire ($\alpha = .73$). A sample item from this scale is "All in all, I am satisfied with my job."

Control Variables

In our analyses we controlled three different variables. The first control variable was the *organization*. Even though empirical tests suggested that the samples were combinable, we controlled for organization to eliminate any differences in the results that were a function of either organization. The second and third control variables were *tenure* and *performance*. Tenure was measured in number of years, while performance was measured using an eight-item scale ($\alpha = .81$) adapted from the scale used by Wright, Kacmar, McMahan, and DeLeeuw (1995). A sample item is "I always get things done on time." We controlled for these variables based on the extant literature (e.g., Spector, 1997), which provides evidence that both of these variables have strong impacts on individuals' levels of job satisfaction.

Analyses

We used hierarchical moderated regression analysis (HMRA) (Cohen & Cohen, 1983) to test our hypothesis. There were four steps in the HMRA. In the first step, the three control variables were entered. Perceptions of politics, quality of leader-member exchange, and information received from the organization were entered on the second step. In the third step, we entered the three different two-way interaction terms, POPS*LMX,

POPS*Information, and LMX*Information. In the fourth and final step, the three-way interaction term between POPS, LMX, and Information was entered.

RESULTS

Means, standard deviations and intercorrelations are presented in Table 1. As can be seen, the correlations between each of the control variables and job satisfaction were significant. More specifically, organization, and job satisfaction were positively and significantly related ($r = .234$, $p < .001$), tenure was negatively and significantly related to job satisfaction ($r = -.057$, $p < .05$), and performance and job satisfaction were positively and significantly related ($r = .263$, $p < .001$). This means that individuals who were in the second organization (state government), who were newer to the firm, and reported higher levels of performance, all indicated higher levels of job satisfaction than their counterparts. In sum, the results support the inclusion of each of the control variables in the study.

A number of intercorrelations are high, especially those between POPS, LMX, information, and job satisfaction. Although the correlations between POPS and information ($r = -.554$), job satisfaction and LMX ($r = .518$), and job satisfaction and information ($r = .535$) are all above .50, they are in line with previous research (e.g., Ferris et al., 1993; Gerstner & Day, 1997; Spector, 1997). To further examine whether these variables were distinct from one another, we conducted an exploratory factor analysis using a principal components analysis with an oblimin (oblique) rotation (acknowledging

TABLE 1
Means, Standard Deviations, and Intercorrelations

	Mean	S.D.	1	2	3	4	5	6	7
1. Organization	.75	.97	-						
2. Tenure	3.05	2.05	-.04	-					
3. Performance Appraisal	4.07	.56	-.13	-.08	-				
4. Perceptions of Politics	3.36	.76	.04	.08	-.05	-			
5. Leader-Member Exchange	3.53	1.02	.06	-.05	.25	-.44	-		
6. Information	3.15	.92	.09	-.10	.19	-.55	.42	-	
7. Job Satisfaction	3.64	.74	.23	-.06	.26	-.48	.52	.54	-

Notes: N = 1256; listwise deletion of cases.

$r > .05$ $p < .05$; $r > .07$ $p < .01$; $r > .10$ $p < .001$.

the correlations among the variables). The results produced unique factors for each variable, with no cross loads over .24.

Regression Analyses

Results from the HRMA are shown in Table 2. In the first step, the organization and the individual's performance ratings were significantly related to job satisfaction ($p < .01$), while tenure was not. In total, step 1 explained 14% of the variance in job satisfaction. In step 2, the main effects for POPS, LMX, and information were found to be significant ($p < .01$) and in total, they explained an additional 32% of the variance, thus showing their robust impacts on job satisfaction. In step 3, all three of the

TABLE 2
Results of Hierarchical Moderated Regression
Analyses of the Three-Way Interaction

		DV = Job Satisfaction	
	Beta	ΔR^2	*Adjusted R^2*
Step 1:			
Organization	.18**		
Tenure	.01		
Performance	.16**	.14	.14**
$F(3,1252) = 69.54**$			
Step 2:			
POPS	.57**		
LMX	.83**		
Information	1.16**	.32	.46**
$F(6,1249) = 186.82**$			
Step 3:			
POPS × LMX	-.17**		
POPS × Information	-.26**		
LMX × Information	-.20**	.01	.47**
$F(9,1246) = 128.32**$			
Step 4:			
POPS × LMX × Information	.06**	.01	.48**
$F(10,1245) = 117.53**$			

Notes: $N = 1256$; unstandardized betas provided from the final step.

  $**p < .01$; $*p < .05$.

two-way interactions were significantly related to job satisfaction and explained an additional 1% of the variance. Finally in the fourth step, the three-way interaction between POPS, LMX, and information was significant ($\beta = .06$, $p < .01$) and explained an additional 1% of the variance, providing support for our hypothesis. A graphical representation of the three-way interaction is provided in Figure 1.

Closer examination of Figure 1 offers further confirmation of our hypothesis. Turning first to conditions of high perceptions of politics, we can see that either high information or high relationship quality produced a moderate, and almost identical, level of satisfaction. Further, this level of

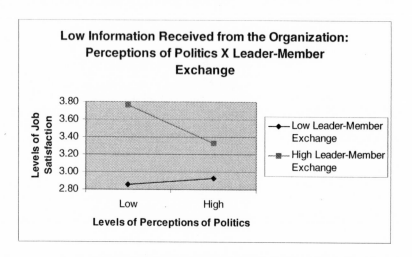

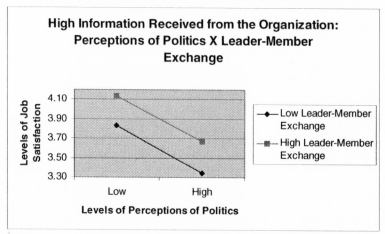

Figure 1.   Three-way interaction of POPS, LMX, and information on Job Satisfaction

satisfaction is lower than that observed by individuals who had a high quality LMX relationship and a high level of information and higher than those who had a low quality LMX relationship and limited information. A similar pattern of results was found when looking at the low perceptions of politics points on the two graphs. When either relationship quality or information were high, but not both, subordinates reported a moderate and almost identical level of job satisfaction. When both relationship quality and information were high, the highest level of job satisfaction was reported while the lowest level was reported when both relationship quality and information were low.

Explaining only 1 percent of the variance in job satisfaction raises the question of the practical significance of our findings. As previously research has noted, small amounts of variance explained by interactions in non-laboratory organizational research are to be expected (Champoux & Peters, 1987; Chaplin, 1991), especially three-way interactions (Jex, Bliese, Buzzell, & Primeau, 2001; Parker & Sprigg, 1999). Additionally, before the final two steps in the HRMA, 46% of the variance in job satisfaction already had been explained. Therefore, when factoring in variables not investigated in this study as well as error variance, explaining 1% of the variance in each of the third and fourth steps is reasonable.

CONCLUSION

This chapter offered five suggestions for future directions of perceptions of politics research. These included:

1. expanding and clarifying the variables that have been shown to predict, moderate, or are predicted by perceptions of politics; more critically examining the
2. measurement,
3. dimensionality, and
4. discriminant validity of perceptions of politics; and
5. exploring the value of alternative statistical analyses when examining perceptions of politics.

In an effort to illustrate the usefulness of at least one of our suggestions, we tested for the three-way interaction of perceptions of politics, leader-member exchange quality, and information on job satisfaction. Results showed that when political perceptions exist and information is high, leader-member exchange makes little difference, but when political perceptions exist and information is low, leader-member exchange makes a considerable difference. We are hopeful that by illustrating that one of our suggestions was a fruitful direction for perceptions of politics researchers to follow, that at least some of our other suggestions will be incorporated into future research efforts in this area.

REFERENCES

Anderson, T. P. (1994). Creating measures of dysfunctional office and organizational politics: The DOOP and short for DOOP scales. *Psychology, 31*, 24-34.

Andrews, M. C., & Kacmar, K. M. (2001a). Discriminating among organizational politics, justice, and support. *Journal of Organizational Behavior, 22*, 347-366.

Andrews, M. C., & Kacmar, K. M. (2001b). Further examination of the sources of feedback scale. *Journal of Business Communication, 38*, 206-226.

Biberman, G. (1985). Personality and characteristic work attitudes of persons with high, moderate, and low political tendencies. *Psychological Reports, 57*, 1303-1310.

Blau, P. M. (1964). *Exchange and power in social life*. New York: Wiley.

Cammann, C., Fichman, M., Jenkins, D., & Klesh, J. (1979). *The Michigan organizational assessment questionnaire*. Ann Arbor, MI: University of Michigan.

Champoux, J. E., & Peters, W. S. (1987). Form, effect size, and power in moderated regression analysis. *Journal of Occupational Psychology, 60*, 243-255.

Chaplin, W. F. (1991). The next generation of moderator research in personality psychology. *Journal of Personality, 59*, 143-178.

Cohen, J., & Cohen, P. (1983). *Applied multiple regression/correlation analysis for the behavioral sciences*. Hillsdale, NJ: Erlbaum.

Cropanzano, R. S., Howes, J. C., Grandey, A. A., & Toth, P. (1997). The relationship of organizational politics and support to work behaviors, attitudes, and stress. *Journal of Organizational Behavior, 18*, 159-181.

Cropanzano, R. S., & Kacmar, K. M. (1995). *Organizational politics, justice, and support: Managing the social climate of the workplace*. Westport, CT: Quorum Books.

Dansereau, F., Graen, G. B., & Haga, W. J. (1975). A vertical dyad approach to leadership within formal organizations. *Organizational Behavior and Human Performance, 13*, 46-78.

Dienesch, R. M., & Liden, R. C. (1986). Leader-member exchange model of leadership: A critique and further development. *Academy of Management Review, 11*, 618-634.

Drory, A. (1993). Perceived political climate and job attitudes. *Organizational Studies, 14*, 59-71.

DuBrin, A. J. (1978). *Winning at office politics*. New York: Van Nostrand Reinhold Company.

DuBrin, A. J. (1988). Career maturity, organizational rank, and political behavioral tendencies: A correlational analysis of organizational politics and career experiences. *Psychological Reports, 63*, 531-537.

Duffy, M. K., Ganster, D. C., & Shaw, J. D. (1998). Positive affectivity and negative outcomes: The role of tenure and job satisfaction. *Journal of Applied Psychology, 83*, 950-959.

Fedor, D., Ferris, G. R., Harrell-Cook, G., & Russ, G. S. (1998). The dimensions of politics perceptions and their organizational and individual predictors. *Journal of Applied Social Psychology, 28*, 1760-1797.

Ferris, G., Adams, G., Kolodinsky, R., Hochwarter, W., & Ammeter, A. (2003). Perceptions of organizational politics: Theory and research directions. In F. Dansereau & F. Yammarino (Eds.), *Multi-level issues in the organizational sciences.* Oxford, UK: JAI Press.

Ferris, G. R., Frink, D. D., Bhawuk, D. P. S., Zhou, J., & Gilmore, D. C. (1996). Reactions of diversity groups to politics in the workplace. *Journal of Management, 22,* 23-44.

Ferris, G. R., Frink, D. D., Galang, M. C., Zhou, J., Kacmar, K. M., & Howard, J. L. (1996). Perceptions of organizational politics: Prediction, stress-related implications, and outcomes. *Human Relations, 49,* 233-266.

Ferris, G. R., & Kacmar, K. M. (1992). Perceptions of organizational politics. *Journal of Management, 18,* 93-116.

Ferris, G. R., Russ, G. S., & Fandt, P. M. (1989). Politics in organizations. In R. A. Giacalone and P. Rosenfeld (Eds.), *Impression management in organizations* (pp. 143-170). Newbury Park, CA: Sage.

Gandz, J., & Murray, V. V. (1980). The experience of workplace politics. *Academy of Management Journal, 23,* 237-251.

Ganzach, Y. (1998). Nonlinearity, multicollinearity and the probability of type II error in detecting interaction. *Journal of Management, 24,* 615-622.

Gerstner, C. R., & Day, D. V. (1997). Meta-analytic review of leader-member exchange theory: Correlates and construct issues. *Journal of Applied Psychology, 82,* 827-844.

Gilliland, S. W., Groth, M., Baker, R. C., Dew, A. F., Polly, L. M., & Langdon, J. C. (2001). Improving applicants' reactions to rejection letters: An application of fairness theory. *Personnel Psychology, 54,* 669-703.

Graen, G. B., & Scandura, T. A. (1987). Toward a psychology of dyadic organizing. In L. L. Cummings & B. M. Staw (Eds.), *Research in organizational behavior* (Vol. 9, pp. 175-208). Greenwich, CT: JAI Press.

Herold, D. M., Liden, R. C., & Leatherwood, M. L. (1987). Using multiple attributions to assess sources of performance feedback. *Academy of Management Journal, 30,* 826-835.

Hochwarter, W. A., Perrewé, P. L., Ferris, G. R., & Guercio, R. (1999). Commitment as an antidote to the tension and turnover consequences of organizational politics. *Journal of Vocational Behavior, 55,* 277-297.

Hochwarter, W. A., Witt, L. A., & Kacmar, K. M. (2000). Perceptions of organizational politics as a moderator of the relationship between conscientiousness and job performance. *Journal of Applied Psychology, 85,* 472-478.

Homans, G. C. (1958). Social behavior as exchange. *American Journal of Sociology, 63,* 597-606.

Jex, S. M., Bliese, P. D., Buzzell, S., & Primeau, J. (2001). The impact of self-efficacy on stressor-strain relations: Coping style as an explanatory mechanism. *Journal of Applied Psychology, 86,* 401-409.

Kacmar, K. M., & Baron, R. A. (1999). Organizational politics: The state of the field, links to related processes, and an agenda for future research. In G. R. Ferris (Ed.), *Research in personnel and human resources management* (Vol. 17, pp. 1-39). Stamford, CT: JAI Press.

Kacmar, K. M., Bozeman, D. P., Carlson, D. S., & Anthony, W. P. (1999). An examination of the perceptions of organizational politics model: Replication and extension. *Human Relations, 52,* 383-416.

Kacmar, K. M., & Carlson, D. S. (1997). Further validation of the Perceptions of Politics Scale (POPS): A multi-sample approach. *Journal of Management, 23,* 627-658.

Kacmar, K. M., & Ferris, G. R. (1991). Perceptions of organizational politics scale (POPS): Development and construct validation. *Educational and Psychological Measurement, 51,* 193-205.

Lee, T. W., & Mitchell, T. R. (1994). An alternative approach: The unfolding model of voluntary employee turnover. *Academy of Management Review, 19,* 51-89.

Liden, R. C., Sparrowe, R. T., & Wayne, S. J. (1997). Leader-member exchange theory: The past and potential for the future. In G. R. Ferris (Ed.), *Research in personnel and human resources management* (Vol. 15, pp. 47-119). Greenwich, CT: JAI Press.

MacCallum, R., & Mar, C. (1995). Distinguishing between moderator and quadratic effects in multiple regression. *Psychological Bulletin, 118,* 405-421.

Maslyn, J., & Fedor, D. B. (1998). Perceptions of politics: Does measuring different foci matter? *Journal of Applied Psychology, 84,* 645-653.

Nye, L. G., & Witt, L. A. (1993). Dimensionality and construct validity of the Perceptions of Politics Scale (POPS). *Educational and Psychological Measurement, 53,* 821-829.

Parker, C. P., Dipboye, R. L., & Jackson, S. L. (1995). Perceptions of organizational politics: An investigation of antecedents and consequences. *Journal of Management, 21,* 891-912.

Parker, S. K., & Sprigg, C. A. (1999). Minimizing strain and maximizing learning: The role of job demands, job control, and proactive personality. *Journal of Applied Psychology, 84,* 925-939.

Porter, L. W., Allen, R. W., & Angle, H. L. (1981). The politics of upward influence in organizations. In L. L. Cummings & B. M. Staw (Eds.), *Research in organizational behavior* (Vol. 3, pp. 109-149). Greenwich, CT: JAI Press.

Randall, M. L., Cropanzano, R., Bormann, C. A., & Birjulin, A. (1999). Organizational politics and organizational support as predictors of work attitudes, job performance, and organizational citizenship behavior. *Journal of Organizational Behavior, 20,* 159-174.

Scandura, T. A., Graen, G. B., & Novak, M. A. (1986). When managers decide not to decide autocratically: An investigation of leader-member exchange and decision influence. *Journal of Applied Psychology, 71,* 579-584.

Shore, L. M., & Shore, T. H. (1995). Perceived organizational support and organizational justice. In R. S. Cropanzano & K. M. Kacmar (Eds.), *Organizational politics, justice, and support: Managing the social climate of the workplace* (pp. 149-164). Westport, CT: Quorum.

Spector, P. E. (1997). *Job satisfaction: Application, assessment, causes, and consequences.* Thousand Oaks, CA: Sage.

Valle, M., & Witt, L. A. (2001). The moderating effect of teamwork perceptions on the organizational politics—job satisfaction relationship. *Journal of Social Psychology, 141,* 379-388.

Wayne, S. J., Shore, L. M., & Liden, R. C. (1997). Perceived organizational support and leader-member exchange: A social exchange perspective. *Academy of Management Journal, 40,* 92-111.

Wheaton, B., Muthen, B., Alwin, D., & Summers, G., (1977). Assessing reliability and stability in panel models. In D. R. Heise (Ed.), *Sociological methodology*. San Francisco: Jossey-Bass.

Witt, L. A. (1998). Enhancing organizational goal congruence: A solution to organizational politics. *Journal of Applied Psychology, 83*, 666-674.

Witt, L. A., Andrews, M. C., & Kacmar, K. M. (2000). The role of participation in decision-making in the organizational politics-job satisfaction relationship. *Human Relations, 53*, 341-358.

Wright, P. M., Kacmar, K. M., McMahan, G. C., and DeLeeuw, K. (1995). Ability as a moderator of the relationship between personality and job performance. *Journal of Management, 21*, 1129-1139.

Zahra, S. A. (1989). Executive values and the ethics of company politics: Some preliminary findings. *Journal of Business Ethics, 8*, 15-29.

Zhou, J., & Ferris, G. R. (1995). The dimensions and consequences of organizational politics perceptions: A confirmatory analysis. *Journal of Applied Social Psychology, 25*, 1747-1764.

CHAPTER 5

COMPLEX, NONLINEAR RELATIONSHIPS BETWEEN GROUP INCENTIVE CONTEXT, DESIGN, AND EFFECTIVENESS

Edilberto F. Montemayor
University of Redlands

ABSTRACT

This study examines the relationships between organizational climate, three design features (formula type, formula complexity, and payout frequency), and two effectiveness dimensions (outcome alignment and behavioral alignment) for group incentive plans. The theoretical framework used has three major building blocks. First, sociological and economic views of organizations are used to understand the effectiveness consequences of organizational context. Second, "macro psychological" modeling (Staw & Sutton, 1993) applied to motivation theory is used to understand the effectiveness consequences of incentive plan design. Third, non-linear thinking is used to understand the net effectiveness consequences that opposing mechanisms have. Results indicate the relationships under study are more complex than previously assumed involving quadratic and interaction terms. For example,

New Directions in Human Resource Management
A Volume in: Research in Management, pages 111–137.
Copyright © 2003 by Information Age Publishing, Inc.
All rights of reproduction in any form reserved.
ISBN: 1-59311-099-5 (hardcover), 1-59311-098-7 (pbk.)

> group incentive contributions to organizational performance seem greater the more an organization resembles either a control-oriented or a commitment-oriented setting. Also, medium formula complexity and medium payout frequency correlate with greater effectiveness, which contradicts simple heuristics that are typically found in the applied literature.

Group incentive plans, which offer a group of eligible employees the opportunity to earn variable bonuses contingent on measurable results of their collective performance, are becoming quite common; the majority of large- and medium-sized firms offer some group incentive (Belcher, 2000). Further, group incentive plans are a key element in strategic human resource management (Pfeffer, 1998), and research spanning more than fifty years has shown that group incentive effectiveness is related to organizational performance. This research stream has been reviewed elsewhere (see Bullock & Tubbs, 1990; Graham-Moore, 1995; Gowen, 1990; Jones, Kato, & Pliskin, 1997; Kruse, 1993; Lawler, 1988; Welbourne & Gomez-Mejia, 1995; White, 1979). Additionally, other research has confirmed that group incentives are an essential element in organizational change to the so-called high performance work systems, human resource management bundles, or configurations (Appelbaum, Bailey, Berg, & Kalleberg, 2000; Bullock & Tubbs, 1990).

Establishing an effective group incentive plan is difficult. More than one third of the attempts to deploy a group incentive fail (Altmansberger, 2000; Heneman, Ledford, & Gresham; 2000). Although we still lack a clear understanding of the factors associated with group incentive effectiveness (Mangel & Useem, 2000), models in the literature concur in that a suitable organizational context, appropriate plan features, and the interplay between context and plan features all contribute to the effectiveness of group incentive plans (De Matteo, Eby, & Sundstrom, 1998; Hammer, 1988; Hanlon & Taylor, 1991).

This study makes three contributions to the literature on group incentive effectiveness. First, while past research has failed to recognize its multi-dimensional nature, this study considers two distinct dimensions of group incentive effectiveness: *outcome alignment* and *behavioral alignment*. These two dimensions correspond to the consequences group incentives have for organizational performance and change, respectively. The first effectiveness dimension, outcome alignment, is defined as the extent to which a group incentive plan helps improve organizational performance. Group incentive plans facilitate collective performance by increasing employee awareness of organizational goals and priorities, and by aligning employee effort with such goals and priorities. Research shows that group incentives can lead to productivity gains ranging from a low of ten percent for profit-sharing plans to a high of twenty-five, even thirty-five percent for single-site gainsharing plans (Cooke, 1994; Jones, Kato, & Pliskin, 1997; Kaufman, 1992, McGrath, 1993). The second effectiveness dimension, behavioral alignment, is defined as the extent to which a group incentive plan stimulates desired organizational change (cf., Doherty, Nord, & McAdams, 1989). Group incentive plans facilitate organizational change, foster teamwork, and advance employee involvement initiatives (McAdams & Hawk, 1992). It is important to distinguish these two effectiveness dimensions because their correlates may differ, which would suggest the need to make trade-offs depending on the relative importance each of the two effectiveness dimensions has for a particular organization.

Second, this study focuses on a set of explanatory variables that have not been examined together. Models used in previous research have concurred in that group incentive effectiveness depends on a supportive organizational context, a suitable plan design, and the interaction between organizational context and plan design (De Matteo, Eby, & Sundstrom, 1998; Lawler, 1988; Welbourne & Gomez-Mejia, 1995). Contextual and design factors, and their interaction, determine the extent to which group incentives have a positive impact on communication, cooperation, motivation, and organizational commitment, which, in turn, facilitate organizational performance and change (Hanlon & Taylor, 1991; Welbourne, Balkin, & Gomez-Mejia, 1995). This study examines the relationship between group incentive effectiveness and two organizational climate dimensions: *participation* and *openness*. Other things being equal, climate differences across organizations should correlate with differences in the effectiveness of group incentive plans because organizational climate provides the immediate context for employee activity (Hoefstede, 1998; Schneider, 2000). Additionally, this study examines relationships between group incentive effectiveness and three plan design features: *plan type, formula complexity,* and *payout frequency.* These factors are critical to incentive plan success (Belcher, 1996; Heneman, Ledford, & Gresham, 2000) but have received little attention in previous research.

Third, the conceptual framework for this study differs significantly from those used in previous studies. The conceptual framework for this study combines sociological and economic views of organizations to understand organizational context effects. The literature contains two contradictory views, one social and the other economic, regarding how organizational context and group incentives relate to each other (Shaw, Gupta, & Delery, 2000; Wright & Mukherji, 1999). The social view has dominated the group incentive literature and contends that employee motivation arises from social norms and interactions while financial incentives help by reinforcing social motivation effects. The economic view has received considerably less attention in the group incentive literature and is illustrated best by Agency Theory. This economic view contends that group incentives align employee financial self-interest with organizational goals regardless of any social influence processes.

Additionally, the conceptual framework for this study uses "macro psychological" modeling (Staw & Sutton, 1993) to understand the effects of plan design features. Staw and Sutton (1993) suggested a "macro psychological modeling" approach to the study of organizational phenomena. This entails using individual-level psychological models to explain organization-level behavior. Staw and Sutton argued that individual-level models provide useful metaphors when thinking about organizations because organizations exhibit quasi-rational, utility-maximizing, goal-directed behavior. In this study, notions from individual motivation theories will be applied to understand the relationship between design features and group incentive effectiveness.

Lastly, the conceptual framework for this study considers the possibility that some of the relationships examined may be nonlinear. Although there seems to be a bias against nonlinear models in management research, nonlinear relationships between independent and dependent variables may be more prevalent than extant research suggests (Ganzach, 1998). Group incentive research is not different. Previous research published in scholarly journals has only estimated linear models, which assume the sign of the relationship between an independent variable and group incentive effectiveness remains constant over the entire independent variable range. That is, prior research has assumed that "more is always better (or worse)" when it comes to the effectiveness consequences of any significant independent variable. However, some results reported by Abernathy (1999) suggest the relationship between incentive plan features and group incentive effectiveness may not be linear.

This study specifies models involving quadratic relationships among the variables of interest because quadratic models are sufficient to describe non-linear relationships involving many organizational and behavioral phenomena (Cortina, 1993). Quadratic models are used for conceptual reasons. Quadratic models allow the possibility of changing signs in the relationship between an independent variable and group incentive effectiveness over different portions of the independent variable range. As discussed below, a quadratic form can reconcile opposing theoretical propositions and may help explain conflicting findings from previous studies. Finding significant nonlinear relationships would indicate that intermediate levels of the corresponding independent variable correlate with maximum (or minimum) incentive effectiveness. Quadratic models are used here for methodological reasons as well. This study considers interaction effects and several recent publications have suggested that estimating interaction effects requires the inclusion of quadratic terms for the interacting variables. Failing to include quadratic terms may reduce statistical power for detecting significant interaction effects and/or may lead to spuriously finding significant interaction effects where none exist (Cortina, 1993; Ganzach, 1997, 1998; MacCallum & Mar, 1995).

CONCEPTUAL BACKGROUND AND HYPOTHESES

Organizational Climate and Group Incentive Effectiveness

Organizational culture and climate represent distinct constructs. Organizational culture concerns values and assumptions that are shared by (many?) members of a given organization (Schein, 1990). In contrast, organizational climate consists of the policies, practices, and behavior expectations that guide employees in organizations (Kopelman, Brief, & Guzzo, 1990). The debate over the distinction between these two constructs notwithstanding (cf. Denison, 1996), there is substantial agreement that culture and climate affect different kinds of organizational phenomena. Organizational culture has influence mostly on structural phenomena such as formalization, centralization, and competitive strategy because culture concerns values and assumptions about problems of internal integration and/or external adaptation (Hofstede, 1998; Schein, 2000). In contrast, organizational climate has influence mostly on behavioral phenomena such as motivation, communication, and teamwork because climate depicts the immediate milieu for employee activity (Hoefstede, 1998; Schneider, 2000).

Thus, organizational climate should have more influence on group incentive effectiveness than organizational culture because organizational climate depicts critical features of the context for group incentive plans. The literature suggests that a compatible organizational climate characterizes organizations that use group incentives successfully (Gross & Bacher, 1993; Hale & Bailey, 1998; Lawler, 1988; Welbourne & Gomez-Mejia, 1988).

There are multiple dimensions of organizational climate. However, two climate dimensions appear frequently in the literature on group incentives: participation, which concerns the extent to which employees are involved in problem solving and decision-making, and openness, which concerns the degree to which employees receive information regarding organizational issues and problems. Prior research supports construct validity for these two climate dimensions. For example, Tesluk, Vance, and Mathieu (1999) showed that the extent to which employees participate in decision-making is an important dimension of organizational climate. Additionally, factor analyses have generally found that information openness is a distinct facet of organizational climate that impacts the effectiveness of multiple management initiatives (Poole, 1985). Further, these two climate dimensions can help distinguishing between "commitment-oriented" and "control-oriented" settings (cf., Arthur, 1994), which represent qualitatively different contexts for group incentives. High levels of employee participation and information openness characterize "commitment-oriented" settings. Conversely, low levels of employee participation and little information openness characterize "control-oriented" settings.

Relationship between Organizational Climate and Outcome Alignment

This distinction between "commitment-oriented" and "control-oriented" settings can help ascertain the applicability of two apparently contradictory perspectives, the sociological and the economic view of organizations, regarding the relationship between organizational context and outcome alignment (the organizational performance consequences of group incentives). On one side, the social view of organizations regards group incentives as a complement to "commitment-oriented" settings. According to the social view of organizations, a "commitment-oriented" setting promotes intrinsic motivation and problem-solving competence among employees, which lead to improved organizational performance; incentive bonuses, in turn, close the cycle sustaining employee commitment (Hammer, 1988). On the other side, the economic view of organizations regards group incentives as a complement to "control-oriented" settings. According to the economic view employee interests tend to conflict with those of the organization. Consequently, organizations need to use explicit contracts, close monitoring and supervision, and/or incentives to align employee and organizational interests and to obtain superior organizational performance (Deckop, Mangel, & Cirka, 1999; Wright, Mukherji, & Kroll, 2001).

There is empirical support for both views. Multiple studies have supported the positive relationship between high levels of employee participation and/or high levels of information openness and the first dimension of group incentive effectiveness (outcome alignment). A review of 33 published case studies concluded that group incentive plans contribute more to organizational performance among organizations with a highly participative climate than in organizations without such a climate (Bullock & Tubbs, 1990). However, the experience of firms using a particular type of gainsharing known as IMPROSHARE is consistent with the economic view. IMPROSHARE incentive plans have contributed to organizational performance even in "control-oriented" settings because these group incentives align employee self-interest with organizational priorities such as improving efficiency and reducing waste (Kaufman, 1992).

This study takes a composite view assuming that both the social and economic views may be valid depending on the organizational context. That is, depending on the level of the climate variables. This assumption is consistent with recent research, which has suggested combining the social and economic views in order to understand better the consequences of compensation practices (Deckop, Mangel, & Cirka, 1999; Shaw, Gupta, & Delery, 2000). Using such a composite view, this study contends that the sign of the relationship between each of the two climate dimensions and outcome alignment may be different for the left and right portions of the climate range. Consistent with the economic view, which implies that group incentives can complement a "control-oriented" setting, we expect a negative relationship between climate and outcome alignment within the left portion of the climate range (low participation and openness). That is, group incentives may contribute more to organizational performance the more an organization resembles a "control-oriented" setting. Consistent with the social view, which implies that group incentives can complement a "commitment-oriented" setting, we expect a positive relationship between climate and outcome alignment within the right portion of the climate range (high participation and openness). That is, group incentives may contribute more to organizational performance the more an organization resembles a "commitment-oriented" setting. Therefore,

H: 1.   the relationship between each of the two climate dimensions (participation and openness) and the first dimension of group incentive effectiveness, outcome alignment, will be curvilinear (U-shaped). The relationship will be negative in the left portion of the climate range and then will become positive.

Relationship between Organizational Climate and Behavioral Alignment

Behavioral alignment, the second effectiveness dimension considered here, relates to the role group incentives play in organizational change. It concerns the extent to which a group incentive stimulates desired changes in employee behavior. In this regard, there is substantial consensus within the group incentive literature that there is an organizational development synergy between "commitment-oriented" settings and the use of group incentives. Organizations with a highly participative climate enjoy high levels of employee commitment to organizational goals, individual self-monitoring, and mutual monitoring between co-workers. These attitudes and behaviors, in turn, enhance the organizational change capability of group incentives (Jones, Kato, & Pliskin, 1997; Lawler, 1988; Welbourne & Gomez-Mejia, 1995). Further, a climate characterized by open communication among organizational members also predicts positive organizational change when group incentives are used (Doherty, Nord, & McAdams, 1989).

Empirical research supports the positive relationship between each of the two organizational climate dimensions, participation and openness, and the second dimension of group incentive effectiveness (behavioral alignment). In the first large-scale review of case research on group incentives, White (1979) concluded that a high level of employee participation is one of the few definite predictors of group incentive effectiveness in promoting organizational change. Thus,

H: 2.   the relationship between each of the two climate dimensions and
the second dimension of group incentive effectiveness, behavioral
alignment, will be linear and positive with behavioral alignment
being higher in organizations with more participative and open
climates.

Plan Design Features

This study examined the relationship between group incentive effectiveness and three plan design features: plan type, payout frequency, and formula complexity. Decisions concerning these three features have strategic
consequences (Belcher, 1996). However, no prior empirical research has
been published that address the effectiveness of different types of group
incentive plans. In addition, research published to date and cited below
regarding the consequences of formula complexity and payout frequency
has produced conflicting results. Additional evidence on the consequences
of these three design features should complement the literature.

Plan Type

In terms of measurement system and incentive formula, there are two
types of group incentive plans: gain-based and goal-based group incentive
plans. As discussed below, these two plan types may differ significantly in
terms of their motivational effects. Goal-based formulas stipulate the size
of individual bonuses as a function of achieving specific objectives. For
example, Guthrie and Cunnigham (1992) describe a goal-based plan. This
incentive plan includes "basic" and "stretch" (more difficult) goals in four
result areas: safety, quality, waste, and transformation costs. For each results
area, achieving the "basic" goal has a value of 0.5 percent and achieving
the "stretch" goal yields has a value of 1 percent . The incentive bonus for
eligible employees depends on the number and difficulty of plant operations goals accomplished each quarter. In contrast, gain-based formulas
stipulate the total amount of money that will be awarded as incentive
bonuses (for the entire group) as a function of the difference between
"expected" and actual results (profits and/or costs). The class of
gain-based group incentives includes labor cost gainsharing (like the
oft-cited Scanlon, Rucker, and Improshare plans), multi-cost gainsharing
plans, and cash profit sharing (which offer employees the opportunity to
earn annual bonuses contingent on the firm's profitability level). Deferred
profit sharing plans do not represent a group incentive in the sense of the
term used here because employees do not receive any payout from such
plans until they retire.

Payout Frequency

Group incentive plans also differ in terms of the frequency with which
bonuses are paid. Group incentive plans may pay weekly, monthly, quar-

terly, biannually, or annually. Payout frequency may affect group incentive effectiveness through its impact on bonus size and timing.

Formula Complexity

Group incentive plans also vary in terms of formula complexity, which relates to the formula elements. The following six elements can add to the complexity of incentive plan formulas:

1. the use of "qualifier" factors that establish additional financial conditions, besides achieving the goal or gains specified in the incentive formula, which must exist before any payout may be awarded;
2. the use of payout "multiplier" factors, which modify the size of bonuses awarded depending on results accomplished in non-cost measures such as quality or customer service;
3. having a "cap" that limits maximum payouts;
4. keeping a portion of the gains in a "reserve" to offset financial losses during poor performance periods;
5. a provision for periodic (annual) adjustments to baselines (targets); and
6. a provision for periodic (annual) changes in the specific measures included in the incentive formula.

Several or all of the elements listed above may be warranted, even necessary, for a particular organization to deploy a group incentive plan suitable for the organization's industry, product life cycle stage, demand trends, etc. However, formula complexity may affect group incentive effectiveness through its impact on employee understanding and acceptance. The more of these elements are used (that is, the more complex the incentive formula), the more difficult it becomes for employees to understand and respond positively to the incentive plan.

Individual motivation theory provides a useful lens for thinking about the relationships between plan design features and outcome alignment. Individual-level motivation theories can serve as metaphors for organizational-level phenomena because organizations, like individuals, respond to external reinforcement (consequences) and exhibit utility-maximizing, goal-directed behaviors (Staw & Sutton, 1993).

Relationships between Plan Features and Outcome Alignment

Notions adapted from Expectancy Theory can help understand the relationship between incentive plan features and outcome alignment. As defined here, outcome alignment concerns the role group incentives play in organizational performance, and Expectancy Theory is a useful paradigm for understanding the motivational effects of performance-reward relationships at the organizational level (Ambrose & Kulik, 1999).

Extending Expectancy Theory to a collective level suggests the two plan types, gainsharing and goalsharing, should differ significantly in terms of their motivation power. From an Expectancy Theory point of view, gain-based plans provide a greater (Performance → Reward) Instrumentality because bonuses in gain-based incentives are directly proportional to the level of results achieved. That is, any increment in organizational performance will yield a proportional increment to the bonus employees receive. Conversely, goal-based plans provide a lower (Performance → Reward) Instrumentality because goal-based bonuses are calculated using pass/fail criteria. Once they meet a lower level productivity goal (say a 5% improvement), employees may not continue to strive for higher productivity because they find the next higher goal (say 10% improvement) fairly difficult and, to make things worse, there would be no additional monetary payoff if results improved somewhat beyond the first goal but failed to satisfy the next higher goal. Although no research has been published that compares the relative effectiveness of gainsharing and goalsharing plans, the preceding considerations lead to the following hypothesis:

H: 3.   Gain-based plans will be significantly more effective than goal-based plans in terms of the outcome alignment criterion.

The applied literature has advocated frequent payouts (Gross & Bacher, 1993; Imberman, 1996; Masternak, 1997). Even academics have suggested that frequent payouts deliver timely reinforcement and lead to plan effectiveness (Mawhinney & Gowen, 1991). However, there is conflicting empirical evidence regarding the relationship between payout frequency and outcome alignment. An earlier review of 33 published case studies concluded that incentive plans that paid monthly tended to be more successful than plans paying less frequently (Bullock & Tubbs, 1990). In contrast, an empirical analysis of the experience with 269 group incentives found that increased payout frequency correlated with poorer outcomes (Kim, 1996).

Expectancy Theory also suggests a negative relationship between payout frequency and the motivational power of group incentive plans. Other things being equal, increases in payout frequency lead to reductions in reward Valence. The more frequent the payout the smaller the associated bonus. For example, an incentive plan with annual payouts of $600 per employee would result (on average) in $12 bonuses if paying weekly, $50 bonuses if paying monthly, $150 bonuses if paying quarterly, $300 bonuses if paying twice a year, and a $600 bonus if paying annually. Accordingly,

H: 4.   there will be a negative relationship between payout frequency and outcome alignment.

Heuristic criteria found within the applied literature contend that group incentive plans with simpler formulas tend to be more effective (Gross & Bacher, 1993; Hale & Bailey, 1998). However, there is conflicting empirical evidence regarding the relationship between formula complexity and outcome alignment. An analysis of experience with four group incentive plans concluded that plan complexity is negatively related to plan effectiveness (Doherty, Nord, & McAdams, 1989). Another study, using data from more than 600 group incentive plans, also concluded that complex incentive formulas are less effective (Zenger & Marshall, 2000). In contrast, a recent study found a curvilinear relationship between plan complexity and effectiveness (Abernathy, 1999).

These findings thus suggest a curvilinear, inverted-U relationship between formula complexity and outcome alignment. The combined (Effort → Performance → Reward) Expectancy may be lower in low and high complexity plans than in plans with a medium complexity level. By failing to reflect the idiosyncratic conditions in each organization, the performance bonus in very simple plans may not be effective because participating employees may regard such plans as simplistic and subject to factors outside their control (Lawler, 1988). Conversely, very complex plans may not provide an effective means for collective goal setting and feedback (Zenger & Marshall, 2000). Moreover, high complexity plans may lack motivating power because employees find them difficult to understand and follow (Ledford, Heneman, & Gresham, 2000). These ideas suggest the following hypothesis:

H: 5.   the relationship between formula complexity and outcome alignment will have an "inverted U" shape with outcome alignment being highest for medium complexity levels

Plan Features—Behavioral Alignment Relationships

Notions adapted from Reinforcement Theory can help understand the relationship between incentive plan features and behavioral alignment, the second effectiveness dimension studied here. As defined here, behavioral alignment concerns the role group incentives play in organizational change. Further, the behavioral alignment associated with the deployment of a group incentive plan represents continuous and incremental organizational change, which is best understood as a learning phenomenon (Weick & Quinn, 1999); Reinforcement Theory is regarded as a useful paradigm for understanding the effects of reward contingencies on behavioral change (Luthans & Stajkovic, 1997; Ambrose & Kulik, 1999).

Neither plan type nor formula complexity should have any relationship with behavioral alignment (which concerns the influence group incentives have on organizational change). The degree and speed of organizational learning depends mostly on the reinforcement of appropriate behavioral changes but does not depend as much on the complexity of the mechanism that generates such reinforcement. That is, the type and complexity of the incentive formula should not have any impact on changes in communication, coordination, and mutual monitoring between co-workers associated with the use of a group incentive plan. Therefore,

Expectation 1: Plan type and formula complexity will not have any significant relationship with behavioral alignment. (Note: Although one cannot statistically support a null hypothesis, formal a priori statement of this expectation seems desirable.)

In contrast, payout frequency should correlate with the second effectiveness dimension behavioral alignment. Differences in payout frequency should have consequences for organizational learning and change, which are reflected in the behavioral alignment effectiveness dimension. Bonuses (or their absence) reinforce (or fail to reinforce) employee efforts to improve communication, coordination, and cooperation. Moreover, increases in payout frequency shorten the time lapsed between behavior and reinforcement (but also reduce reinforcement size). Plans with low payout frequency may not convey a clear behavior-reinforcement linkage. Conversely, plans with very frequent payouts may not provide noticeable rewards. Therefore, plans with annual (low frequency) payouts and plans with weekly (high frequency) payouts may be significantly less effective in terms of the behavioral alignment criterion than plans with a medium (quarterly or biannual) frequency payouts. These ideas suggest the following hypothesis:

H: 6.   the relationship between payout frequency and behavioral alignment will have an "inverted U" shape, with behavioral alignment being highest for medium payout frequency levels.

Participation Climate and Payout Frequency Interaction

An organization's climate regarding participation should affect the relationship between payout frequency and behavioral alignment. The literatures on high performance work systems and strategic human resource management make a convincing case for qualitative differences between organizations with a highly participative climate ("commitment-oriented" settings) and organizations whose climate does not favor employee participation in decision-making ("control-oriented" settings). A "commitment-oriented" setting should amplify the relationship between payout frequency and behavioral alignment because employees should be more able and willing to learn and adjust in response to the feedback provided through bonus payouts. Conversely, a "control-oriented" setting should muffle the relationship between payout frequency and behavioral alignment because employees may not be afforded the opportunity to learn and make adjustments in response to the feedback received through bonus payouts. Therefore,

H: 7.   The more participative an organization's climate, the steeper the relationship between payout frequency and behavioral alignment. That is, there will be a positive interaction between participation climate and payout frequency when predicting behavioral alignment.

No interaction effects were expected on outcome alignment because Hypothesis 1 proposed a curvilinear (U-shaped) relationship that implies that the sign of the relationship between climate and outcome alignment should change over the range of climate values. Therefore, one cannot to expect that climate may have a stable moderating influence, either magnifying or attenuating the relationship between plan design features and outcome alignment.

METHOD

Sample

We randomly chose a group of one thousand organizations registered with WorldatWork. Then we sent, via US mail, a questionnaire to the top management employee from each organization that was a member of WorldatWork. The questionnaire requested information about a group incentive plan for non-executive employees. One hundred and seven questionnaires were returned with all the information required for this study. The one hundred and seven usable questionnaires comprise a diverse random sample with forty-three percent of manufacturing organizations and the rest in services. Twenty-two percent of the organizations in this sample were unionized. These statistics are very similar to those reported recently for another sample of WorldatWork member organizations (cf., Shaw, Gupta, & Delery, 2000). The apparently low response rate should be judged within the context of this study. It seems reasonable to estimate that no more than one half of the organizations receiving the questionnaire actually had a group incentive plan. Recent surveys suggest between forty and seventy percent of large firms have adopted group incentives (Hansen, 1998; *HR Focus*, 2000). Further, the fraction of small and medium firms with a group incentive is considerably lower. Moreover, WorldatWork membership is comprised of small, medium, and large organizations. Therefore, the one hundred and seven returned questionnaires represent approximately twenty percent of the estimated five hundred organizations that had a group incentive in place and received the questionnaire.

Measuring Incentive Plan Effectiveness

The notion of effectiveness concerns the extent to which a group incentive plan achieves its objectives. We obtained a list of six objectives that organizations may pursue when deploying a group incentive plan from a previous study by McAdams and Hawk (1992). We expected that these objectives would fall into the two group incentive effectiveness dimensions we discussed earlier. The six items appeared in random order within the appropriate questionnaire section. Questionnaire respondents rated the extent to which their group incentive helped achieve each objective using a Likert-type format with the following anchors: 1 = "no effect"; 2 = "minimal success"; 3 = "somewhat successful"; 4 = "successful"; and 5 = "very successful".

Exploratory factor analysis, retaining factors with an eigenvalue greater than one and using varimax rotation, suggested that the six items belong in two distinct dimensions. Three items comprised the outcome alignment dimension:

i.   "Focus employees on key business priorities";
ii. "Link employee rewards to business results"; and
iii. "Improve business results (performance)".

The other three items comprised the behavioral alignment dimension:

i.   "Motivate desired behavioral and/or organizational changes";
ii. "Promote teamwork"; and
iii. "Support employee involvement initiatives".

Internal consistency (Cronbach's alpha) for these two effectiveness measures was estimated at 0.74 and 0.69 respectively. The average response to the corresponding three items was used as the effectiveness score for each dimension.

Measuring Organizational Climate

As stated above, the practices and expectations guiding employee behavior create an organization's climate (Kopelman, Brief, & Guzzo, 1990), which may correlate with the effectiveness of group incentive plans. We obtained a list of eight organizational practices from the inventory used by Hoefstede, Bond, and Luk (1993). We expected these practices would depict the two organizational climate dimensions discussed earlier. The eight items appeared in random order within the appropriate question-naire section. Respondents used a seven-point Likert-type format (with the following anchors: 1 = "strongly disagree"; 4 = "neither agree nor disagree"; and 7 = "strongly agree") to indicate the extent to which these items described their organization.

Exploratory factor analysis, retaining factors with eigenvalue greater than one and using varimax rotation, suggested that the eight items belonged in two distinct dimensions. Four items comprised the first cli-mate dimension, participation:

i.   "important decisions are made in groups";
ii.   "employees are free to organize their work";
iii.   "changes are established by decree"; and
iv.   "managers resent being contradicted."

The last two items were reverse-scored. Four items comprised the second climate dimension, openness:

i.   "managers encourage different opinions";
ii.   "we appreciate people who act assertively";
iii.   "everyone knows the purpose of their work"; and
iv.   "people are told when they are doing a good job".

Internal consistency (Cronbach's alpha) for these two climate measures was estimated at 0.73 and 0.88, respectively. The average response to the corresponding four items was used as the climate score for each dimen-sion.

Measuring Incentive Plan Features

Three plan features were considered in this study: formula type, payout frequency, and formula complexity. Formula type was coded as a 0/1 dummy variable with 0 representing goal-based formulas and 1 represent-ing gain-based formulas (the difference between these two formula types was explained in the previous section). Payout frequency was measured as the potential number of bonuses per year. That is, annual plans were char-acterized by a payout frequency of one; quarterly plans by a payout fre-quency of four, monthly plans by a payout frequency of twelve, and so on. Formula complexity was measured by counting how many of six elements were part of a given plan:

1.   use of "qualifier" factors;
2.   use of payout "multiplier" factors;

TABLE 1
Sample Descriptive Statistics[a]

Variable	Range	M	SD
Outcome alignment (DV)	1-5	3.63	0.90
Behavioral alignment (DV)	1-5	2.63	0.95
Participation climate	1-7	4.18	1.11
Openness climate	1-7	4.90	0.95
Formula type	0/1	26% gain-based	
Formula complexity	0-6	3.18	1.28
Payout frequency (per year)	1-52	3.00	5.85

Note: [a] $n = 107$

3. having a "cap";
4. keeping a "reserve";
5. annual adjustment to baselines; and
6. annual revision of measures in the formula.

The complexity measure used here gives equal weight to each of the formula elements listed above. Equal weighting seemed appropriate because the notion of complexity relates to the difficulty for employees to understand the incentive plan, and explanations concerning the role and need for each of these formula elements tend to be similarly complicated in the author's consulting and teaching experience. Moreover, formula complexity has not been included in prior published research. Therefore, no other measurement approach could be found in the literature.

Table 1 presents descriptive statistics for the measures discussed above. These statistics show that there is considerable diversity among sample organizations for all measures. The coefficient of variation, the mean-to-standard deviation ratio, exceeds one-fourth for all measures except openness climate. Thus, sample diversity should help in detecting empirical relationships among the variables considered in this study.

ANALYSIS AND RESULTS

In order to examine non-linearity hypotheses, this study used quadratic (squared) terms and interaction (cross-product) terms involving the climate, formula complexity and payout frequency measures. These quadratic and interaction terms were constructed from mean-centered scores to reduce multicollinearity between measured and constructed variables (Cohen & Cohen, 1983). Moreover, interaction analyses considered linear and quadratic interaction terms for formula complexity and payout frequency. The use of quadratic interaction terms allows for differential inter-action effects at various levels of the climate measure. However, interaction variables were limited to those involving the participation dimension of cli-mate because of the relatively small sample size.

Table 2 shows the correlations among all variables, measured or con-structed, which were used in subsequent analyses. The information sug-gests that multicollinearity should not be a serious problem in the analyses that follow. Except for nonlinear terms involving payout frequency, corre-lations between independent variables tend to fall below 0.70, the oft-used heuristic to diagnose potential multicollinearity.

Busemeyer and Jones (1983), Feucht (1989), and more recently Krom-rey and Foster-Johnson (1999) have raised concerns regarding the escala-tion of measurement error when using variables created by multiplying other variables that were measured with error. However, MacCallum and Mar (1995) concluded this error escalation is likely to be a problem only under high multi-collinearity and low reliability conditions. As stated above, high multi-collinearity is not apparent in this study. Unreliability is not a concern either. It should be noted that plan features such as formula complexity and payout frequency are tangible attributes and, thus, include minimal measurement error. In addition, the two climate measures used here exhibited moderate-to-satisfactory reliability levels (0.73 and 0.88 respectively). Therefore, the analyses reported below should not have suf-fered from the statistical power reduction that results from measurement error amplification in constructed variables.

This study reports the results from two multiple regression analyses using each of the two effectiveness measures as the dependent variable respectively. The estimated multiple regression models included all qua-dratic and interaction terms regardless of whether there was a hypothesis concerning these terms. This was done to examine whether the two dimen-sions of group incentive effectiveness are differentially related to each of the various independent variables under study. Such an empirical finding would support the notion that the two dimensions of group incentive effec-tiveness are distinct from each other, which is an important premise behind this research. Such differential relationships would also allay con-cerns regarding common source biases in this study.

Table 3 reports key statistics, standardized regression (beta) coefficients and the multiple coefficient of determination, and indicates the signifi-cance level for each of these statistics. Regression models estimated in pre-vious studies, such as Cooke (1994) and Kaufman (1992), typically explain between five and thirty five percent of the variance in group incentive effectiveness. Accordingly, the coefficients of determination, reported in Table 3, bottom row confirm that the independent variables examined in this study are important correlates of group incentive effectiveness.

Hypothesis 1 was supported. This hypothesis proposed a curvilinear (U-shaped) relationship between the first effectiveness dimension (out-

TABLE 2

Sample Correlations (×100)[a,b]

Variable	1	2	3	4	5	6	7	8	9	10	11	12	13	14	15
1. Outcome alignment	100														
2. Behavioral alignment	54	100													
3. Participation climate	32	26	100												
4. Participation climate²	04	04	-02	100											
5. Openness climate	42	41	40	-12	100										
6. Openness climate²	04	-16	-27	17	-47	100									
7. Formula type	27	14	00	10	10	03	100								
8. Formula complexity	16	16	07	-28	08	-12	00	100							
9. Formula complexity²	-18	-01	20	21	04	-02	-12	-30	100						
10. Payout frequency	-29	-06	-18	10	-04	10	01	-07	-06	100					
11. Payout frequency²	-28	-14	-17	12	-18	17	-06	-08	-03	90	100				
12. Particip × Complexity	-27	-07	-33	-03	-11	04	-07	24	-05	09	12	100			
13. Particip × Complexity²	33	22	60	08	29	-17	06	-01	33	-07	-08	-65	100		
14. Particip × Pay frequency	22	13	10	-14	11	-13	06	07	01	-83	-96	-12	02	100	
15. Particip × Pay frequency²	25	14	18	-14	19	-18	06	09	01	-82	-98	-13	08	98	100

Notes: [a] $n = 107$
[b] $p < 0.10$ for absolute values greater than 16
$p < 0.05$ for absolute values greater than 19
$p < 0.01$ for absolute values greater than 25
$p < 0.001$ for absolute values greater than 3

come alignment) and the two climate dimensions, participation and openness. The squared term for participation, and both the linear and squared terms for openness were significantly related to outcome alignment. Additionally, the regression coefficients for both quadratic terms are positive indicating U-shaped relationships.

Hypothesis 2 proposed a linear relationship between the second effectiveness dimension (behavioral alignment) and the two climate dimensions. Table 3 results suggest there is no relationship between participation climate and behavioral alignment. In contrast, the linear term for openness climate is significantly related to behavioral alignment while the quadratic term is not. Thus, Hypothesis 2 was supported only for one of the two climate dimensions.

Further, the statistics in Table 3 support Hypotheses 3, 4 and 5. As stated in Hypothesis 3, and confirmed by the significant positive regression coefficient for the plan type dummy variable, gain-based plans performed better than goal-based plans in terms of outcome alignment. This is consistent with the theorized stronger Instrumentality in gain-based formulas. As stated in Hypothesis 4, and confirmed by the significant negative regression coefficient, group incentive effectiveness measured by the outcome alignment criterion declines as payout frequency increases. This is consistent with the theorized negative relationship between payout frequency

TABLE 3
Multiple Regression Results[a,b]

Independent Variable	Outcome Alignment	Behavioral Alignment
Participation climate	.066	.188
Participation climate^2	.138†	.107
Openness climate	.459***	.344**
Openness climate^2	.212*	.029
Formula type	.169*	.042
Formula complexity	.108	.133
Formula complexity^2	-.280**	-.073
Payout frequency	-.478†	.633*
Payout frequency^2	.123	-1.524*
Particip × Complexity	-.092	.119
Particip × Complexity^2	.193	.167
Particip × Pay frequency	.109	1.211*
Particip × Pay frequency^2	-.212	-2.100**
R^2	.484***	.296***

Notes: [a] $n = 107$
[b] $^\dagger p < .10$; * $p < .05$; ** $p < .01$; *** $p < .001$

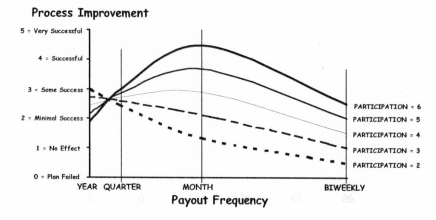

Figure 1.   Behavioral Alignment v. Payout Frequency for Various Levels of Participation Climate

and reward Valence. Hypothesis 5 was also supported. The quadratic term for formula complexity is significant and negative, which indicates the inverted-U relationship proposed in Hypothesis 5. This is thus consistent with the theorized conflicting impact that formula complexity has on incentive plan realism and understandability.

Furthermore, the statistics in Table 3 also support Expectation 1 and Hypotheses 6 and 7. Consistent with Expectation 1, the results in Table 3 suggest that there is no relationship between formula type or formula complexity and behavioral alignment. Hypothesis 6 proposed an inverted-U relationship between payout frequency and behavioral alignment. In addition, Hypothesis 7 proposed a positive interaction, by which the relationship between payout frequency and behavioral alignment would be steeper the more participative an organization climate is. The statistics reported in Table 3 confirm these two hypotheses. The Table 3 results show that the quadratic and quadratic-interaction terms involving payout frequency are significant and negative, confirming the hypothesized inverted-U relationship. Moreover, The patterns in Figure 1 further support Hypothesis 7. Figure 1, which was created using regression coefficient estimates from Table 3, shows the regression-fitted relationship between behavioral alignment and payout frequency for selected values that span the range of participation climate.

DISCUSSION

This study improves our understanding of the group incentive effectiveness construct. First, this study shows there are (at least) two dimensions of group incentive effectiveness. These two dimensions are called outcome alignment and behavioral alignment and correspond to the consequences group incentives have for organizational performance and change respectively. Second, this study demonstrates that these two effectiveness dimensions are distinct from each other. This study reveals qualitative differences in the relationships that organizational climate and incentive plan features have with each of the two effectiveness dimensions. For example, support for Hypotheses 3 and 5 and Expectation 1 confirms that formula type and formula complexity are related to the first effectiveness dimension (outcome alignment), but are not related to the second effectiveness dimension (behavioral alignment). Moreover, the results reported in Table 3 indicate an interaction between participation climate and payout frequency when predicting behavioral alignment, but fail to find any interaction effects when predicting outcome alignment. Hence, the empirical results provide some evidence in support of the notion that the two dimensions of group incentive effectiveness studied here are distinct from each other.

This study also provides new specific insights regarding factors correlated with group incentive effectiveness. First, this study confirms the value of combining the social and economic views of organizations when thinking about the consequences of group incentives for organizational performance. This study provides empirical support for Hypothesis 1, which proposed a "U-shaped" relationship between outcome alignment and two climate dimensions (participation and openness). This study found a negative relationship between climate and outcome alignment for the left portion of the climate range. That is, the argument from the economic view that financial incentives can serve as a motivational alternative to methods stressing social and intrinsic motivation seems valid within "control-oriented" settings, which are characterized by low climate scores. At the same time, this study found a positive relationship between climate and outcome alignment for the right portion of the climate range. That is, the argument from the social view that social and intrinsic motivation are essential pre-requisites for group incentives to have a motivational effect seems valid within "commitment-oriented" settings, which are characterized by high climate scores.

Second, this study supports explanations of the organizational change effects of group incentives that are consistent with the literatures on high-performance work systems and on strategic human resource management. Partial support for Hypothesis 2 confirms that extensive information flow, associated with the openness climate dimension, is critical to the contribution group incentives make to behavioral alignment.

In addition, support for Hypothesis 7 augments our understanding of the consequences of employee participation in organizations with group incentives. Using values computed with regression coefficient estimates in Table 3, Figure 1 shows the estimated relationship between behavioral alignment and payout frequency for selected values that span the range of participation climate. Figure 1 depicts how the interaction between participation climate and payout frequency relates to behavioral alignment. This is a complex relationship. The patterns in Figure 1 show that changes in participation climate scores are associated with qualitative changes in the relationship between payout frequency and behavioral alignment. Figure 1 indicates a complete "inverted-U" relationship between payout frequency and behavioral alignment in "commitment-oriented" settings (medium-to-high climate scores). It seems monthly payouts result in an optimum balance between the behavior-reinforcement time lapse and reinforcement size in "commitment-oriented" settings. In contrast, Figure 1 also indicates a negative relationship between payout frequency and behavioral alignment in "control-oriented" settings (low-to-medium climate scores). This suggests frequent payouts introduce "noise", not useful reinforcement, in "control-oriented" settings.

Third, this study provides initial evidence of differential effects for goal-based and gain-based formulas. Results reported here confirm a slight motivational advantage for gain-based formulas when compared with goal-based formulas. It is worth repeating that the motivational effectiveness of these two types of formulas had not been contrasted empirically in research published previously.

Fourth, in support of Hypotheses 5 and 6, this study finds "inverted-U" relationships between formula complexity and outcome alignment, and between payout frequency and behavioral alignment. These results indicate that intermediate levels of these two features correlate with optimum plan effectiveness, which means that balancing formula realism and understandability enhances the motivational effectiveness of group incentive plans, and that balancing feedback amount and salience enhances the contribution of group incentives to organizational development.

In sum, the results reported here indicate that the relationships outcome alignment and behavioral alignment have with organizational climate and with incentive plan features are more complex than assumed by the linear models typical of past research.

The results reported here also have practical implications. First, this study offers a new perspective on the long-standing debate regarding whether group incentives should be installed before or after developing a "commitment-oriented" climate (see Ledford and Heneman, 2000 vs. Wruck, 2000 for an example). According to the results reported here, the proverbial "it depends" seems to be the answer to this debate. The "U-shaped" relationships between the two climate measures and outcome alignment indicate that group incentives can lead to better organizational outcomes in "control-oriented" as well as in "commitment-oriented" settings. That is, organizations do not need to wait until they develop a "commitment-oriented" climate if the primary reason for deploying a group incentive is its motivational outcome-improvement capability. On the other hand, if the primary reason for deploying a group incentive is to promote organizational change through behavioral alignment, organizations should focus first on building a "commitment-oriented" climate. The linear relationship between openness climate and behavioral alignment found here suggests that the organizational development impact of group incentives will be minimal in "control-oriented" settings but will increase to the extent that the organization resembles a "commitment-oriented" setting.

Second, the results reported here caution against the heuristic that "plans providing for more frequent bonuses are better than plans providing for less frequent bonuses," which assumes a positive linear relationship between payout frequency and effectiveness. Our results contradict this rule of thumb. On one hand, this study found a negative linear relationship between payout frequency and outcome alignment. This means that plans providing for more frequent bonuses result in lower reward Valence than plans providing for less frequent bonuses. On the other hand, this study found the relationship between payout frequency and behavioral alignment differs between "control-oriented" and "commitment-oriented" settings. The interaction depicted in Figure 1 indicates low (annual) payout frequency is best in "control-oriented" settings and medium (monthly) payout frequency is best in "commitment-oriented" settings. Combined, these results clearly contradict the oft-cited rule of thumb in favor of the most frequent payouts possible.

Third, the results reported here caution organizations against the heuristic that "simpler incentive plans are better than complex plans", which assumes a negative linear relationship between formula complexity and effectiveness. The results reported here, indicating an "inverted-U" relationship, imply that moderately complex formulas are more associated with superior performance than are extremely simple or complex plans. Presumably, moderately complex formulas would offer an appropriate balance between realism and understandability.

Although it presents a novel perspective and distinct findings, this study suffers from two limitations. First, this study represents the first use of the effectiveness measures (outcome alignment and behavioral alignment) and the climate scales (participation and openness) described above within the context of group incentive research. Obviously, further studies, using the same or equivalent scales, are needed to replicate or challenge the validity and significance of our findings. Second, although seemingly representative of WorldatWork member organizations, this study examined a somewhat small sample. Sample size limitations prevented the inclusion of additional control and/or explanatory variables, which may correlate with group incentive effectiveness. Prior research, cited here, has reported effectiveness differences associated with economic sector (manufacturing vs. services), unionization status of participating employees, and number of participating employees. Ancillary analyses, not reported here, failed to find any significant relationship between these three factors and the effectiveness measures used here. However, such ancillary analyses may have suffered from limited statistical power resulting from a small sample size. It is hoped that future studies will obtain larger samples in order to incorporate a broader array of control and/or explanatory factors.

CONCLUSION

Despite its limitations, this study illustrates the need for non-linear thinking in the study of human resource management practices and their relationship to organizational level phenomena. As done here, non-linear thinking can reconcile the seemingly competing economic and social views of employee motivation within organizations. Also, non-linear thinking may help to reconsider widely accepted rules of thumb, which assume linear relationships between key variables. In addition, this study illustrates the value of "macro psychological modeling", suggested by Staw and Sutton (1993), which entails applying individual-level psychological models to organizational phenomena. This study applied notions from motivation theories to the study of group incentive effectiveness. The positive findings reported here strengthen Staw and Sutton's argument that individual-level models can provide useful metaphors when thinking about organizations because organizations exhibit quasi-rational, utility-maximizing, goal-directed behavior. In addition to the study of organizational-level phenomena, the study of smaller collectivities (such as teams and groups) may also benefit from a similar metaphorical approach to modeling collective motivation and performance.

REFERENCES

Abernathy, W. B. (1999). Evaluating organization scorecards and incentive-pay plans. *Employment Relations Today, 25*(4), 83-96.

Altmansberger, H. N. (2000). Variable pay: An overview. In L.A. Berger & D.R. Berger (Eds.), *The compensation handbook: A state-of-the-art guide to compensation strategy and design* (4th Ed., pp. 199-207). New York: McGraw-Hill.

Ambrose, M. L., & Kulik, C. T. (1999). Old friends, new faces: Motivation research in the 1990s. *Journal of Management, 25,* 231-292.

Appelbaum, E., Bailey, T., Berg, P., & Kalleberg, A. (2000). *Manufacturing advantage: Why high performance systems pay off.* Ithaca, NY: ILR Press.

Arthur, J. (1994). Effects of human resource systems on manufacturing performance and turnover. *Academy of Management Journal, 37,* 670-687.

Belcher, Jr., J. G. (1996). *How to design & implement a results-oriented variable pay system.* New York: Amacom.

Belcher, Jr., J. G. (2000). Variable pay: New perspectives. In L. A. Berger & D. R. Berger (Eds.), *The compensation handbook: A state-of-the-art guide to compensation strategy and design* (4th Ed., pp. 209-216). New York: McGraw-Hill.

Bullock, R. J., & Tubbs, M. E. (1990). A case meta-analysis of gainsharing plans as organizational development interventions. *Journal of Applied Behavioral Science, 26*, 383-404.

Busemeyer, J. R., & Jones, L. E. (1983). Analysis of multiplicative combination rules when the causal variables are measured with error. *Psychological Bulletin, 93*, 549-562.

Cohen, J., & Cohen P. (1983). *Applied Multiple Regression-Correlation Analysis for the Behavioral Sciences* (2nd Ed.). Hillsdale, NJ: Erlbaum.

Cooke, W. N. (1994). Employee participation programs, group-based incentives and company performance: A union-nonunion comparison. *Industrial and Labor Relations Review, 47*, 594-609.

Cortina, J. M. (1993). Interaction, nonlinearity, and multicollinearity: Implications for multiple regression. *Journal of Management, 19*, 915-922.

Deckop, J. R., Mangel. R., & Cirka, C. C. (1999). Getting more than you pay for: Organizational citizenship behavior and pay-for-performance plans. *Academy of Management Journal, 42*, 420-428.

DeMatteo, J. S., Eby, L. T., & Sundstrom, E. (1998). Team-based rewards: Current empirical evidence and directions for future research. *Research in Organizational Behavior, 20*, 141-183.

Denison, D. R. (1996). What is the difference between organizational culture and organizational climate? A native's point of view on a decade of paradigm wars. *Academy of Management Review, 21*, 619-654.

Doherty, E. M., Nord, W. R., & McAdams, J. L. (1989). Gainsharing and organizational development: A productive synergy. *Journal of Applied Behavioral Science, 26*, 209-230.

Feucht, T. E. (1989). Estimating multiplicative regression terms in the presence of measurement error. *Sociological Methods and Research, 17*, 447-472.

Ganzach, Y. (1997). Misleading interaction and curvilinear terms. *Psychological Methods, 2*, 235-247.

Ganzach, Y. (1998). Nonlinearity, multicollinearity and the probability of Type II Error in detecting interaction. *Journal of Management, 24*, 615-622.

Gowen, C. R. III. (1990). Gainsharing programs: An overview of history and research. *Journal of Organizational Behavior Management, 11*(2), 77-99.

Graham-Moore, B. (1995). Review of the literature. In B. Graham-Moore & T. L. Ross (Eds.), *Gainsharing and Employee Involvement* (pp. 15-44). Washington, DC: Bureau of National Affairs.

Gross, S. E., & Bacher, J. P. (1993). The new variable pay programs: How some succeed, why some don't. *Compensation and Benefits Review, 25*(1), 51-56.

Guthrie, J. P., & Cunnigham, E. P. (1992). Pay for performance for hourly workers: The Quaker Oats alternative. *Compensation and Benefits Review, 24*(2), 18-23.

Hale, J., & Bailey, G. (1998). Seven dimensions of successful reward plans. *Compensation and Benefits Review, 30*(4), 71-77.

Hammer, T. H. (1988). New developments in gainsharing, profit sharing, and employee ownership. In J. P. Campbell, R. J. Campbell, & Associates (Eds.), *Productivity in organizations* (pp. 328-366). San Francisco: Jossey-Bass.

Hanlon, S. C., & Taylor, R. R. (1991). An examination of changes in work group communication behaviors following installation of a gainsharing plan. *Group and Organization Studies, 16*, 238-267.

Hansen, F. (1998). Percentage of companies using variable pay raises by ten points. *Compensation and Benefits Review, 30*(2), 7.

Heneman, R. L., Ledford, G. E., & Gresham, M. T. (2000). The changing nature of work and its effects on compensation design and delivery. In S. L. Rynes & B. Gerhart (Eds.), *Compensation in organizations: Current research and practice* (pp. 195-240). San Francisco: Jossey-Bass.

Hoefstede, G. (1998). Attitudes, values and organizational culture: Disentangling the concepts. *Organization Studies, 19,* 477-492.

Hoefstede, G., Bond, M. H., & Luk, C. (1993). Individual perceptions of organizational cultures: A methodological treatise on levels of analysis. *Organization Studies, 14,* 483-503.

HR Focus. (2000). The real value of variable pay plans. *77*(5), 3-4.

Imberman, W. (1996). Gainsharing: A lemon or lemonade? *Business Horizons,* (January-February), 36-40.

Jones, D., Kato, T., & Pliskin, J. (1997). Profitsharing and gainsharing: A review of theory, incidence and effects. In D. Lewin, D. J. B. Mitchell, & M. Zaidi (Eds.), *The human resource management handbook—Part I* (pp. 153-173). Greenwich, CT: JAI Press.

Kaufman, R. T. (1992). The effect of IMPROSHARE on productivity. *Industrial and Labor Relations Review, 45,* 311-325.

Kim, D. (1996). Factors influencing organizational performance in gainsharing programs. *Industrial Relations, 35,* 227-244.

Kopelman, R. E., Brief, A. P., & Guzzo, R. A. (1990). The role of climate and culture in productivity. In B. Schneider (Ed.), *Organizational culture and climate* (pp. 282-318). San Francisco: Jossey-Bass.

Kromrey, J. D., & Foster-Johnson, L. (1999). Statistically differentiating interaction and nonlinearity in multiple regression analysis: A Monte Carlo investigation of a recommended strategy. *Education and Psychological Measurement, 59,* 392-413.

Kruse, D. L. (1993). *Profit sharing: Does it make a difference?* Kalamazoo, MI: Upjohn Institute for Employment Research.

Lawler, III, E. E. (1988). Gainsharing theory and research: Findings and future research. *Research in Organizational Change and Development, 2,* 323-344.

Ledford, Jr., G. E., & Heneman, R. L. (2000). Compensation: A troublesome lead system in organizational change. In M. Beer & N. Nohria (Eds.), *Breaking the code of change* (pp. 307-322). Boston: Harvard Business School Press.

Luthans, F., & Stajkovic, A. D. (1997). A meta-analysis of the effects of Organizational Behavior Modification on task performance, 1975-95. *Academy of Management Journal, 40,* 1122-1149.

MacCallum, R. C., & Mar C. M. (1995). Distinguishing between moderator and quadratic effects in multiple regression. *Psychological Bulletin, 118,* 405-421.

Mangel, R., & Useem, M. (2000). The strategic role of gainsharing. *Journal of Labor Research, 21,* 327-343.

Masternak, R. (1997). How to make gainsharing successful: The collective experience of 17 facilities. *Compensation and Benefits Review, 29*(5), 43-52.

Mawhinney, T. C., & Gowen, III., C. R. (1991). Gainsharing and the law of effect as the matching law: A theoretical framework. *Journal of Organizational Behavior Management, 11,* 61-75.

McAdams, J. L., & Hawk, E. (1992). *Capitalizing on human assets.* Scottsdale, AZ: American Compensation Association.

McGrath, T. C. (1993). How three screw machine companies are tapping human productivity through gainsharing. *Employment Relations Today, 19,* 437-446.

Pfeffer, J. (1998). *The human equation: Building profits by putting people first.* Boston, MA: Harvard Business School Press.

Poole, M. S. (1985). Communication and organizational climates: Review, critique and a new perspective. In R. D. McPhee & P. K. Tompkins (Eds.), *Organizational communication* (pp. 79-108). Beverly Hills, CA: Sage.

Schein, E. (1990). Organizational culture. *American Psychologist, 45,* 109-119.

Schein, E. (2000). Sense and nonsense about culture and climate. In N. M. Ashkanasy, C. P. M. Wilderom, & M. F. Peterson (Eds.), *Handbook of organizational culture and climate* (pp. xxiii-xxx). Thousand Oaks, CA: Sage.

Schneider, B. (2000). The psychological life of organizations. In N. M. Ashkanasy, C. P. M. Wilderom, & M. F. Peterson (Eds.), *Handbook of organizational culture and climate* (pp. xvii-xxi). Thousand Oaks, CA: Sage.

Shaw, J. D., Gupta, N., & Delery, J. E. (2000). Empirical organizational-level examination of agency and collaborative predictions of performance-contingent compensation. *Strategic Management Journal, 21,* 611-623.

Staw, B. M., & Sutton, R. I. (1993). Macro organizational psychology. In J. K. Murnighan (Ed.), *Social psychology in organizations: Advances in theory and research* (pp. 350-383). Englewood Cliffs, NJ: Prentice-Hall.

Tesluk, P. E., Vance, R. J., & Mathieu, J. E. (1999). Examining employee involvement in the context of participative work environment. *Group & Organization Management, 24,* 271-299.

Weick, K. E., & Quinn, R. E. (1999). Organizational change and development. *Annual Review of Psychology, 50,* 361-386.

Welbourne, T., Balkin, D. B., & Gomez-Mejia, L. R. (1995). Gainsharing and mutual monitoring: A combined agency-organizational justice interpretation. *Academy of Management Journal, 38,* 881-899.

Welbourne, T., & Gomez-Mejia, L. R. (1988). Gainsharing revisited. *Compensation and Benefits Review, 20*(4), 19-28.

Welbourne, T., & Gomez-Mejia L. R. (1995). Gainsharing: A critical review and future research agenda. *Journal of Management, 21,* 559-609.

White, J. K. (1979). The Scanlon Plan: Causes and correlates of success. *Academy of Management Journal, 22,* 292-312.

Wright, P., & Mukherji, A. (1999). Inside the firm: Socioeconomic versus agency perspectives on firm competitiveness. *Journal of Socio-Economics, 28,* 295-307.

Wright, P., Mukherji, A., & Kroll, M. J. (2001). A reexamination of agency theory assumptions: extensions and extrapolations. *Journal of Socio-Economics, 30,* 413-429.

Wruck, K. H. (2000). Compensation, incentives and organizational change: Ideas and evidence from theory and practice. In M. Beer & N. Nohria (Eds.), *Breaking the code of change* (pp. 269-305). Boston: Harvard Business School Press.

Zenger, T. R., & Marshall, C. R. (2000). Determinants of incentive intensity in group-based rewards. *Academy of Management Journal, 43,* 149-163.

CHAPTER 6

EVALUATING RECRUITING EFFECTIVENESS IN A NEW MILLENIUM

Kevin D. Carlson
Virginia Polytechnic Institute and State University

ABSTRACT

This chapter reviews the evaluation of recruitment processes by organizations, classifies measures of recruiting effectiveness, and discusses their strengths and weaknesses. A new approach to recruitment evaluation is proposed, emphasizing the development of value measures by the use of utility analysis. Examples are provided of how this new framework may be used to assess recruiting outcomes, and an evolutionary model of recruitment evaluation is presented. The chapter ends with implications and suggestions for future research and practice.

> If you don't measure it, you can't manage it
> —*Deming, 1986.*

New Directions in Human Resource Management
A Volume in: Research in Management, pages 139–163.
Copyright © 2003 by Information Age Publishing, Inc.
All rights of reproduction in any form reserved.
ISBN: 1-59311-099-5 (hardcover), 1-59311-098-7 (pbk.)

Let me begin with the bottom-line. The most important step that can be taken to improve the effectiveness of recruitment and recruitment research is to develop and use fine-grained assessments of the quality of applicants attracted. This single assessment is the basis for evaluating the effectiveness of current recruitment efforts, determining whether modifications of recruitment tactics is likely to be worth the effort, and if meaningful improvement is possible, identifying where those efforts should be placed.

Organization assessment is in the midst of a paradigm shift. The increasing use of integrated human resource information systems (HRIS) permits greater access to data than has ever been possible while dramatically reducing the marginal costs of assessment activities. This new capability has triggered increased interest in HR analytics. However, as a review of recruitment evaluation measures will show, more extensive use of current measures is unlikely to lead to meaningful improvement in recruitment effectiveness. It is time to reevaluate recruitment evaluation. In this chapter, I review the range of measures that have been used to assess recruitment effectiveness and discuss the consequences of their use. I then offer an alternative approach to evaluating recruitment effectiveness that can be used to support more aggressive management of the recruitment function and provide two examples of its application. In the final section, I discuss the evolution of recruitment evaluation and management and offer a perspective on how the changes suggested here may influence future research and practice.

RECRUITMENT AND ITS EVALUATION

Rynes (1991) defines recruitment as encompassing "all organizational practices and decisions that affect either the number, or types, of individuals who are willing to apply for, or accept, a given vacancy" (p. 429). Similarly, Barber (1998) describes recruitment as "a set of activities conducted by an organization in hopes of identifying and attracting suitable employees, with the implicit distal goal of improving organizational performance" (p. 124). Contributions to recruitment theory by Rynes (1991), Rynes and Barber (1990), Breaugh (1992), Taylor and Giannantonio (1993[AU: pls. cite in refs.]), Barber (1998), Breaugh and Starke (2000) and Carlson and Connerley (2003) have extended our understanding and shaped current conceptualizations of recruitment as organizations' attempts to influence three pre-hire decisions by prospective employees. These are:

1. the decision to apply for a position,
2. the decision to maintain their status as an applicant until the organization determines if they will receive a job offer, and
3. the decision to accept an offer.

The actions of organizations designed to influence these three decisions are described respectively as attraction, status maintenance and gaining job acceptance.

Research interest in recruitment effectiveness can be traced at least as far back as Raphael's (1937) discussion of the use of the recommendations of past staff members as a method of recruiting administrative personnel from outside the organization. Yet, while rhetorical (Barber, 1998; Boudreau & Rynes, 1985; Rynes, 1991) and empirical arguments (e.g., Grossman, 2000; Huselid, 1995; Terpstra & Rozell, 1993) demonstrate the importance of recruitment to organization success, few organizations formally evaluate the effectiveness of their recruitment efforts (e.g., Davidson, 1998; Grossman, 2000; Rynes & Boudreau, 1986). A SHRM/CCH (1999) survey of recruiting practices found that less than half of 279 organizations surveyed engaged in any type of formal evaluation. When organizations do evaluate, they typically assess only a fraction of their recruitment efforts using a limited number of measures. These results are even more interesting because they were collected during a period of tight labor markets when organization interest in recruitment generally increases (Guion, 1976).

Given its importance, the lack of systematic evaluation of recruitment effectiveness should at least pique the interest of recruitment scholars. There are several reasons why organizations may choose not to engage in more extensive evaluation of recruitment outcomes. Some of the more commonly offered reasons suggest decision-makers may still be unconvinced that recruitment adds significant value. These managers may believe that simply attracting a "sufficiently large" number of applicants for open positions leaves little to be gained through more aggressive management of recruitment or that emphasizing effective selection and post-hire management of new employees can compensate for poor recruitment. Others may believe that outcomes are driven primarily by factors outside of recruiters' control, i.e., favorableness of the economy, fluctuations in labor supply and demand (Becker, 1989); and organization and job characteristics (Barber, Wesson, Roberson & Taylor, 1999; Cable, Aiman-Smith, Mulvey & Edwards, 2000). If recruitment tactics have only limited effects on outcomes, evaluation would seem to be of limited value. Existing research, though, does not support these arguments.

How organizations recruit does make a difference. Boudreau and Rynes (1985) and Murphy (1986) demonstrated that even relatively small changes in recruitment outcomes can have significant dollar-valued consequences for organizations. Research indicates a variety of recruitment tactics influence recruitment decisions, e.g., choice of recruitment tactics (Garman & Mortensen, 1997; Lavigna, 1996; Rynes & Barber, 1990); source of recruits (Griffith, Hom, Fink & Cohen, 1997; Werbel & Landau, 1996); content of recruiting messages (Belt & Paolillo, 1982; Highhouse, Stierwalt, Bachiochi, Elder, & Fisher, 1999; Mason & Belt, 1986). Finally, organization decision-makers have demonstrated their belief that recruiting tactics make a difference through their rapid adoptions of Internet-based recruitment (Starcke, 1996).

Another possible explanation for the lack of recruitment evaluation is that current measures of recruitment effectiveness do not provide organization decision-makers the information they need to support more aggressive recruitment management. As will be shown in the following section, this argument has merit. It may also explain, in part, why human resources management as a field has been described as metric-averse (Crouse, 2002).

MEASURES OF RECRUITING EFFECTIVENESS AND THEIR CONSEQUENCES

Measures of recruitment effectiveness can be organized according to timing of the assessment (i.e., pre-hire versus post-hire) and the type of information gathered (i.e., intervening psychological variables versus outcomes). Table 1 offers a sampling of each of the resulting four types of measure and instances where each has appeared in the recruitment literature.

Pre-hire recruitment measures refer to assessments that occur prior to the time that individuals begin their employment with an organization. The use of pre-hire measures is common in research investigating how recruiting tactics influence individual applicants (e.g., Cable & Judge, 1994; Turban, Forret, & Hendrickson, 1998). Pre-hire measures gather data related to individuals' decisions to apply for positions, to continue pursuing employment, or to accept a job offer. An advantage of pre-hire measures is that they can be aligned with specific recruitment actions and, therefore, may capture purer (i.e., less contaminated) assessments of the effects of targeted recruitment tactics. On a practical note, because they can be assessed concurrent to ongoing recruitment efforts, the use of pre-hire measures also offers organizations an opportunity to intervene when it is still possible to influence outcomes if current tactics appear to be ineffective. The primary disadvantage of pre-hire measures is that they represent intermediate outcomes that are further influenced by subsequent staffing decisions. As a result, what may appear to be significant improvements in one or more pre-hire recruitment outcomes may, as a result of subsequent decisions, have only modest effects on the ultimate outcomes achieved by the organization.

Post-hire measures are assessed after the individual has started working. Post-hire measures are common in several areas of recruitment research. Recruiting source research has examined whether specific sources of recruits (e.g., walk-ins, referrals) are associated with greater on-the-job performance or lower rates of turnover (Blau, 1990; Breaugh, 1981; Williams, Labig, & Stone, 1993). Turnover is one of several post hire measures exam-

TABLE 1
Framework of Recruitment Outcome Measures with Examples from the
Research Literature

	Intervening Psychological Variables	*Outcomes*
Pre-Hire	Applicant Impressions of Recruiters (e.g., Harn & Thornton, 1985; Rogers & Sincoff, 1978; Schmitt & Coyle, 1976) Attractiveness of Job or Organization (e.g. Fisher, Ilgen, & Hoyer, 1979; Rynes & Miller, 1983) Intention to Apply/Intent to Accept an Offer (Herriot & Rothwell, 1981; Liden & Parson, 1986) Expectancy of Receiving an Offer (Alderfer & McCord, 1970; Powell, 1984; Schmitt & Coyle, 1976) Probability of Accepting an Offer (Alderfer & McCord, 1972; Schmitt & Coyle, 1976; Taylor & Bergmann, 1987)	Job Acceptance Decisions (Taylor & Bergman, 1987) Number of Applicants Attracted (Gersen, 1976; Willams & Dreher, 1992) Applicant Quality/Qualifications (Blau, 1990; Breaugh & Mann, 1984; Dreher & Sackett, 1982; Gersen, 1976; Griffith, Hom, Fink, & Cohen, 1997; Kirnan, Farley, & Geisinger, 1989; Taylor & Bergmann, 1987; Werbel & Landau, 1996; Williams, Labig, & Stone, 1993) Percent of Offers Accepted (Williams & Dreher, 1992) Time Required to Fill Open Positions (Williams & Dreher, 1992)
Post-Hire	Job/Work Satisfaction (Breaugh, 1981; (Latham & Leddy, 1987) Organization Commitment (Latham & Leddy, 1987) Turnover/Tenure Intentions (Taylor & Bergmann, 1987) Perceptions of organizational climate, organizational commitment, coping, initial/ expectations/met expectations, job satisfaction (Premack & Wanous, 1985)	Absenteeism (Breaugh, 1981; Taylor & Schmidt, 1983) Turnover within 12 months (Caldwell & Spivey, 1983; Conard & Ashworth, 1986; Reid, 1972; Taylor & Schmidt, 1983; Ullman, 1966; Werbel & Landau, 1996; Williams, Labig, & Stone, 1993) Performance rating (Blau, 1990; Breaugh, 1981; Breaugh & Mann, 1984; Hill, 1970; Swaroff, Barclay & Bass, 1985; Taylor & Schmidt, 1983; Werbel & Landau, 1996; Williams, Labig, & Stone, 1993) Diversity (Caldwell & Spivey, 1983; Kirnan, Farley, & Geisinger, 1989; Vecchio, 1995)

ined in realistic job preview research (e.g., Premack & Wanous, 1985; Wanous, Poland, Premack & Davis, 1992). An advantage of post-hire measures is that they can be more directly tied to organization outcomes and they offer convenience—most organizations already gather these data for other purposes. A disadvantage of post-hire measures is that they are only available after the fact, too late to intervene to improve poor outcomes.

Post-hire assessments also only include data for those individuals that are hired. The vast majority of individuals involved in and influenced by recruitment processes are ignored. Finally, post-hire measures capture the combined effects of several staffing processes making the diagnosis of problems in recruitment practices difficult. Poor results on post-hire assessments could be due to poor attraction, status maintenance, or job acceptance; but they could just as easily be due to poor selection, orientation, training, job design, or supervision.

Measures of intervening psychological states or outcomes can be assessed pre- or post-hire. Measures of intervening psychological states capture assessments of individuals' affect, attitudes, knowledge, beliefs, or intentions that are believed to be correlates or antecedents of individuals' recruitment decisions. Some examples include attitude toward recruiters, intent to apply, intent to accept a job offer, or job satisfaction. An advantage of assessments of intervening psychological states is that they not only add to our understanding of why individuals make the decisions they do, but they also provide insight into the tactics organizations could use to influence decision-makers. Assessments of psychological states are relatively easy to administer and have the capacity to be assessed outside of actual recruitment decision contexts (i.e., in controlled laboratory settings). A limitation of intervening psychological variables is that they capture dynamic states that may have only modest associations with actual recruitment decisions.

Measures of outcomes are assessments of the consequences of actual recruitment/staffing decisions (e.g., applying for a position, number or quality of applicants attracted, choosing to withdraw from consideration before receiving an offer, accepting an offer, absenteeism, functional/dysfunctional voluntary/involuntary turnover, job performance, contribution, or cost). Assessments of outcomes are more common in recruitment evaluation practice than are measures of intervening psychological variables. No psychological variables are listed among the ten most frequently used recruitment measures in the SRHM/CCH (1999) survey (i.e., time to fill, retention rates, turnover rates, cost per hire, number of applicants generated, job performance of new hires after a specified time, EEO/diversity impact, total cost of recruiting, average length of employment, and offers extended compared to offers accepted). An advantage of observable outcomes is they focus on what has been achieved. They directly assess the targeted outcomes that recruitment practices are designed to influence. Data on outcomes can often be gathered from records of human resource management transactions. Assuming appropriate measures are adopted to ensure privacy, these assessments are less invasive and require fewer organizational resources than psychological assessments. A disadvantage of outcome measures is they are also influenced by environment or contextual factors that can make it difficult to determine the effects of recruitment tactics.

Each of the four types of measures has utility, but pre-hire measures of outcomes are best positioned to form the foundation of recruitment evaluation systems. Recruitment is a system of actions designed to influence a sequence of decisions. Using multiple pre-hire measures assessing outcomes at different points during recruitment (i.e., when the applicant pool is developed, when offers are extended, after offers have been accepted or rejected) offers greater conceptual clarity for understanding and disentangling the effects of recruitment tactics than is possible with post-hire measures. Further, assessments of post-hire outcomes can be interpreted more accurately if we understand the effects that recruitment actions have on each of the pre-hire recruitment decisions. Outcome measures are preferred to psychological assessments because they can be interpreted directly. This is not to say that assessments of pre-hire psychological states are not meaningful; an emphasis on outcomes is simply a matter of logical priority. Before we can focus effort on how to manipulate psychological variables we first need to understand how various psychological states work together to influence recruitment decisions. This requires an integrated model of these relationships that does not currently exist and cannot be developed without first understanding the properties of the outcomes these variables are expected to predict.

Pre-hire measures of outcomes can be further organized into assessments of cost, quantity, time, quality, and value. A targeted review of recruitment evaluation measures (i.e., Cascio, 1991, 1998; Fitz-Enz, 1990, 1993, 2002; Hawk, 1967; Sullivan, 1999) identified 46 unique outcome measures that have been specifically suggested for evaluating recruitment effectiveness. Of these, 21 were assessments of pre-hire outcomes and 22 were quantity measures. Table 2 offers a breakdown of pre-hire and post-hire examples of these five types of outcome measures.

Forty-eight percent of organizations in the SHRM/CCH (1999) survey reported the use of a post-hire measure of costs (i.e., cost per hire). An emphasis on costs reflects both the relative ease of gathering cost information and the reality that recruitment processes are a direct source of costs, but can only affect revenue indirectly, once new hires are on the job. Where the benefits of recruitment—the greater contributions of higher performing employees—are often considered difficult to estimate, organizations' accounting systems already track cost data and can make it readily accessible to managers. Minimizing recruitment costs is a desired organizational outcome and cost reduction has been an important driver of HRIS investments. But intense management of recruitment costs can produce undesired outcomes. If only costs are considered, the optimal strategy is cost minimization. But recruitment tactics have cost and benefit consequences. Reducing recruitment costs without also recognizing any potentially negative consequences on benefits can harm, rather than help, organizations.

TABLE 2
Recommended Assessments of Observable
Recruitment Outcomes and Source

PRE-HIRE MEASURES

Cost

- Total Cost of Recruiting (Hawk 1967; SHRM/CCH, 1999)

Quantity

- Number of applicants or resumes generated (Fitz-Enz, 1990, 2002; Hawk, 1967; SHRM/CCH, 1999) by source or geography (Hawk, 1967)
- Interview/invitation ratio: Number of interviews conducted/Number of individuals offered the opportunity to interview (Hawk, 1967)
- Invitation/resume input ratio: Number of individuals offered the opportunity to interview/Number of resumes or candidates generated (Hawk, 1967)
- Offer acceptance ratio: Number of offers accepted/Number of offers extended (Fitz-Enz, 1993; Hawk, 1967; SHRM/CCH, 1999).
- Offer to Interview Ratio: Number of Offers Extended/Number of candidates interviewed (Hawk, 1967)
- Hiring rates or selection ratio: Number of individuals hired/Number of candidates considered (Fitz-Enz, 1993)
- Recruiter Activity: Analysis of number of resumes handled, the number of interviews conducted, the number of offers made, and the number of offers accepted for each recruiter (Hawk, 1967)
- Recruiter efficiency: Number of hires generated by a recruiter/Total costs of employing the recruiter including salary and benefits plus operating expenses (Hawk, 1967) or by some combination of interview time, hire ratio, hit rate by recruiter (Fitz-Enz, 2002)
- Recruiting Source Effectiveness-assessed by some combination of cost per hire, response rate, and hit rate by source (Fitz-Enz, 2002)
- Referral Rate: Total number of candidate referrals received (by source)/Total number of recruiting events (uses of a source) (Fitz-Enz, 2002)

Time

- Response time or Average Response Time: Total response time/Number of hiring requisitions received (Fitz-Enz, 2002)
- Time lapse between recruiting stages by acceptance versus rejection (analysis of accept versus reject decisions according to how long candidates spent in each stage of the recruiting process (Hawk, 1967)
- Time lapse between recruiting stages by source (Hawk, 1967)
- Time to fill or Average Time to Fill: Total time that filled positions remained vacant/Number of positions filled (Fitz-Enz, 2002, 1993; SHRM/CCH, 1999)
- Time to fill Requisitions: Days from time requisitions are received until positions are filled/Number of requisitions filled (Fitz-Enz, 1993)

Quality

- Comparison of placement test scores (Hawk, 1967)
- Biographical data analyses of candidates (Hawk, 1967)

(continued)

TABLE 2

Continued

- Quality/assessment of Resumes (Hawk, 1967, Sullivan, 1999)
- Percent of qualifications met (Sullivan, 1999)
- Manager prediction (at the time of job offer) of the quality of a hire (Sullivan, 1999)

Value

[No Measures Identified]

POST HIRE MEASURES

Cost

- Cost per hire: Total Hiring Costs/Number Hired (Fitz-Enz, 2002; 1991; Grossman, 2000; Hawk, 1999; SHRM/CCH, 1999)
- Total Compensation Revenue Percent: [Compensation cost + Benefit Cost]/Revenue (Grossman, 2000)
- Turnover Costs: Cost to terminate + Total costs of lost production + Total impact of wage differentials for replacement workers + Total costs of recruiting new workers + Total costs of lost production and training costs associated with orienting new employee and getting them up to the level of the prior employee (Grossman, 2000)
- Total Labor Cost Revenue Percent: [Compensation cost + Benefit Cost + Other labor Costs]/Revenue (Grossman, 2000)

Quantity

- Absentee percentage: Number of days workers/new hires were absent/Number of work days for all workers/all new hires (Fitz-Enz, 1993)
- Total Days missed due to illness (Fitz-Enz, 1990)
- EEO/Diversity Impact (SHRM/CCH, 1999)
- Percent of new hire retained after one year (Fitz-Enz, 2002).
- Percent of new hires promoted (Fitz-Enz, 2002)
- Personnel head count: Total Employees, Number in Human Resources (Fitz-Enz, 1990)
- Retention Rates (SHRM/CCH, 1999) of top performers (Sullivan, 1999)
- Source Yield: Number hired by source (Hawk, 1967)
- Source Efficiency: Number hired by source/Total costs associated with the use of that source (Hawk, 1967)
- Transfer rates: Number of individuals transferred to positions at a comparable level in other units, departments of divisions/Total number of hires (Fitz-Enz, 1990)
- Voluntary Turnover Rate: Number of individuals leaving the organization during a given period of time/Total head count (Fitz-Enz, 1990, 1993; Grossman, 2000; SHRM/CCH, 1999).
- Involuntary turnover rate or percentage: Number of individuals leaving positions involuntarily/Total head count (Fitz-Enz, 1993; Grossman, 2000)

Time

- Time to productivity: The number of days until the minimum expected level of output is reached for a new hire (Sullivan, 1999)
- Average length of employment (SHRM/CCH, 1999)

(continued)

TABLE 2
Continued

Quality

- Job performance rating or average job performance rating of new hires: Sum of all performance ratings for new hires across all evaluation periods considered/Number of evaluations completed (Fitz-Enz, 2002; SHRM/CCH, 1999, Sullivan, 1999)
- Quality of Hire: Quality of hire + average performance rating + percent of new hires promoted + percent of new hires retained after 1 year/Number of indices. (Fitz-Enz, 2002)
- Placement test scores of hires versus observed performance (Hawk, 1967)
- Subjective ratings of managers, co-workers, or subordinates (Sullivan, 1999)

Value

- Human Capital ROI: [Revenue - (Operating expense - (Compensation cost + Benefits cost))]/(Compensation cost - Benefits cost) (Grossman, 2000)
- Human Capital Value Added: [Revenue - (Operating expense - (Compensation cost + Benefits cost))]/Total FTE (Grossman, 2000)
- Revenue Factor: Revenue/Total FTE (Grossman, 2000)

Where costs are naturally reported in a dollar metric, this is not the case for recruitment benefits. In the absence of direct measures of recruitment benefits, organizations have employed alternative measures, or proxies, for more direct assessments of benefits. These include measures of quantity, time, and quality. As might be expected, the use of these measures limits what can be learned from existing recruitment evaluation efforts.

Examples of quantity outcome measures include number of applicants attracted, percent of applicants that withdraw prior to receiving an offer, percent of individuals that receive offers that accept them, rate of absenteeism, and tenure or rate of turnover. Measures of the number of applicants at various stages of recruitment are indirect measures of applicant quality and cost. The more applicants an organization is able to attract relative to the number of positions to be filled the more selective the organization can be in choosing new hires. If we assume applicant pools are random draws from the underlying applicant population greater selectivity should lead to higher quality hires and greater organizational effectiveness. But since the actual distribution of applicant quality in applicant pools is generally unknown, the actual contribution of greater selectivity cannot be determined. Further, at some point the costs of screening and processing increasing larger applicant pools will outpace the added benefits of greater selectivity.

Applicants that withdraw prior to receiving offers or who fail to accept offers when they receive them can also affect quality. The greater the rate of withdrawal or non-acceptance of offers the greater the potential loss to the organization because individuals perceived to have less performance potential are being hired. Withdrawal of candidates or their failure to accept offers can also result in recruiting failures (i.e., when no applicants are hired) and increases costs if recruiting activities must be repeated.

Time assessments measure how long it takes to complete recruitment processes. Time to fill positions was the most commonly reported recruitment evaluation metric in the SHRM/CCH (1999) survey; assessed by 72 percent of organizations. Other common pre-hire time measures include assessments the number of days positions remain vacant and the number of days between closing of applications and making offers. With the exception of organization tenure, longer periods of time are generally associated with higher costs or greater reductions in productivity. The longer positions remain open, the longer any loss of productivity caused by the vacancy is extended. The longer it takes to make hire decisions, the greater the likelihood that applicants will withdraw or be able to generate alternative offers. Time measures offer an indication of the magnitude of lost production or increased costs by providing a multiplier that can be applied to daily loss or cost estimates; but they offer no insight into the magnitude of the daily loss or cost estimate. Further, minimizing the time required to complete recruitment activities may be sub-optimal if filling positions quickly results in lower quality hires.

Quality measures assess the characteristics of individuals (KSAs) that are predictive of future job performance. Examples of measures of applicant quality include direct scoring of resumes or application blanks, ratings of training and experience (e.g., McDaniel, Schmidt, & Hunter, 1988), or scores on employment tests or interviews. Measures of applicant quality can provide fine-grained data that can be captured at multiple points in the recruitment process, even at the earliest stages of attraction. Also, quality measures are direct assessments of applicant potential making them more precise assessments of recruitment benefits than quantity or time measures; in fact, nothing is provided in measures of quantity or time that is not more meaningfully captured by directly assessing applicant quality or recruitment costs.

Surprisingly, measures of applicant quality are used infrequently in research and practice. No measure of applicant quality was reported in the findings of the SHRM/CCH (1999) survey of evaluation practices. Breaugh and Starke (2000) identified only two instances where researchers assessed the quality of applicants attracted (e.g., Kirnan, Farley, & Geisinger, 1989; Williams, Labig, & Stone, 1993). Expanding the definition of quality measures to include assessments or ratings of education and qualifications, as was done in the development of Table 1, added only seven additional studies to this list.

Measures of applicant quality are preferred over measures of quantity or time, but even these are not ideal benefits measures. The most common approach used to evaluate new tactics in organizations is cost-benefit analysis—an examination of the expected benefits derived from new tactics in comparison to the projected costs. However, none of the recruitment benefits measures discussed to this point provide benefits data in a dollar metric. Using existing quantity, time, or quality measures results in awkward mixed-metric cost-benefit analyses. For example, should an organization undertake a change in recruiting tactics estimated to cost $1000 if it results in a 20 percent increase in the number of applicants? What if it reduced the amount of time positions remain vacant by 15 days? What if it could increase the average quality of applicants by 10 percent? These are the types of questions that recruitment decision-makers face, yet none of the measures of recruitment benefits discussed so far leads to definitive answers to any of these questions.

The missing component in current approaches to recruitment evaluation is measures of value. As noted in Table 1, no pre-hire measure of value was identified. The only value measures that were identified were for post-hire outcomes and these measures were based on organization level estimates of revenue that also incorporate compensation and other cost components. Value assessments provide dollar-valued estimates of benefits derived from recruitment activities that can be combined with cost data in meaningful cost-benefit analyses. In situations where recruitment activities generate revenue (i.e., recruiting agencies), direct estimates of changes in revenue are possible. In most organizations, though, recruitment contributes to revenue indirectly. Therefore, methods of estimating value from other forms of data are needed.

RETHINKING RECRUITMENT EVALUATION

In an effort to address the limitations noted above, Carlson, Connerley, and Mecham (2002) offered a new recruitment evaluation framework. In it they argued that a practicable approach to recruitment evaluation could be achieved by

a. isolating and evaluating attraction outcomes,
b. directly assessing the quality (i.e., job performance potential) of each applicant, and then
c. using utility analysis to convert differences in applicants' job performance potential to a dollar metric.

This final step produces an estimate of the value of alternative attraction activities that can be compared to their costs.

Attraction is the first phase of recruitment and is a critical determinant of recruitment and staffing success. Attraction activities establish the pool of applicants from which new hires will eventually be chosen. The maximum potential value of a recruiting event (i.e., the contribution the best applicants could make to organizational effectiveness) is fixed once the applicant pool is established. If top candidates do not apply, an organization has no chance of hiring them. That potential, though, is realized only if the best applicants in the pool are offered, and then accept, positions. Any other outcome (i.e., the failure to retain top candidates in the pool or to gain their acceptance of offers of employment) represents a loss of potential value. Status maintenance and gaining job acceptance activities influence the effectiveness of recruitment by reducing or avoiding the loss of potential that can occur when the best applicants do not join organizations. However, neither status maintenance nor efforts to influence job choice can raise the potential contribution of a recruitment cycle beyond that initially present in the applicant pool. Therefore, the first priority of recruitment is to attract the best possible applicants. Assessments of applicant quality measure this outcome directly. Once attraction outcomes are assessed, evaluating the effectiveness of status maintenance and job acceptance outcomes follows naturally by examining whether top candidates are lost during status maintenance or job acceptance activities. The magnitude of the loss can be estimated by examining the reduction in applicant quality that occurs during each decision event.

Carlson et al. (2002) provides a six-step procedure for assessing attraction outcomes that produces benefit value and cost data. This procedure includes the following steps:

1. Determine the positions to be evaluated; high volume and high impact (i.e., high autonomy and responsibility) positions are likely targets.

2. Identify what mechanisms are currently used for screening candidates in the organization and determining their assessment properties. Some organizations may need to formalize existing screening procedures.

3. Determine a procedure for producing scores for each applicant and adapting existing measures. Usually organization's current screening devices will not produce scores with ideal properties (i.e., fine-grained, high validity for predicting job performance, known population parameters). Organizations need to decide if and to what extent they may want to modify current screening practices. Scores with more optimal properties provide more accurate estimates, but developing measures with more optimal properties is likely to increase costs.

4. Assess the quality of each applicant. Scores are developed for all applicants. Comparisons of recruitment events can be conducted

using data on the level and distribution of quality scores for entire applicant pools or for some subset of high scoring applicants. Archiving applicant quality score data can facilitate the development of population norms (e.g., Sackett & Ostgaard, 1994) that permit meaningful comparisons of outcomes across recruiting events.

5. Match recruitment activities to recruitment decisions and estimate recruitment costs. In order to evaluate the cost effectiveness of various recruitment practices, recruitment costs must be identified and mapped to the appropriate phase of recruitment (i.e., attraction, status maintenance, gaining job acceptance).

6. Use utility analysis (UA) to develop estimates of the value of differences in applicant quality. This can be done using the following equation:

$$\Delta U_{\text{benefits}} = r_{xy} \times SD_y \times \Delta Z_x \times T \times N \tag{1}$$

Using UA requires several values to be estimated including the validity of screening devices (r_{xy}), the standard deviation of performance in dollars for the job in question (SD_y), the number of individuals to be hired or the subset of applicants to be evaluated (N), and the average expected tenure of applicants in their positions once hired (T). Methods of estimating these values are discussed in Boudreau (1991) and Carlson et al. (2002). The effect of recruitment efforts on applicant quality can be examined by comparing the change in average standardized quality scores (ΔZ_x) of top candidates across recruiting events.

Some individuals have raised concerns about relying on organizations' existing procedures for screening applicants as the basis for any form of evaluation. In some instances the screening methods organizations currently employ have unknown or questionable validity. The use of low validity selection devices is neither recommended nor desired. But irrespective of the validity or other properties of current screening procedures, these are the procedures the organization is using. If they are adequate for supporting current organization decision-making, it is illogical to argue they are insufficient to support evaluation (Carlson et al. 2002). Other concerns may center on the need to estimate unknown values required to develop utility estimates, SD_y for instance. While this is a concern, it should not deter use of the methodology. As organizations develop more experience and expertise, methods for estimating these values will improve. Until that time, it is important to recognize that in the absence of another methodology for estimating the dollar value of differences in applicant quality, reasonable, though imperfect, estimates of value are better than no estimate at all.

This methodology supports more aggressive management of the recruiting function than is otherwise possible. Using this methodology, organizations can

a. pursue independent evaluations of attraction, status maintenance, and gaining job acceptance practices,
b. perform concurrent evaluations of attraction outcomes,
c. conduct cost-benefit analyses of alternative recruitment processes, and
d. compare applicants from different recruitment events.

EXAMPLES OF RECRUITING OUTCOME ASSESSMENTS USING THIS FRAMEWORK

These methods have been employed in two studies comparing attraction outcomes for organizations recruiting individuals for the same or very similar job titles. Carlson et al. (2002) examines the extent to which attraction outcomes differ across organizations that compete head-to-head in a narrowly defined labor market. This study compared the results of attraction outcomes for five organizations recruiting for the position of associate engineer at the same university. In this analysis, grade point average was used as a simple estimate of applicant quality. The advantage of using grade point average is that an estimate of its validity for predicting job performance exists in the research literature (e.g., Roth, BeVier, Switzer, & Schippmann, 1996). Assuming top down hiring, the top 2 applicants from each applicant pool are compared using utility analysis to estimate the value of differences across organizations. This analysis found meaningful differences did exist in the quality of applicants attracted by these five firms. Comparing the applicant pools with the highest and lowest average quality scores produced an estimated difference in utility of $4,473.59. That is to say, if these two organizations were to hire the top two individuals from their respective applicant pools, the difference in the expected contribution in favor of the organization with superior attraction outcomes is estimated to be over $4,400 for this one recruitment event.

Perhaps even more illuminating is the subsequent analysis of the potential effects of status maintenance and job acceptance activities. Beginning with the actual attraction data for each job posting, the effects of nine combinations of status maintenance and job acceptance outcomes on utility (i.e., value) were examined for each applicant pool. Three status maintenance outcomes (i.e., ideal—all applicants are retained; moderate—applicants ranked 2, 7, and 12 withdraw; and poor—applicants ranked 1, 3, 5, 7, 9, 11, and 13 withdraw) were fully crossed with three sets of job acceptance outcomes (i.e., ideal—all top candidates accept offers, moderate—the second best candidate refuses the job offer; poor—applicants ranked 1, 2, and 4 refuse job offers). For the highest ranked applicant pool, a pool containing many high-scoring applicants, even poor status maintenance and job acceptance had little impact on utility (i.e., -$323.70). But where attraction resulted in few high scoring applicants and greater variance in applicant quality scores, the effects of poor status maintenance and job acceptance were dramatic. In the worst case scenario, where attraction alone resulted in an estimated difference in utility of $4,473.59, the addition of poor status maintenance and poor job acceptance outcomes resulted in an additional reduction in utility of $7,827.15 (i.e., a total of over -$12,300) for this one event.

Connerly, Carlson, & Mecham (2003) examined the generalizability of these findings using data on the quality of applicants attracted for more than 400 positions representing 18 narrowly defined job families. The results of this analysis, which is also based on hiring two applicants who are expected to remain in their positions for one year, mirrored those above. Within job families, comparisons of the top ranked, second ranked, median, and bottom-ranked applicant pools in each job family according to average applicant quality scores produced a consistent pattern of results. Comparisons of the two best applicant pools in each job family resulted in very little if any difference in utility (i.e., M_{diff} = $135.24). However, comparing the top-ranked applicant pool to the median and lowest ranked applicant pool in each family produced far greater differences in utility (i.e., M_{diff} = $1270.62 and M_{diff} = $6394.45, respectively). The differences in utility between the highest and lowest ranked applicant pools were greatest for the job families of mechanical engineers (M_{diff} = $13.880.96) and general engineers (M_{diff} = $15,069.60). These data suggest that organizations that are already among the best at attracting applicants may not have much to gain by attempting to improve attraction efforts. But organizations whose attraction outcomes rank in the lower half for a job family could increase recruitment utility by as much as several thousand dollars by improving the effectiveness of their attraction efforts.

Conducting this type of analysis requires that organizations be willing to assess the quality of every applicant attracted. Developing quality scores for all applicants is time consuming and prohibitively expensive if done using paper and pencil methods. Harnessing the capacity of today's computing systems allows this process to be conducted at minimal cost and concurrent to on-going recruitment activities. Several integrated HRIS software packages and stand-alone applicant tracking programs available on the market today offer tools that will perform these calculations automatically. It is hard to look forward and not be optimistic.

AN EVOLUTIONARY VIEW OF RECRUITMENT EVALUATION

I would like to end this chapter by attempting to place current recruitment evaluation practices in the context of an evolutionary model of recruiting evaluation and management consisting of three distinct phases. These phases represent our recruitment evaluation past, our changing present and a look at what the future might offer. I briefly discuss each phase and discuss how continued progress in recruitment evaluation may affect research and practice.

Phase I: It is Broken?

It can be argued that recruitment's primary contribution to organization success is simply ensuring that open positions are filled. If this is done well, the organization is adequately staffed to carry out its business day in and day out. The lack of formal evaluation of recruitment efforts does not necessarily mean organizations are not concerned about the effectiveness of their recruitment efforts. Managers acknowledge the importance of recruitment activities, particularly when turnover is high and the organization is experiencing recruitment failures—when attraction efforts fail to produce enough qualified applicants to fill open positions. The focus of their attention, though, is adequacy, rather than optimization. Monitoring indicators of recruitment adequacy is Phase I recruitment evaluation.

Phase I evaluation does not require sophisticated measures or formalized evaluation procedures, though both would be preferred. The purpose of Phase I evaluation is to simply assure that recruitment activities do not jeopardize the continued viability of the organization. Phase I evaluation, therefore, can be accomplished by a limited number of high impact indices of recruitment success (i.e., number of recruitment failures, number of applicants attracted, amount of time positions remain vacant, rated performance or survival of new hires on the job). Coarse-grained measures or even "eye-ball" estimates may be sufficient for these purposes.

Every organization likely engages in some form of Phase I recruitment evaluation. In fact, most if not all of the organizations responding to the SHRM/CCH (1999) survey of recruitment evaluation practices would fall in this category. This is an initial assessment of the effectiveness of organization recruitment efforts and success at this level of evaluation will generally be required before more aggressive evaluation and management would be appropriate. If an organization is struggling to meet its day-to-day staffing needs, the organization's first priority must be to solve these problems. Managers would be likely to choose to forego more aggressive or fine-grained evaluation until Phase I problems are resolved.

Phase II: Fine Tuning Recruitment Processes

Where Phase I evaluation assesses the general health of recruitment, Phase II evaluation can be thought of as fine-tuning healthy recruitment processes for peak performance. The purpose of Phase II recruitment evaluation is to assure that the organization is optimizing its attraction, status maintenance and job acceptance practices. Phase II evaluation requires fine-grained measures and formalized procedures for assessing decision outcomes for each recruitment decision outcome that few organizations currently employ. To conduct Phase II recruitment evaluation organizations would need to (1) conduct assessments of the quality of applicants attracted as well as status maintenance and job acceptance outcomes and (2) be able to estimate both the magnitude and value of available opportunities to enhance performance for each of these outcomes. The methods described in Carlson et al. (2002) are an example of Phase II evaluation. Combining these methods with the greater access to data and the computing capacity of HRIS greatly enhances organizations' capacity to perform Phase II recruitment evaluation.

The potential benefits from Phase II evaluation in otherwise healthy recruitment systems can be substantial. But, as can be seen in Carlson et al. (2002) and Connerley et al. (2003) and in the application of UA to recruitment issues in Boudreau and Rynes (1985) and Murphy (1986), opportunities for improvement may not be obvious to the naked eye. Without Phase II evaluation techniques, which employ more systematic analysis, fine-grained measures of costs and benefits, and tools for converting differences in applicant quality to a dollar metric, managers may not recognize or effectively evaluate subtler opportunities for improving recruitment practices.

How effectively organizations can employ Phase II evaluation is determined by the validity of their screening practices and how effectively they can estimate the parameters required by utility analysis for specific positions within their organizations. Treatments of utility analysis generally use population level parameters of the required inputs. The use of actual applicant quality data instead of estimated Z_x scores greatly enhances the accuracy of utility estimates, but improving our capacity to estimate other parameters required by utility analysis, like SD_y will enable further refinement of Phase II evaluation capabilities (i.e., increasing the accuracy of cost and benefit estimates).

Phase III: Integrated Management of the Recruitment System.

Optimizing the individual components of recruitment systems is important, but additional opportunities exist if organizations can optimize their entire recruitment systems within the context of existing environmental factors, job design and selection system components. Optimizing attraction, status maintenance, and job acceptance individually is equivalent to the mathematical concept of reaching local optima. However, this may not simultaneously maximize the entire system. Phase III evaluation focuses on the effectiveness of the entire recruitment system. Consequently, Phase III evaluation requires a comprehensive set of fine-grained pre-hire and post-hire outcome measures as well as assessments of environment (i.e., labor market size and characteristics, competitive factors) and job design variables that influence those outcomes.

Effective management of recruitment based on Phase III evaluation requires a comprehensive understanding of the effects of environmental factors and recruitment activities on outcomes as well as the relationships between immediate and distal recruitment outcomes. The objective of Phase III recruitment management is to adjust recruitment tactics in concert with job design and other staffing decisions in order to continually maximize recruitment effectiveness in response to changes in labor markets, competitive circumstances or organization strategy. Job design decisions (e.g., Campion & Stevens, 1991) have important influences on recruitment. Job characteristics influence how difficult it will be to attract applicants, where qualified applicants are likely to be found, what selection devices will have validity for predicting high performers, and how difficult it will be to gain job acceptance and retain high performers after hire. Attraction outcomes also affect the utility of selection devices. If attraction efforts succeed in producing an applicant pool that only contains high scoring applicants (i.e., no low scoring applicants applied) the validity of selection devices is much less consequential; the effect of less than perfect validity is mitigated.

The capacity to manage all recruitment practices as an integrated system and deploy them in ways that allow the organization to respond to changes in organization strategy or the environment are the capabilities that define strategic human resource management (Schuler & Jackson, 1999). Unfortunately, we do not currently possess the knowledge or assessment expertise required for truly strategic HRM, but developing the capacity for strategic management of recruitment is attainable. Building our Phase II recruitment evaluation capabilities is a necessary first step toward the goal of Phase III recruitment evaluation and management.

IMPLICATIONS FOR RESEARCH AND PRACTICE

The deployment of integrated HRIS in most large organizations will accelerate the rate of growth in our understanding of recruitment systems. Greater access to data will occur as organizations begin to develop their own HR analytics capabilities (i.e., these differ from the management of transaction systems which have occupied HRIS professionals to this point) and methods emerge for addressing privacy concerns. Leading organizations have overcome both hurdles and researchers are likely to be able to negotiate access to more fine-grained data about organizations than has ever been available. Access to fine-grained outcome data at multiple points in the recruitment process (e.g., Taylor & Bergmann, 1987) provides an enhanced capacity to study both the effects of recruitment tactics on both the level and distribution of applicant quality (e.g., Williams & Dreher, 1992). These data also enhance researchers' capacity to understand the competing influences of intervening psychological variables on recruitment decisions in "real" organization settings subject to changing environmental influences.

Research is also needed to support enhanced Phase II evaluation capabilities. Priorities include:

a.   Developing methods of initially screening applicants that have high validity and produce fine-grained estimates of applicant quality;

b.   estimating the effects of the selection device choice, sequencing, and cut-scores on validity and utility in multiple hurdle selection systems; and

c.   developing practical tools for directly estimating SD_y (e.g., Becker & Huselid, 1992).

Phase III evaluation will require that we also develop an understanding how job design influences attraction, status maintenance, selection, gaining job acceptance, job performance and retention and tools for measuring assessing these effects.

The Staffing Cycles Framework (Carlson & Connerley, 2003) can support researchers' efforts to develop more systematic views of recruitment and staffing. The Staffing Cycles Framework adopts a broad definition of staffing that extends from the decision of an individual to enter the work force and an organization to create a position, to the matching of individual and position, to employment where that match is ended by either the individual or the organization. It depicts staffing as a sequence of seven decision events controlled alternately, not mutually by individuals seeking jobs and organization decision makers that are subject to the effects of environment and the direct and indirect influence actions of interested stakeholders. The Staffing Cycles Framework is particularly relevant for studying staffing systems because it depicts the flow of decision outcomes that combine to determine the impact of staffing systems on organization success. These dynamics determine the extent to which utility gains in recruitment will eventually affect the organization's bottom-line.

Implications for Recruitment Practice

The availability of cost effective methods of recruitment evaluation will make it easier for organizations to pursue more extensive and more diverse forms of recruitment evaluation. The capacity to evaluate attraction, status maintenance and gaining job acceptance as separate practices will provide decision-makers the tools to more aggressively manage recruitment efforts.

Examining differences in attraction outcome value can help managers understand how effective their recruitment efforts are and not only where opportunities for improvement exist, but also the potential return for those efforts. These data can also be used to evaluate attraction efforts over time or from different sources (i.e., different universities in college recruitment).

Assessing attraction outcomes also provides insight into the effects of other recruitment practices. As was apparent in the comparison of college attraction outcomes, excellent attraction outcomes diminish the importance of status maintenance and job acceptance efforts. Organizations with excellent attraction outcomes have less incentive to engage in expensive applicant communication efforts or for those organizations to pay large signing bonuses. Conversely, less effective attraction increases the importance of status maintenance and job acceptance efforts.

Access to greater amounts of information becomes more valuable if it is matched with expertise in organization research and assessment. Therefore, it is likely that organizations may once again look to employ industrial and organizational psychologists and other individuals trained in measurement and the analysis of people and how they function in organizations. Effectively utilizing the large amounts of data that are available in organizations requires more than building a data warehouse and data mining capabilities. The vast amounts of data available can overwhelm decision-makers. Rather, organizations will need individuals who know what data are most appropriate for addressing key organization efforts and how to develop and interpret appropriate metrics. This will provide organizations an unprecedented opportunity to understanding of their own systems. As this expertise is developed, the unique knowledge of an organization's recruitment systems and the capacity to manage them aggressively can become a source of competitive advantage.

CONCLUSION

Recruitment is a critical organization function. Assessing measures of pre-hire recruitment outcomes is necessary for organizations to move beyond the adequacy assessments of Phase I recruitment evaluation. The first and most important step in this evolution is developing and using fine-grained measures of the quality of applicants attracted. Using utility analysis to convert these data into dollar valued estimates of recruitment benefits and combining them with already existing recruitment cost data offers organizations a powerful set of recruitment evaluation and management tools that can also be used for supporting recruitment research. The future looks bright indeed.

REFERENCES

Alderfer, C. P., & McCord, C. G. (1970). Personal and situational factors in the recruitment interview. *Journal of Applied Psychology, 34*, 377-385.

Barber, A. E. (1998). *Recruiting employees: Individual and organizational perspectives.* Thousand Oaks, CA: Sage Publications.

Barber, A. E., Wesson, M. J., Roberson, Q. M., & Taylor, M. S. (1999). A tale of two job markets: Organizational size and its effects on hiring practices and job search. *Personnel Psychology, 52*(4), 841-867.

Becker, B. E. (1989). The influence of labor markets on human resources utility estimates. *Personnel Psychology, 42*, 461-489.

Becker, B. E., & Huselid, M. A. (1992). Direct estimates of SD_y and the implications for utility analysis. *Journal of Applied Psychology, 77*, 227-233.

Belt, J. A & Paolillo, J. G. (1982). The influence of corporate image and specificity of candidate qualifications on response to recruitment advertisement. *Journal of Management, 8*(1), 105-112.

Blau, G. (1990). Exploring the mediating mechanisms affecting the relationship of recruitment source to employee performance. *Journal of Vocational Behavior, 45*, 738-752.

Boudreau, J. (1991). Utility analysis for decisions in human resource management. In M. D. Dunnette & L. M. Hough (Eds.), *Handbook of industrial and organizational psychology* (Vol. 2, pp. 621-752). Palo Alto, CA: Consulting Psychologists Press.

Boudreau, J. W., & Rynes, S. L. (1985). Role of recruitment in staffing utility analysis. *Journal of Applied Psychology, 70*, 354-366.

Breaugh, J. A. (1981). Relationships between recruiting source and employee performance, absenteeism, and work attitudes. *Academy of Management Journal, 24*, 142-147.

Breaugh, J. A. (1992). *Recruitment: Science and practice.* Boston: PWS-Kent.

Breaugh, J. A., & Mann, R. B. (1984). Recruiting source effects: A test of two alternative explanations. *Journal of Occupational Psychology, 57*, 261-267.

Breaugh, J. A., & Starke, M. (2000). Research on employee recruitment: So many studies, so many remaining questions. *Journal of Management, 26*(3), 405-434.

Cable, D. M., & Judge, T. A. (1994). Pay preferences and job search decisions: A person-organization fit perspective. *Personnel Psychology, 47*, 317-348.

Cable, D. M., Aiman-Smith, L., Mulvey, P. W., & Edwards, J. R. (2000). The sources and accuracy of job applicants' belief about organizational culture. *Academy of Management Journal, 43*(6), 1076-1085.

Caldwell, D. F., & Spivey, W. A. (1983). The relationship between recruiting source and employee success: An analysis by race. *Personnel Psychology, 36*, 67-72.

Campion, M. A., & Stevens, M. J. (1991). Neglected questions in job design: How people design jobs, tasks, job predictability, and influence of training. *Journal of Business and Psychology, 6*, 169-191.

Carlson, K. D., & Connerley, M. L. (2003). The staffing cycles framework: Viewing staffing as a system of decision events. *Journal of Management, 29*(1), 51-78.

Carlson, K. D., Connerley, M. L., & Mecham, III., R. L., (2002). Recruitment evaluation: The case for assessing the quality of applicants attracted. *Personnel Psychology, 55*(2), 461-490.

Cascio, W. F. (1998). *Applied Psychology in human resource management*. Upper Saddle River, NJ: Prentice-Hall.

Cascio, W. F. (1991). *Applied psychology in personnel management*. (4th Ed.). Englewood Cliffs, NJ: Prentice Hall.

Conard, M. A., & Ashworth, S. D. (1986). Recruiting source effectiveness: A meta-analysis and re-examination of two rival hypotheses. A paper presented at the annual meeting of the Society for Industrial and Organizational Psychology. Chicago, IL.

Connerley, M. L., Carlson, K. D., & Mecham, III, R. L. (2003). Evidence of differences in applicant pool quality. *Personnel Review, 32*(1), 22-39.

Crouse, R. (2002). Creating business cases: ROI for human resources. *IHRIM Journal, 6*(2), 17-21.

Davidson, L. (1998). Measuring what you bring to the bottom line. *Workforce, 77*(9), 34.

Deming, W. E. (1986). *Out of the crisis*. Cambridge, MA: Massachusetts Institute of Technology.

Dreher, G. F., & Sackett, P. R. (1982). *Perspectives on employee staffing and selection*. Homewood, IL: Irwin.

Fisher, C. D., Ilgen, D. R., & Hoyer, W. D. (1979). Source credibility, information availability, and job offer acceptance. *Academy of Management Journal, 22*, 94-103.

Fitz-enz, J. (1990). *Human Value Management: The value adding human resource strategy for the 1990s*. San Francisco: Jossey-Bass.

Fitz-enz, J. (1993). *Benchmarking staff performance: How staff departments can enhance their value to the customer*. San Francisco: Jossey-Bass.

Fitz-enz, J. (2002). *How to measure human resource management* (3rd Ed.). New York: McGraw-Hill, Inc.

Garman, A. N., & Mortensen, S. (1997). Using targeted outreach to recruit minority students into competitive service organizations. *College Student Journal, 31*(2), 174-179.

Gersen, W. F. (1976). The effects of a demanding application process on the applicant pool for teaching positions. (Doctoral Dissertation, University of Pennsylvania, 1975) *Dissertation Abstracts International, 36*, 7773A.

Griffith, R. W., Hom, P. W., Fink L. S., & Cohen, D. J. (1997). Comparative tests of multivariate models of recruiting source effects. *Journal of Management, 23*, 19-36.

Grossman, R. J. (2000). Measuring up: Appropriate metrics help HR prove its worth. *HR Magazine, 45*(1), 28-35.

Guion, R. M. (1976). Recruiting, selection and job placement. In M. D. Dunnette (Ed.) *Handbook of industrial and organizational psychology* (pp.777-828). Chicago: Rand McNally.

Harn, T. J., & Thornton, G. C., III. (1985). Recruiter counseling behaviors and applicant impressions. *Journal of Occupational Psychology, 58*, 57-65.

Hawk, R. H. (1967). *The recruitment function*. New York: American Management Association.

Herriot, P., & Rothwell, C. (1981). Organizational choice and decision theory: Effects of employers' literature and selection. *Journal of Occupational Psychology, 54*, 17-31.

Highhouse, S., Stierwalt, S.L., Bachiochi, P., Elder, A.E., & Fisher, G. (1999). Effects of advertised human resource management practices on attraction of African American applicants. *Personnel Psychology, 52,* 425-442.

Hill, R. E. (1970). New look at employee referrals as a recruitment channel. *Personnel Journal, 49,* 144-148.

Huselid, M. A. (1995). The impact of human resource management practices on turnover, productivity, and corporate financial performance. *Academy of Management Journal, 38,* 635-672.

Kirnan, J. P., Farley, J. A., & Geisinger, K. F. (1989). The relationship between recruiting source, applicant quality, and hire performance: An analysis by sex, ethnicity, and age. *Personnel Psychology, 42,* 293-308.

Latham, V. M., & Leddy, P. M. (1987). Source of recruitment and employee attitudes: An analysis of job involvement, organizational commitment, and job satisfaction. *Journal of Business and Psychology, 1,* 230-235.

Lavigna, R. J. (1996). Innovation in recruiting and hiring: Attracting the best and brightest to Wisconsin state government. *Public Personnel Management, 25*(4), 423-437.

Liden, R. C., & Parsons, C. K. (1986). A field study of job applicant interview perceptions alternative opportunities, and demographic characteristics. *Personnel Psychology, 39,* 109-123.

Mason, N. A., & Belt, J. A. (1986). Effectiveness of specificity in recruitment advertising. *Journal of Management, 12,* 425-432.

McDaniel, M. A., Schmidt, F. L., & Hunter, J. E. (1988). A meta-analysis of the validity of methods for rating training and experience in personnel selection. *Personnel Psychology, 41,* 283-314.

Murphy, K. R. (1986). When your top choice turns you down: Effect of rejected offers on the utility of selection tests. *Psychological Bulletin, 99,* 133-138.

Powell, G. N. (1984). Effects of job attributes and recruiting practices on applicant decisions: A comparison. *Personnel Psychology, 37,* 71-732

Premack, S. L., & Wanous, J. P. (1985). A meta-analysis of realistic job preview experiements. *Journal of Applied Psychology, 70*(4), 706-719.

Raphael, W. (1937). Sources of recruitment and methods of selection of personnel suitable for high administrative positions. *Conference Internationale de Psychotechnique (Prague). Comptes Rendus, 1935,* 175-177.

Reid, G. L. (1972). Job search and the effectiveness of job-finding methods. *Industrial and Labor Relations Review, 25,* 479-495.

Rogers, D. P., & Sincoff, M. Z. (1978). Favorable impression characteristics of the recruitment interviewer. *Personnel Psychology, 31,* 495-504.

Roth, P. L., BeVier, C. A., Switzer III, F. S., & Schippmann, J. S. (1996). Meta-analyzing the relationship between grades and job performance. *Journal of Applied Psychology, 81,* 548-556.

Rynes, S. L. (1991). Recruitment, job-choice, and post-hire consequences. In M. D. Dunnette (Ed.), *Handbook of industrial and organizational psychology* (2nd Ed., pp. 399-444). Palo Alto, CA: Sage Publications.

Rynes, S. L., & Barber, A. E. (1990). Applicant attraction strategies: An organizational perspective. *Academy of Management Review, 15,* 286-310.

Rynes, S. L., & Boudreau, J. W. (1986). College recruiting in large organizations: Practice, evaluation, and research implications. *Personnel Psychology, 39,* 729-757.

Rynes, S. L., & Miller, H. E. (1983). Recruiter and job influences on candidates for employment. *Journal of Applied Psychology, 68,* 146-154.

Sackett, P. R., & Ostgaard, D. J. (1994). Job-specific applicant pools and national norms for cognitive ability tests: Implications for range restriction corrections in validation research. *Journal of Applied Psychology, 79,* 680-684.

Schmitt, N., & Coyle, B. W. (1976). Applicant decisions in the employment interview. *Journal of Applied Psychology, 61,*184-193.

Schuler, R. S., & Jackson, S. E. (Eds.) (1999). *Strategic human resource management.* Malden, MA: Blackwell Publishers.

SHRM/CCH (1999, Summer). *Human resources management: Ideas and trends in personnel.* St. Petersburg, FL: CCH Incorporated.

Starcke, A.M. (1996). Internet recruiting shows rapid growth. *HRMagazine, 41*(8), 61.

Sullivan, J. (1999). Personal communication. HRNet discussion on staffing evaluation. October.

Swaroff, P. G., Barclay, L. A., & Bass, A. R. (1985). Recruiting sources: Another look. *Journal of Applied Psychology, 70,* 720-728.

Taylor, M. S., & Bergman, T. J. (1987). Organizational recruitment activities and applicants' reactions at different stages of the recruitment process. *Journal of Management, 40,* 461-515.

Taylor, M. S., & Giannantonio, C. M. (1992). Forming, adapting, and terminating the employment relationship: A review of the literature from individual, organizational, and interactionist perspectives. *Journal of Management, 19*(2) 461-515.

Taylor, M. S., & Schmidt, D. W. (1983). A process-oriented investigation of recruitment source effectiveness. *Personnel Psychology, 36,* 343-354.

Terpstra, D. E., & Rozell, E. J. (1993) The relationship of staffing practices to organizational level measures of performance. *Personnel Psychology, 46,* 27-48.

Turban, D. B, Forret, M. L., & Hendrickson, C. L. (1998). Applicant attraction to firms: Influences of organization reputation, job and organizational attributes, and recruiter behaviors. *Journal of Vocational Behavior, 52*(1), 24-44.

Ullman, J. C. (1966). Employee referrals: A prime tool for recruiting workers. *Personnel, 43,* 30-35.

Vecchio, R. P. (1995). The impact of referral sources on employee attitudes: Evidence from a national sample. *Journal of Management, 21,* 953-965.

Wanous, J. P., Poland, T. D., Premack, S. L., & Davis, K. S. (1992). The effects of met expectations on newcomer attitudes and behaviors: A review and meta-analysis. *Journal of Applied Psychology, 77,* 288-297.

Werbel, J. D., & Landau, J. (1996). The effectiveness of difference recruitment sources: A mediating variable analysis. *Journal of Applied Psychology, 26,* 1337-1350.

Williams, M. L., & Dreher, G. F. (1992). Compensation system attributes and applicant pool characteristics. *Academy of Management Journal, 35,* 571-595.

Williams, C. R., Labig, C. E., & Stone, T. H. (1993). Recruitment sources and posthire outcomes for job applicants and new hires: A test of two hypotheses. *Journal of Applied Psychology, 78,* 163-172.

AUTHOR BIOGRAPHIES

H. John Bernardin is a University Research Professor in the College of Business at Florida Atlantic University in Boca Raton. He earned his PhD in industrial/organizational psychology from Bowling Green University, and is the former director of doctoral studies in I/O psychology at Virginia Tech. He is past Chair of the Division of Personnel/Human Resources of the Academy of Management. Dr. Bernardin was editor of Human Resource Management Review and has served on the editorial boards of numerous journals, including the *Academy of Management Review, Human Resource Management Journal,* and the *Journal of Organizational Behavior.* He is the author of six books and over 100 articles related to human resource management. His paper on employment discrimination was cited as the best paper of the year by the Society of Human Resource Management in 2001. Dr. Bernardin has consulted for many of the most successful companies in the world and he has served as an expert witness in numerous employment discrimination lawsuits.

Michael G. Bowen earned an AB in Economics from the University of Michigan in 1971. After several years of work and self-employment, he earned an MBA at the University of Detroit in 1981, and a PhD in Organizational Behavior (Minor Area: Strategic Management) at the University of

New Directions in Human Resource Management
A Volume in: Research in Management, pages 165–170.
Copyright © 2003 by Information Age Publishing, Inc.
All rights of reproduction in any form reserved.
ISBN: 1-59311-099-5 (hardcover), 1-59311-098-7 (pbk.)

Illinois at Urbana-Champaign in 1987. He has been a member of the Management Department at the University of South Florida, Tampa, since 2002.

Professor Bowen has published a number of scholarly articles, chapters, reviews, and cases in the management, small business/entrepreneurship, and business ethics literatures. His main research interest lies in "escalating commitment" (the tendencies for people to, perhaps, throw "good money after bad"). Other research areas are leadership and organizational development; organizational culture change; business ethics, accountability, spirituality and managing; and systems thinking, strategy, and managing.

Kevin D. Carlson (PhD, University of Iowa) is an associate professor of Management in the Pamplin College of Business at Virginia Polytechnic Institute and State University where he teaches and does research in the areas of recruitment, training and development, productivity and quality management, and human resource information systems. Dr. Carlson's work has been published in the *Journal of Applied Psychology, Personnel Psychology, Journal of Management* and *Personnel Review* and he has presented papers at the meetings of the Academy of Management, the Society for Industrial and Organization Psychology, the International Association for Human Resource Information Management, and the Nation Institute for Staff and Organizational Development. His current research interests include evaluating recruitment and staffing effectiveness, the application of human resource information systems, modeling the determinants of performance outcomes, knowledge structures and the development of competence.

Gerald R. Ferris is the Francis Eppes Professor of Management and Professor of Psychology at Florida State University. Formerly, he held the Robert M. Hearin Chair of Business Administration, and was Professor of Management and Acting Associate Dean for Faculty and Research in the School of Business Administration at the University of Mississippi from 1999-2000. Before that, he served as Professor of Labor and Industrial Relations, of Business Administration, and of Psychology at the University of Illinois at Urbana-Champaign from 1989-1999, and as the Director of the Center for Human Resource Management at the University of Illinois from 1991-1996. Ferris received a PhD in Business Administration from the University of Illinois at Urbana-Champaign. He has research interests in the areas of social influence processes in human resources systems, and the role of reputation in organizations. Ferris is the author of articles published in such journals as the *Journal of Applied Psychology, Organizational Behavior and Human Decision Processes, Personnel Psychology, Academy of Management Journal,* and *Academy of Management Review.* Ferris served as editor of the annual series, *Research in Personnel and Human Resources Management,* from 1981-2003.

Dwight D. Frink obtained his AM and PhD degrees in Labor and Industrial Relations from the University of Illinois at Urbana-Champaign in 1994, where he majored in Human Resources Management. He currently is Associate Professor, PMB and William King Self Chair of Free Enterprise, and Management Department chair at the University of Mississippi. Frink worked for nearly 20 years in production, systems design, supervision, and management, which led to his research interests in social and personal influences on workplace outcomes. These include such things as accountability in organizations, various diversities, dispositions, organizational politics, and political skill. He has published approximately 30 articles in various academic journals and books, including the *Journal of Management, Academy of Management Journal, Journal of Applied Social Psychology, Human Relations,* and *Research in Personnel and Human Resources Management,* among others, and presented in various academic conferences.

Christine M. Hagan received a PhD degree in Management from Florida Atlantic University. She is currently a Lecturer at the University of Miami's School of Business. Her research interests include performance appraisal, human resource management in service settings, compensation, and human resource effectiveness. Her research has been published in a variety of journals including *Administrative Science Quarterly, Human Resource Management Review,* and the *Journal of Applied Behavioral Science.* Prior to pursuing a doctoral degree, she spent over 20 years in human resource management positions with such organizations as General Electric, RKO General Entertainment, Montefiore Medical Center, and First Jersey Financial Services.

Angela T. Hall is a doctoral candidate at the College of Business, Florida State University. She received a Juris Doctor degree from Florida State University in 1993, and has been a member in good standing of the Florida Bar since her admittance in 1994. Her research interests include accountability, ethics, workplace accommodations, and organizational politics. She has co-authored several contributed book chapters including a chapter on work-family conflict and family-friendly policies that appeared in *Individual and Organizational Health* (SIOP Organizational Frontiers Series).

Ken Harris is currently a PhD candidate at Florida State University, with an emphasis in Organizational Behavior/Human Resource Management. His research interests are primarily in the areas of dyadic leadership, metaperception, and organizational and individual antecedents to turnover.

Wayne A. Hochwarter (PhD, Florida State University) is currently an Associate Professor of Management and Coordinator of Doctoral programs in Management at Florida State University. His research has been published in the *Journal of Applied Psychology,* the *Journal of Management,* and the *Journal of Vocational Behavior.* His research interests include accountability processes, social influence, and cynicism.

Charles J. Kacmar is an Associate Professor in the MIS Department at Florida State University. He received his PhD in computer science from Texas A&M University. His research interests include behavioral and organizational information systems, human-computer interaction, collaborative systems, and hypertext/hypermedia. His publications may be found in *Academy of Management Journal, Information Systems Research, Journal of Strategic Information Systems, Communications of the ACM, ACM Transactions on Information Systems, Hypermedia, and Behaviour and Information Technology.* He is a member of the Association for Information Systems and ACM.

K. Michele (Micki) Kacmar is the Charles A. Rovetta Professor of Management and the Director of the Center for Human Resource Management at Florida State University. She received her PhD in Human Resource Management from Texas A&M University. Her research interests include impression management and organizational politics. She has published over 50 articles in journals such as *Journal of Applied Psychology, Organizational Behavior and Human Decision Processes,* and *Human Relations.* Dr. Kacmar served as Editor of the *Journal of Management* from 2000-2003 and on the Board of Directors of the Society for Human Resource Management Foundation from 1993-2000.

Angela K. Miles is an assistant professor at North Carolina A&T University. She earned a BA in Economics/Psychology from the University of Virginia, an MBA in Finance from the University of Wisconsin—Madison, and a PhD in Management from Florida State University. She also holds an Associate in Risk Management designation. Her research focuses on organizational stress, ergonomics, and work life initiatives. These research interests extend into her teaching areas of Organizational Behavior, Human Resource Management, and Cross-cultural Management. Dr. Miles is published in numerous journals and conference *Proceedings* and is the recipient of several conference best paper awards and scholarships. Her professional experiences have included responsibilities in finance, management, operations, marketing, and academia. She was previously employed in the banking, automotive, and telecommunications industries.

Edilberto (Ed) Montemayor (Ed_Montemayor@redlands.edu) received a PhD in Industrial Relations from the University of Minnesota. He currently teaches graduate and undergraduate courses in Management and in Human Resource Management at the University of Redlands, School of Business. Ed has considerable teaching, work, and consulting experience dealing with performance management and compensation matters. His current research interests include: employee reactions to pay systems, and the interplay between organizational culture, business strategy, compensation strategy, and firm performance. Ed has made multiple research presentations at Conferences organized by the Academy of Management, the

Michigan Council of the Society for Human Resource Management, the American Compensation Association, and the Industrial Relations Research Association. Among other periodicals, Ed's manuscripts have also appeared in *The Journal of Management, Management Research, Human Resource Management Review, The Academy of Management Best Paper Proceedings, The American Compensation Association Journal,* and *The Journal of Psychology.*

Linda L. Neider (PhD, State University of New York at Buffalo, 1979) is a Professor and chairman of the Department of Management. Her teaching and research interests lie in the fields of leadership, motivation, human resource management, and other areas of organizational behavior. Dr. Neider has published in a variety of journals, including the *Academy of Management Journal, Leadership Quarterly, Organization Behavior,* and *Human Decision Processes.* She is the co-author of the textbook *The Human Relations of Organizations.* Dr. Neider has also received several outstanding teaching awards, including the University of Miami Teaching Excellence Award. She is a member of the Academy of Management, and the American Psychological Association.

Pamela L. Perrewé (PhD) is the Jim Moran Professor of Management in the College of Business at Florida State University. She received her Bachelor's degree in Psychology from Purdue University and her masters and PhD degrees in Management from the University of Nebraska. Dr. Perrewé has focused her research interests in the areas of job stress, coping, organizational politics, and personality. Dr. Perrewé has published over 70 book chapters and journal articles in journals such as *Academy of Management Journal, Journal of Management, Journal of Applied Psychology, Journal of Organizational Behavior, Journal of Vocational Behavior, Human Relations* and *Journal of Applied Social Psychology.* She serves as a member of the Editorial Review Board for *Journal of Occupational Health Psychology, Human Resource Management Review* and *Journal of Management.* Finally, she is the co-editor of an annual series entitled, *Research in Occupational Stress and Well Being* published by Elsevier, Inc.

Chester A. Schriesheim, a professor at the University of Miami, received his PhD from The Ohio State University (1978). He was previously a tenured Professor at the University of Florida (1982-1986) and a tenured Associate Professor at the University of Southern California (1978-1982). Dr. Schriesheim's primary interests are in organizational behavior and human resource management, and he is the author or co-author of numerous publications (his scientific writings have appeared in *Psychological Bulletin, Administrative Science Quarterly, Academy of Management Journal,* and *Journal of Applied Psychology,* among others). Dr. Schriesheim is a Fellow of the American Psychological Association and a Fellow of the Southern Management

Association; he is also a past President of the Southern Management Association, and a winner of several awards for excellence in teaching and research productivity

Printed in the United States
1426700001B/148-177